ROBERT SCHUMANN

A SUPPLEMENTARY AND CORRECTIVE BIOGRAPHY

AMS PRESS
NEW YORK

ROBERT SCHUMANN

ROBERT SCHUMANN

BY

FREDERICK NIECKS

Mus.D., LL.D.

EDITED BY

CHRISTINA NIECKS, Mus.B.

MCMXXV

LONDON & TORONTO

J. M. DENT & SONS LTD.

NEW YORK: E. P. DUTTON & CO.

Library of Congress Cataloging in Publication Data

Niecks, Frederick, 1845-1924.
    Robert Schumann.

    Reprint of the 1925 ed. published by Dent,
London; E. P. Dutton, New York, in series: Dent's
international library of books on music.
    "List of the published works of Robert
Schumann": p.
    Includes index.
    1. Schumann, Robert Alexander, 1810-1856.
ML410.S4N53 1978   780'.92'4 [B]   74-24167
ISBN 0-404-13065-8

Reprinted from the edition of 1925, London and New York
First AMS edition published in 1978
Manufactured in the United States of America

AMS PRESS INC.
NEW YORK, N.Y.

"And so it is throughout human life—the goal we have attained is no longer a goal, and we yearn, and strive, and aim ever higher and higher, until the eyes close in death, and the storm-tossed body and soul lie slumbering in the grave."

(ROBERT SCHUMANN *to his mother, April* 28, 1828.)

". . . Certain it is that I have spared no pains, and for twenty years, regardless of praise and blame, have striven for one object—to be called a true servant of art . . ."

(SCHUMANN *to Franz Brendel, September* 18, 1849.)

PREFACE

THE author of this book, which for conscientious research and accuracy deserves a place in every music-lover's library beside the *Life of Chopin*, was prevented by declining strength from completing the latter chapters with his own hand. Their subject-matter, however, and his intentions concerning it, he discussed fully with his wife, who had collaborated with him throughout, entrusted the completion to her, and sanctioned the manner of presentation.

As the work (then appearing in article form) had to be finished within a given time and space, great condensation, chiefly towards the end, was inevitable, but needs less excuse since biographical details regarding the unhappy close of the poet-composer's life are sufficiently—even painfully—complete. The book as it stands seems to me to offer the most minute and exhaustive record of Robert Schumann's character and the development of his genius that has yet appeared.

The composer's open-hearted letters (and copious literary productions), proving him to be his own best biographer, should be read and studied in that sense. And in this connection, it is within my own knowledge that Frederick Niecks —had he lived—would have commented at greater length upon certain influences which left a deep impression upon their gifted writer.

Among them, the attitude of Schumann's father-in-law towards a somewhat wayward young student and unwelcome aspiring son-in-law ; the effect of Mendelssohn's intimacy upon the mind of the mature man—or better said, their mutual influence upon each other : and, more particularly, would he have dwelt on the interesting report of an extremely uncomfortable situation from the official pen of the assistant *Bürgermeister* Wortmann.

While many sidelights thrown upon the conditions and progress of music and its makers illuminate these pages, the final chapters dealing with Schumann's slowly developing mental deterioration and the resulting disagreements regarding his fitness—or otherwise—to continue in office as conductor are of special significance, since the matter is put in a fresh light with abundance of reliable detail.

My late friend was keenly desirous of clearing Julius Tausch's memory from unworthy insinuations and aspersions which prejudice and bias cast upon Schumann's willing assistant at the time. And having known him personally I gladly chime with the author's wish. Tausch (a composer of considerable merit) was of much too simple (a mild term) a nature to be an intriguer, far less a successful one.

There must be few, if any, now living who can speak from a personal experience of those days. Niecks told me that when a boy he saw Schumann walking, evidently in deep thought, in the Public Garden, his lips pursed as if in the act of whistling. Some of his portraits convey the same impression.

I came too late upon the scene to have that privilege; but soon enough to know Düsseldorf while the sad story— a common subject of gossip—was still fairly fresh in men's minds, and even to meet one or two of the dramatis personæ— the once famous artist Hildebrandt, then an old man of weakened intellect, among others; and I had previously met the genial Gottfried Hermann, to whom Schumann addressed an inquiry regarding the possibility of occupying his vacated position, when he came from Lübeck to visit his successor (my master) Stein at Sondershausen.

These facts, and a long friendship with the late occupant of the Edinburgh Reid Chair of Music, alone induce me to add these few—although unnecessary—introductory lines to a book which speaks authoritatively for itself.

Niecks, Leopold Auer's pupil and Ferdinand Hiller's admiring disciple, expressed (somewhere in 1868) a desire to come to this country; and just at a time when we were greatly in need of a competent viola player to take part in a series of chamber concerts in my native city.   By a fortunate chance I was soon able to secure a modest position for him as organist and teacher in Dumfries.   Thus, to our mutual advantage, the difficulty was overcome, and the little band of " Schumannianer " was enabled to offer hearings of such works as the pianoforte quartet and quintet (also *Paradise and the Peri*) at a time when these masterpieces—although making their way—had hardly yet been found wholly acceptable in the metropolis.

The remainder of Frederick Niecks's career, culminating in a prominent Professorship, was patiently carved out by himself, and is too well known to require extended reference here.   He rapidly acquired a masterly command of our language which astonished even the few who best knew his intellectual attainments, studious habits and persistent thirst for knowledge.   A retiring, modest disposition, added to an enviable gift of silence, prevented the many from readily arriving at an adequate appreciation of an exceptionally well-stored mind and evenly-balanced power of judgment.

It is to be regretted that so eminently capable a thinker was not permitted to add those technical and æsthetical criticisms on the works of the great composer, with which he intended to conclude this volume.   As it is, he leaves a valuable legacy to us and to the history of our art at the close of a long life of ceaseless industry and far-reaching usefulness.

A. C. Mackenzie.

London, *September* 1924.

NOTE

For many years my husband had collected information and documents for a *Life and Work of Robert Schumann* on a large scale, but other work continuously prevented the execution of the project. War conditions made its possibility still more remote. In 1920, however, feeling that the time had passed by for him to begin the enterprise of a systematic full biography, he resolved to produce at least the main features of his material in the form of articles, the scope of which he defined in the title : *Supplementary and Corrective to Biography of Robert Schumann.* The series appeared in the *Monthly Musical Record* from February 1921 to December 1923, and was intended for subsequent publication in book-form.

The chief sources drawn upon are acknowledged in the Introductory Chapter : others, as they arise in the course of the book.

The translations were made throughout from the original German.

It was my husband's wish that I should revise the text of the articles before their appearance in book-form, and this I have done—as far as it could be done without him and the knowledge that has died with him.

Except for some completions and expansions which for want of space had to be forgone in the articles, no change has been made as to the subject-matter.

I wish to express my warm thanks to those who helped me by valuable suggestions and by reading the proofs ; and to Dr. Otto Schlapp of the University of Edinburgh for the loan of the silhouette which appears as frontispiece. Thanks are also due to Messrs. Augener Ltd. for permission to use the articles.

CHRISTINA NIECKS.

EDINBURGH, *March* 1925.

CONTENTS

xi

CONTENTS

ROBERT SCHUMANN

ROBERT SCHUMANN

CHAPTER I

INTRODUCTORY

MANY years ago I conceived the idea of writing a life of Schumann. Various reasons induced me thereto. Firstly, my admiration, or, rather, my *Schwärmerei* (then more intense than now) for the Romanticism of the composer; and secondly, the flattering hope that certain advantages of position and disposition—on the one hand, nearness to the hero and his friends (Düsseldorf, 1850–56), and on the other hand, carefulness of research—would fit me for the task. As a little child I sometimes saw the master walking in the Düsseldorf Park and conducting at rehearsals; and my father, a member of the orchestra, did not fail to point out the strangeness of his aspect, especially the rounded mouth and pursed-up lips as if softly whistling to himself, further, a *douceness* of bearing and movement, a languor of gait, and a dreamy self-obliviousness that seemed an inner state behind a veil—in fact, a mystery.

When a few years later, still at a very early age, I joined the Düsseldorf orchestra, and the channels of communication became at once multiplied, the master was no longer with us, having become mentally deranged in 1854 and dying in 1856. All the Düsseldorf facts involved, therefore, fall within the very narrow span of six years, the last two of them, moreover, spent in confinement. Owing to circumstances of time and place, it was at a later—indeed, a very much later—time that I made the acquaintance of most of my informants.

B

Besides the members of the band there have to be mentioned the members of the choral bodies, the amateur instrumentalists, the specially engaged supplementary leading instrumentalists, the committee members of the musical societies, and those of the municipal council charged with the musical affairs. Then there were the two very dissimilar groups, the general musical public, and the particular friends of the Schumanns. Much of this, all that is trifling and unworthy, has, of course, to be ignored. It will suffice to take into consideration the more important witnesses. One of the first must be the pianist and composer, Julius Tausch, the assistant and successor of Schumann, who came to Düsseldorf with a recommendation from Mendelssohn, and under whose baton I served, and whose teaching I enjoyed in after years. Between Mendelssohn and Schumann, Julius Rietz and Ferdinand Hiller occupied the post of conductor, and they subsequently kept more or less in touch with the Düsseldorf doings, more of course Hiller of Cologne, close at hand, than Rietz of Leipzig and Dresden. Fräulein Hartmann, a member of the mixed Choral Society, who as a solo singer often took part in performances of the master's works, also came in frequent personal contact with him and his wife. And there were others like her. Among the special instrumentalists we meet Ruppert Becker, son of E. A. Becker, of Dresden (Finance Secretary), and Freiberg (Mines), the old friend of Robert and Clara Schumann. He became *Concertmeister* in 1852 in succession to W. J. von Wasielewski, and to him I am indebted for letters, extracts from a diary, and other communications. Leading men that ought to be mentioned are the advocate, Dr. Herz, a well-known violinist, who as a committee member negotiated matters with Madame Schumann ; and the assistant Burgomaster, Wilhelm Wortmann, who communicated to me the report which he supplied officially on the Schumann case. Of Madame Schumann's pupils of these days, Fräulein Wittgenstein in after years put me under obligation both by conversation with me and by allowing me to copy some of the master's letters. Of the Düsseldorf friends, that is, of the Düsseldorf time, not of the town, there are especially three that stand by themselves—a discipleship unique in true admiration, devotion, and love, which the master fully and cordially repaid. I mean, of course, Joseph Joachim, Albert Dietrich, and Johannes Brahms. In intimate intercourse with the first I had long and frequent communings about Schumann, communings of the greatest value and interest. Among the recollections I have of this friendship there is not one that is not flawless. No one would think of so describing the communings of Brahms, least of all his best friends, who, of course, were well aware of the shyness and tartness of his nature and his incalculable temper. Nobody could be more exquisitely delicate and kind, nobody could be more decidedly the reverse. Having found him always in good humour when I was in his company, I certainly thought twice before risking biographical questions. But waiting may bring its rewards. At any rate I found Brahms a most amiable gentleman, and most anxious to make himself obliging—his friends specially congratulated me on the favour he showed me. I was very sorry that when I was able to visit the third of the three disciples, Dietrich, his state of health did not admit of my seeing him, and, as Joachim told me at the time, we must content ourselves with what he has recorded in his book, *Erinnerungen an J. Brahms* (1898).

Zwickau, our hero's birthplace, and where he spent the first eighteen years of his life, is not the dwelling-place one would preferably select for a romantic and a man of genius. Leipzig, Heidelberg, Dresden, and Düsseldorf will have no difficulty in proving the superiority of their advantages over it. But Schumann had a soft place for it in his heart. I certainly feel greatly obliged for the kindly way in which the citizens did the honours of the town during my stay there. The most important place of residence was the second, Leipzig (1828–44, with an intervening year at the University of Heidelberg, May, 1829–August, 1830, including travels in North Italy in September and October, 1829). For here was the concentration of Schumann's life in all its branches; here he had his dreams, developments, realizations, loves, deals, the whole of his art before him like a panorama in

-movement; here he learned all that he had to learn from others and himself, here he spread his poetic ideas about music in a paper of his own, here he published his compositions, more and more original, more and more ambitious, and here he formed friendships and rubbed shoulders with ever so many creative and executive artists. Leipzig at that time, when one thinks of those who lived and those who visited there, was an immense place, much more than a little Paris. The town to which Schumann moved next, Dresden (1844–50), could not be compared to it, nor did it make any such impression on him. As a conductor he had neither the ability nor the opportunity to play an imposing part. It really came to mean a restriction of his musical activity to creative work, and it has to be admitted that his creative powers were already on the wane—the occasional successes cannot blind us to the frequent dimnesses. The third and last residence during activity was at Düsseldorf (1850–54), where appearances seemed at first to hold out promise of a fair and varied activity in easy smiling conditions; but in four years came the tragic removal to Endenich, near Bonn, and in 1856 the end.

All these several residences had to be investigated, and not merely to be examined superficially and in passing, but to be lived in. This I did thoroughly with Leipzig, and more or less thoroughly with the other places. But the abodes of artists are shifting, and it may often be impossible to drag the artists at each other's heels from one part of the world to another. Take as instances the composers Stephen Heller and Theodor Kirchner, and the historical painter Eduard Bendemann. The last and his wife, after they had known Mendelssohn at Düsseldorf, formed a close friendship with the Schumanns at Dresden, which was resumed with Madame Schumann at Düsseldorf on Bendemann's appointment as Director of the Academy there in 1859.

Well, I shall enumerate a few more of the informants to whom I have been greatly obliged. About half a century ago I arrived at Leipzig with warm recommendations from a London friend to a Leipzig musical amateur who had been in intimate intercourse with Mendelssohn and

Schumann. At the hospitable board of this dear and amiable friend I was brought into contact with Heinrich Conrad Schleinitz, the lawyer who, as representative of the Committee of the Gewandhaus Concerts, negotiated the engagement of Mendelssohn. Subsequently he became a friend of Mendelssohn and of Schumann, and *Justizrat* and Director of the Conservatorium. He adopted me as part and parcel of the institution, and as long as I stayed in Leipzig he kept his eye upon me both directorially and as a citizen. A very interesting personality whose acquaintance I made in the same house was the pianoforte professor Ferdinand Wenzel, one of the earliest of Schumann's " Davidsbündler," his contributor and friend, allowed to be somewhat eccentric, and the admired of all his pupils, especially the lady pupils. A man after Schumann's heart, one of a newer generation, was Carl Reinecke (1824–1910), who had then become the head of the Leipzig school of the two masters to whose spirit he remained faithful. That excellent musician, Alfred Dörffel, librarian, reader, and editor of musical works, and author of *Die Gewandhausconcerte zu Leipzig*, who knew everybody, and was always equally known by everybody, put his memory at my service.

In Dresden I made the acquaintance of two ladies closely connected with the Schumann family as pupils, choralists, and friends—Frau Emilie Heydenreich and Fräulein Marie von Lindeman, who aided me more systematically than that word generally implies. Ruppert Becker's diary and letters have already been referred to, and Reinhold Becker may be mentioned as one of Schumann's successors at Dresden. Of more importance is Carl Banck (1809–1889) in certain parts of his life, both as a song composer and critical writer, but Schumann was not so intimate with Banck as with some of his other friends. He left in my hands interesting letters and other information. Old Frau Wieck and her daughter Marie Wieck, Madame Clara Schumann's younger half-sister, had much to tell of the father, Friedrich Wieck, the famous teacher, of the other members of the Wieck family, and of Robert Schumann himself.

In Berlin I met no less a man than Schumann's teacher

of composition, Heinrich Dorn, who, as the friend of his
pupil, deserves inquiring about.   There too I made the interesting acquaintance of Woldemar Bargiel, the excellent
composer, Clara Wieck's step-brother (the son of Clara's
mother, who, after her separation from Wieck, married the
music teacher Bargiel).

The names of Hiller, Liszt, Anton Rubinstein, Robert
Franz, Stephen Heller, Gade, Brahms, and others whom I
have known, and who were in various degrees of relationship
with Schumann, remind me that this opens up an important
subject, a vast subject, spreading out more and more exten-
sively till it comprehends all composers of any genuine originality.   The opinions and comments of Schumann on his
contemporaries are characteristic; they throw light on his
own character as well as on theirs.   And the same is of course
true of their judgments of him.   I believe in this mutuality,
and intend to employ this means of exploration exhaustively.
There are in these revelations curious admissions, confessions,
pretensions, etc.

But one thing has to be made clear without the least
ambiguity before the end of this chapter.   The most important
contributor to Schumann's biography is Schumann himself,
and he is so to a considerable extent unconsciously.   He is so,
in the first place, in the *Gesammelte Schriften* (second edition,
Leipzig, Georg Wigands Verlag, 1871 ; third edition, 1883,
translated by Fanny Ritter ; fifth edition, edited by Martin
Kreisig, Leipzig, Breitkopf & Härtel, 1914) which contain
a selection by himself from the articles, reviews, notices,
characterizations, fancies, etc., furnished by him for his paper,
the *Neue Zeitschrift für Musik* (Leipzig, 1834–1844); and, in
the second place, in the several Collections of his Letters, the
chief being *Jugendbriefe von Robert Schumann*, edited by
Clara Schumann (Leipzig, Breitkopf & Härtel, 1885 and
1886, translated 1888); *Robert Schumanns Briefe. Neue
Folge*, edited by F. G. Jansen (Leipzig, Breitkopf & Härtel,
1886—translated by May Herbert, 1890, as *The Life of Robert
Schumann told in his Letters*—second enlarged German edition,
Leipzig, Breitkopf & Härtel, 1904); and the two volumes

of Schumann Letters, under the title *Robert Schumanns Leben. Aus seinen Briefen*, by Hermann Erler (Berlin, Ries & Erler, 1887). *Die Davidsbündler*, by F. G. Jansen (Leipzig, Breitkopf & Härtel, 1883) must also be mentioned. To these invaluable contributions has to be added Berthold Litzmann's *Clara Schumann, Ein Künstlerleben nach Tagebüchern und Briefen* (Leipzig, Breitkopf & Härtel, three vols., first edition 1902, 1905, and 1908 respectively)—translated and abridged from the fourth edition by Grace E. Hadow (two vols., London, Macmillan & Co., Ltd., and Leipzig, Breitkopf & Härtel, 1913). Litzmann's is a wonderfully rich and interesting publication, which would carry off the palm were it not that the master's *Collected Writings* and his Letters proved themselves unique in self-revelation, direct and indirect, and in genius. This last is a distinguishing feature. With his own and Clara's contributions to his biography there are but few mysteries to be met with in it, and the most serious of these are of the discoverers' own making. In drawing on Wasielewski's valuable biography of Schumann I have used the third edition (Bonn, Emil Strauss, 1880).

The great thing to learn from a composer's biography is what training he had in his profession, how he was helped by his colleagues in acquiring it. Beyond names we have hardly any information whatever as to how Schumann was taught in the conventional sense. Indeed, he was not so taught. The masters and their pupil went on together in perfect amity, but only with the understanding that they would not insist on prescribing what work to do and how to do it : in short, the pupil was allowed to dream and please himself. But if Schumann was not, like Mozart and Mendelssohn, one of those perfectly organized natural geniuses who encounter no difficulties, and can express what they want to express, neither was he one of those who believe that originality is obstructed by anything approaching, however little, the old technique and style. We have to learn that our composer is an intelligence, and that consequently he is able to give a guidance to his training which will make this part of our study particularly interesting.

- In more than one respect Schumann will reveal himself in a startlingly unexpected way which may arouse prejudice. For instance, he is not merely a dreamer, a fantast, but a thinker and a reasoner as well; he is not merely an idealist, but a practical man who can make definite terms and perspicuous technical and other arrangements that would do credit to a first-rate man of business.

The unity, the consistency of our hero's life must become apparent to every observant person. At the beginning of this introduction I recalled my childish picture of Schumann in the Park at Düsseldorf. Let me place beside it the recollection of another somewhat older boy. Joseph Joachim saw Schumann first, he told me, at the rehearsal of the Viardot-Garcia concert at Leipzig on August 19, 1843; the master then looked at him through his lorgnette, smiling kindly. On a later occasion, when they knew one another better, Schumann, at an evening party at Mendelssohn's, said (pointing to the clear, starry sky, and patting Joachim on the knee): " I wonder if those up there have heard how prettily the little fellow plays ? " I imagine I hear the soft voice and see the sweet features of the master.

CHAPTER II

INTERESTING for their own sake, the life and character of
Robert Schumann's father become still more so when they
are seen reflected in the son as an author, editor, and printing
expert. There is, fortunately, a short biography of fifty-
six pages by the well-known public-spirited and enterprising
citizen of Zwickau, *Magister* C. E. Richter, from 1819–22
Conrector and teacher of French at the Lyceum (Latin school),
of whose information I have gladly availed myself.

Friedrich August Gottlob Schumann was born at the village
of Entschütz, near Gera in Saxony, on March 2, 1773, the
eldest son of a worthy but poor Protestant parson and a sickly
mother. In the course of time promotion came, but, alas!
with the title *Archidiaconus* did not come the much-needed
increase of salary. Here was not one of the attractive kind
of idylls familiar to readers of Voss, Jean Paul, and others,
picturing the beautiful, peaceful family life of country parsons
and schoolmasters in the good old times, but rather one of
the unfortunately no less true and common cases where
poverty, social degradation, and other miseries were the order
of the day. As the father of August Schumann had no means
to spare for the boy's education, he did what he could himself
with the help of the village schoolmaster, until, in 1783, he
managed to send the ten-year-old boy to his maternal grandmother in the little town of Eisenberg, to attend the Latin
school there. As the teachers here, like those at home,
failed, rightly or wrongly, to discover any particular talents
in the child, the parents decided that the study of the learned

professions was precluded, and destined him for business. However, the important matter at Eisenberg was not the Latin school, poor like all institutions of its kind in the country at the time, but a new acquaintance, whose influence was to affect the whole of the lad's life—an influence of one young soul on another. This was August's own uncle, Böhme, a young brother of his mother, not much older than August himself, and with similar gifts. Böhme was learning to be a manufacturer, but much preferred the reading (and to some extent the writing) of poetry and philosophy. The two youths quickly drew together, the uncle inspiring the nephew with his tastes, with consequences of far-reaching importance, the influence continuing by correspondence after the two separated.

In 1787 August was placed as apprentice with a merchant in the little town of Ronneburg. Four years later, about 1791, he returned home, where, while waiting for a suitable situation, he wrote a rustic drama, *Die Familie Thalheim*. In the same year he went as clerk to a cotton warehouse in the small manufacturing town of Hohenstein, where he found time not only for learning book-keeping by double entry and extending his mercantile knowledge, but also for the reading of German poetry and the study of French and English. He was soon able to read and understand Milton and Young, relating afterwards that on first acquaintance Young's poetry took so strong a hold upon him that he believed himself near madness. During the Hohenstein stay he prepared two little volumes of poems and essays, and corresponded largely on scientific subjects with his uncle.

Böhme, meantime, having inherited some money, had thrown up business and gone to the University of Jena to study Kant's philosophy under Reinhold. Böhme's accounts of Reinhold becoming more and more enthusiastic, Schumann's desire for a University education became less and less resistible. But where were the means to come from for the realization of the desire? He hoped to be able to make a living by his pen, and sent some of his literary work to the novelist Heinse. But Heinse's answer was discouraging, and Schumann reluctantly gave up this idea, contenting himself at Easter, 1792, with an engagement in a grocer's shop at Leipzig. This, however, was a dangerous temptation, and the inevitable happened—half a year later he left the shop and enrolled as a student in arts at the University, attending lectures and studying privately with the greatest assiduity. He lived with a friend, some savings enabling him to defray his modest expenses for a time ; then he made some money by billiard playing ; and as a last resource sent his play, *Die Familie Thalheim,* to a publisher. It was accepted, on condition that the play was transformed into a tale, which was done in a few days, and a small supply of money thereby obtained. But before another work could be got ready the money was finished, and, no other resources remaining, Schumann had to give up his University studies and return home, with the hope, however, of saving money and resuming his studies at Leipzig.

He now began a novel, *Ritterscenen und Mönchsmärchen* (*Scenes of Knighthood and Monkish Tales*), sending this, too, to Heinse for criticism. But if Heinse's judgment was no more favourable than before, his letter had some comfort, for he offered Schumann the post of book-keeper in the book-shop he was about to start in Zeitz. This step proved fateful—first, because it brought him into the business of his life in which he was to distinguish himself, and, further, brought him to the place where he was to meet his future wife, the mother of his five children—the youngest, Robert Schumann, one of the most original composers the world has seen.

Johanna Christiane Schnabel was the daughter of August Schumann's landlord, the municipal surgeon. The father at first favoured a more prosperous suitor, but eventually consented to the engagement on condition that Schumann gave up the book business for grocery. So, to make money to start the new enterprise, he once more returned home, and threw himself into writing with a zeal that knew no respite or moderation, producing in the space of eighteen months a large mass of literature—seven novels and the greater part of a commercial handbook. By this long, incessant labour he ruined his health, but succeeded in earning enough to realize his purpose, making about one thousand thalers, an enormous sum considering the remuneration of literary work at that time, and the author's obscurity and inexperience.

Having decided to settle in Ronneburg, Schumann opened a grocery business there at Michaelmas, 1795, and the marriage took place. To increase his business he used his own not inconsiderable collection of books as the nucleus of a circulating library, his wife attending to the shop and giving out the books so as to enable her husband to devote himself to literary pursuits. But in time, what with the increase of the library, his own literary activity and dislike for grocery, and, above all, his wife's inability to look after the shop any longer on account of the growing family, Schumann resolved, in spite of his father-in-law's opposition, to give up grocery and start a book business, accomplishing this in 1799.

His publications at first consisted mainly of his own productions, which followed each other in quick succession. In spite of his now very bad health the business prospered, necessitating, as the years passed, his looking out for a more favourable place than Ronneburg. Leipzig, Wilna, Odessa, were thought of, but for different reasons had to be abandoned. Then came a proposal from his former principal, Heinse, to publish a work of his, *Napoleon's Campaigns*. Schumann, it so happened, was an admirer of Napoleon, his enthusiasm reaching a high pitch when he saw him at Gera, although his feeling changed later. He therefore welcomed Heinse's proposal. But as conditions were unfavourable, and Schumann was specially anxious to make the book as widely known as possible, he conceived the idea of combining its sale with a lottery. The execution of this plan entailing more work than he could undertake alone, he got his brother Friedrich to enter into partnership with him. There still remained the drawback of the unsuitability of Ronneburg with its poor postal facilities, and Schumann had to seek seriously for a better centre. At last the brothers decided that, of the neighbouring places, none was more suitable than Zwickau.

The most important post roads crossed there ; there was, moreover, a so-called Latin school, which, in spite of its inadequacy, might nevertheless be advantageous for the book business and even for the education of the growing sons. The lottery plan fell through ; but the resolve to exchange Ronneburg for Zwickau was adhered to, and in spite of financial difficulties the removal to Zwickau was carried out. There, in 1808, August Schumann settled finally, and the firm, Schumann Brothers, was established (the brother, however, going in 1810 to Gera).

An important undertaking now begun was a pocket edition of the classics of all nations. These appeared in a very nice size, well printed on good paper—pioneers of the many modern cheap editions. I shall not enumerate the many novels and novelistic works published by Schumann under his own and other names—they are forgotten now, and were probably at no time of great importance. More important were the mercantile, statistical, and geographical works ; but the value of the mercantile books, too, is very unequal— their subjects range from commercial addresses to commercial ideas. Schumann founded and edited a provincial paper for Saxony, *Der Erzgebirgsche Bote*, which appeared under this title from 1808–12, and was followed by the *Erinnerungsblätter*, 1813–26. Noteworthy is his *Vollständige Staats- Post- und Zeitungs-Lexikon von Sachsen* ; and he left an excellent systematic, but incomplete, commercial text-book. Also to be noted are aids to the study of Italian and French—*Repertorio della Letteratura Italiana* (1804), and *Nouveau Dictionnaire français-allemand et allemand-français* (1805). A lucrative enterprise was the publication of portraits of famous military and political celebrities of the time. While the Lexicon was his most engrossing occupation, a new enthusiasm was kindled by his acquaintance with the poetry of Scott and Byron, and he resolved to make these known in Germany by translation. The translating of Scott's romantic poems he left to others ; but by diligent reading he so steeped himself in Byron that he attempted translations of his own, in the original metres. He successfully completed three cantos of

Childe Harold, and also translated *Beppo,* but here his strength failed him. The high enthusiasm he felt for this work was more than his already worn-out body could bear, and these were his last literary achievements.

August Schumann died on August 10, 1826, a man unique in his own walk of life, alike in character and accomplishment. In judging him as a publisher, we have to bear in mind his necessary calculations with regard to commercial reforms and postal and other departments of administration ; and in general we must take into account the difficulties of circumstance and bad health that beset him from the early stages to the end of his strenuous life.

CHAPTER III

Birth of Robert Schumann—His birthplace Zwickau: notes geographical, historical, and social.

THE place in which Robert Schumann was born is mentioned in archives of the early twelfth century. But we need not trouble to determine when it began to play an important part in the history of towns. In fact, like so many German towns in the seventeenth century, after the miseries of the Thirty Years' War, it had for a long time no leisure to think of progress, nor did the Seven Years' War exactly provide such leisure.

Saxony used to be subdivided into several major and minor states, to which it will be well to give some attention. Zwickau was in the Electorate, and since 1806 had been in the Kingdom of Saxony, which also contained the more important towns of Dresden, Leipzig, and Chemnitz, the other major state being the Prussian province of Saxony with the towns of Magdeburg, Erfurt, and Halle; while the minor Thuringian states included the Duchies of Weimar, Coburg-Gotha, Meiningen, Altenburg, and the principalities of Schwarzburg-Sondershausen and Schwarzburg-Rudolstadt, and the two Reuss states. Let us test our musical knowledge by naming the most famous musicians of these parts, say, Heinrich Schütz (1585–1672), G. F. Handel (1685–1759), J. S. Bach (1685–1750), the Bachs in general, and Richard Wagner (1813–83).

Robert Schumann, who first saw the light of day at Zwickau on June 8, 1810, was born under the ruling Napoleonic star, for the *Zwickauer Wochenblatt* announced military movements of troops during the night. But the notice of the birth and especially its style is of more interest. It runs thus: " On the 8th of June to Herr August Schumann, notable citizen and bookseller here, a little son."

The reader will remember that the parents were married in the late autumn, 1795, near Zeitz, where the bride's father, Abraham Gottlob Schnabel, was municipal surgeon. The newly-born babe was baptized on June 14 with the names Robert Alexander. He was the fifth child, having been preceded by three boys and a girl—Eduard (1797), Carl (1801), Julius (1805), and Émilie (1807).

It will now be our duty and pleasure to acquaint ourselves with the town of Zwickau; and the publications of the firm of Schumann Brothers, of Ronneburg, Zwickau, and other places, will help us not a little in this. First of all, let us note the two most fateful political events enacted in these parts—the battles of Jena, October 14, 1806, the Prussian *débâcle*, and Leipzig, October 16, 18, 19, 1813, the crushing defeat of Napoleon, on both which occasions the cannon thunder was heard at Zwickau. Here are some of the events taken from Dr. Emil Herzog's *Chronicle of the County Town of Zwickau* :

1805 and 1806. The pianist and composer Prince Louis Ferdinand of Prussia [who was to die at the battle of Jena] had in his suite the famous Dussek, and before leaving the barracks he not only indulged in much music-making, but gave a masked ball. Marching through. Cannon heard from Jena. Two hundred and fifty lives were lost from plague, typhus, and smallpox in Zwickau.

1807. Prussian prisoners under Saxon escort on the way to France. Contributions levied on servants, journeymen, and day-labourers.

1809. King Jerome with 16,000 troops quartered at Zwickau. At other times the Duke of Brunswick's Blacks and Junot with some French regiments were about.

1812. With this year begins the hardest time of the French war. From March 13 to the end of June 150,000 of Napoleon's troops passed through Zwickau on their way to Russia. On May 16 Napoleon and the Empress Louise themselves, with a suite of 220, arrived at Zwickau on their way to Poland. All imaginable honours were heaped upon them—ringing of bells, firing of guns, music, speeches, parades, roofs uncovered, windows taken out, and a sumptuous *déjeuner* provided by *Hofrath* Ferber. A glorious three-quarters of an hour for Zwickau.

1813. We are now on the threshold of the worst war year. Famine and contagious diseases bring the town to the brink of destruction. At the end of January the ruins of the *Grande Armée* arrive.—King of Saxony in flight before the Russians, February 26. Prussians, April 3.—Cossacks, April 4.—Viceroy Eugène, May 13.—Wittgenstein and Kleist (70,000).—All mills and bakehouses were seized and not a bite of bread was to be had for any amount of money. The cannonading at the battle of Leipzig was audible. Severed arms and legs lay heaped up in front of hospitals, and in the wretchedness of these places a murderous epidemic typhus soon developed and spread devastation through the whole town. In this year 376 citizens died (in 1812 only 183). Of soldiers there died 380 (Russians, Prussians, and Austrians). The epidemic was at its worst in November and December, when no household remained unspared. But, however bad the outlying places, the horrors could reach their height only at Leipzig, the centre of things—the cruelty, the inhumanity make one despair of any noble impulses in mind or heart.

1814. Russian fever continues. Taxes.

1815. Return of the King of Saxony from imprisonment.

Presently we shall scan the Chronicle for a few facts of peace, for small signs of civilization. But before doing so, let us consider the natural and some of the artificial features of the country.

It was said of Zwickau with excusable pride by Robert Schumann's father that the town and its suburbs lie in one of the most romantic counties of Saxony, on the left bank of the Mulde, amongst gardens, meadows, and fertile fields. The banks of the river are conveniently linked by several bridges varying in size. To the east, on the right bank of the Mulde, there rises a pleasant eminence called the Bridge Mount, affording wide and lovely views, especially over the town. West of the town extends the far higher Windberg, covered in the upper parts with fields and woods. The town lies on two main roads, one running from Dresden to Southern Germany, the other from Leipzig to Bohemia and the *Reich* by Schneeberg and Plauen. A third subsidiary road winds its way from Zwickau by Werdau in a westerly direction into Reuss and Weimar. The town lies nine German miles south of Leipzig, twelve west of Dresden, two north of Schneeberg, and four west of Chemnitz.* We thank August Schumann for his kind service.

* A German mile is between four and five English miles.

c

Towards the end of the eighteenth century, the crenellated
walls, keeps, moat, in short, the remains of the obsolete fortified
Zwickau, were either pulled down or drained and turned into
beautiful gardens, forming a girdle to the inner town.   When
this decision was once taken, it was like the pronouncement
of an everlasting blessing.   Besides the Mulde the town can
boast of other waters, chiefly of three ponds, the largest of
them two thousand yards in circumference, surrounded by
shrubs and trees, inhabited by fish and water-fowl—fishing
and shooting being allowed in season.   Let us note that the
Mulde is in some places as broad as seventy yards.

The Castle of Zwickau has sunk to the low level of a prison.
But among the public buildings, warehouses, and more considerable private dwellings, we find a few that are very interesting.   You find them, for instance, in the market-place, where
one of the most noteworthy is the Cloth Hall (*Gewandhaus*).
It is one of those familiar old German buildings with endless
roofs and gables.   We also come across some German
Renaissance and Rococo buildings.   The buildings of greatest
repute are Gothic, the chief being St. Mary's Church, the
next in importance St. Katharine's.   Robert Schumann gives
us an artistic rather than historical recollection of the former
in the course of one of his journalistic contributions.

One of the most remarkable buildings in Saxony, dark and somewhat
fantastic in appearance, it is, if not in the purest style, the work of no
mean master, showing in part the conceptions of a great mind.   A
nave with high columns spreading out into the roof, a great chancel
with pictures by Lucas Cranach, on which the orchestra was erected,
right and left all sorts of pictures and ecclesiastical rarities, gilt carvings,
old treasured banners of war-time, everything not so much overloaded
as neglected, and here and there covered with mighty cobweb, so that
cleaning and beautification seem called for.

After the Thirty Years' War the population of Zwickau
was said to have dropped from 10,000 to 4,000.   At the time
Robert Schumann became a member of the community it
stood pretty much at the same figure.   In 1820 its houses
numbered 900 and its inhabitants 4,000.   At the end of
1824 the number of the latter had crept up to 5,124 only.   It

was long before the population increased at the rapid rate of
modern manufacturing towns. Zwickau had a few industries
—August Schumann speaks in 1826 of a recently founded
chemico-pharmaceutical manufactory, some wool-carding and,
spinning, and the older trades of nailsmiths, tanners, etc.
Nor will I omit the breweries nor deny myself the joy of
boasting of one organ-builder. But Zwickau had not yet
become a manufacturing town. Its population numbered
in 1834 only 7,890; rising in 1855 to 16,052; and in 1867
to 24,509.

Now let me fulfil my promise to quote some facts illustrative of the advance of education and social conditions. Among
these the development and transference to Zwickau of August
Schumann's business play a not inconsiderable part. It is
therefore regrettable that, notwithstanding the excellence
of the sources of my information, some of the dates seem
contradictory. The removal from Ronneburg may have
been a complicated process, and the position of Friedrich,
August Schumann's brother, may have its obscurities.

Richter says quite distinctly that August Schumann removed
from Ronneburg and settled for good in Zwickau in 1808.
The following statement from Dr. Emil Herzog's *Geschichte
des Zwickauer Gymnasiums* may at first sight seem unduly
surprising. "In the year 1802 Schumann's Bookselling
Establishment, since become so famous in the literary world,
was newly founded; up till then only a few bookbinders
and printers had occupied themselves with bookselling."
We may probably accept Richter's date in view of his connection with the Schumann family. And Dr. Emil Herzog,
in the *Chronicle of the County Town of Zwickau* and in his history
of the Gymnasium, on the whole bears out Richter's statement. But an entry in the following table assigns 1802 as
the year of removal:

1791. Foundation of the private Society "Harmony."
1792. The first real Bookselling Establishment and Circulating
Library came into existence in 1792, the former lasting only one year,
the latter continuing for ten years, when Ch. L. Pfändler, the founder,
died (1802).

1802. The first permanent Bookselling Establishment and Circulating Library, started by Friedrich Schumann, a bookseller who came in November from Ronneburg.

1802. *Zwickauer Wochenblatt* founded.

1804. Foundation of the Casino.

1815. From this year dates the excellent *Sammelschule* (private school) of *Archidiaconus* Döhner.

1816. Foundation of a School Library by *Magister* F. T. Friedemann, the object being to provide the pupils with means for the study of their own literature.

1816. A general utility Society was formed in January to provide free lectures in the winter evenings in the rooms of the Latin school (Lyceum) on matters worth knowing in the lives of citizens. It was a great success. *Archidiaconus* Döhner was one of the leading originators.

1817. The Musical Society, of which also Friedemann was a member, had for its object the giving of concerts for the benefit of the poor.

1817. Difficulties of competition with England and Bohemia owing either to scarcity of work or changed systems of working.

1818. Founding of a school for girls.

1820. A cheap Monthly of general utility : *Der Erzgebirgische Volksfreund.* Continued till 1841.

1820. The finding of pit coal, which gradually revolutionized the conditions of Zwickau.

1821. German Greek Societies in sympathy with insurrectionary Greece.

1823. From now onwards the cheaper heating with coal in the stoves became more common.

1823. The hall of the Gewandhaus turned into a theatre.

1823. Execution of a soldier for murder of his foster-parents. Extraordinary sensation. All the world agog. No one would forgo a single detail of the horrible show. High and low were re-immersed in mediævalism. Military and Civil Law, State and Church, vied with each other ; trial in the market-place, immense procession to the scaffold on the Windberg, great multitudes, soldiers and civil guards, declarations and prayers by the representatives of the authorities, singing children, headsman with sword, hurdle conveying the criminal, wheel on which the dead body was to be exhibited, from which the public tore the fingers and toes, and shreds from the clothing to wear as spells and souvenirs. [Several lives and confessions were published in book-form and in magazines, and among the authors and editors we meet some of our Zwickau acquaintances.]

1825. Introduction of street lighting, after failure of the attempt made a hundred years earlier.

1827. C. E. Richter founded the magazine *Die Biene* (1827-33,

with an increase from eight hundred to five thousand subscribers),
and, after a temporary suppression, resumed publication.

1828. A long-felt want of the Zwickau Lyceum was at last satisfied
in this year by the appointment of a mathematician in the person of
Dr. Friedr. Albert Voigt, so that henceforth mathematics and physics
could be included in the curriculum. Up till then the only mathematical
teaching was the weekly hour of elementary mathematics given by C. E.
Richter during the years 1820–22.

1830. At the suggestion of C. E. Richter a social club was founded
in the hotel *Zum Anker*, which subsequently assumed the name of
Ressource, and met in the town property Bellevue.

1830. C. E. Richter with a partner named Gottlob Richter opened
in August of this year a bookshop with a newspaper reading-room and
circulating music library.

1832. Reorganization of the town Latin schools in this (the *Erzge-
birgisch-Voigtländisch*) district.

1835. The Zwickau Lyceum becomes a Gymnasium.

Apart from church music—which seems to be in hiding—
it would be possible to form a picture of the musical life of
Zwickau from newspaper advertisements and the occasional
contents of periodical summaries.   Nothing is heard of motets,
fugues, and the like ; on the other hand, we are not left in
doubt for a moment about the superiority of orchestral music.
There were two bodies that divided the spoils among themselves—the Town Musician with his men, and the military
band.   But there might be a certain amount of competition,
for instance, when the Town Musician of Schneeberg advertised in the Zwickau paper a concert of his men in their own
place.   The Town Musician (*Stadtmusikus*) was a characteristic national institution, flourishing most highly in Saxony.
He was chosen by the municipality, and had the monopoly
of the exploitation of the music-making in the district.   He
had under him his apprentices and his journeymen, taught
and directed them, sending them, according to the number
of players and instruments desired, to concerts, balls, religious
services, weddings, funerals, serenades, etc.   We need not
enter into the details of board, lodging, and pay.   Robert
Schumann mentioned that the Town Musician of Zwickau
had for several decades enjoyed the reputation of having

trained the best brass wind instrument players of the district. Speaking of old institutions, I am reminded of one that still flourished in the time of J. S. Bach, and was dying in the third, and dead in the fourth, decade of the nineteenth century, in the early years of Robert Schumann. I mean the *Currende* (from the Latin for " to run "), the poor scholars, the so-called mendicants, who walked about town at stated times singing and collecting contributions from charitable well-to-do citizens.

But of what is often the most generally cultivated branch of music—accompanied vocal solo and choral music—Zwickau had nothing in number of societies and variety of concerts to compare with what we enjoy in this country.   What have Handel's oratorios not been to us ! What, even, those of the lesser masters, Haydn, Mendelssohn, and Spohr ! The choral societies of the small Saxon towns showed little vigour and spirit, and no enterprise.   We hear only of rare perform- ances of oratorios, often at long intervals, as a general rule one of two appearing alternately—Friedrich Schneider's *Weltgericht* (*Last Judgment*) and Haydn's *Die Schöpfung* (*The Creation*). And when these occasionally crop up it is always as an exceptional effort. The first event of this kind dates back to March 11, 1802, a performance of *The Creation*, in which the garrison teacher, Kuntzsch, lately come to Zwickau, joined the orchestral forces of the Town Musician and the military bandsmen, and combined them with the choral and vocal solo forces, the orchestra consisting of sixty men.   On November 6, 1821, he brought about a performance of the other oratorio, Schneider's *Last Judgment ;* and on October 29, 1822, by desire, *The Creation.* There were some more similar events in Zwickau and in the neighbouring small towns, but nothing unusual. On October 1, 1823, Schumann's town was treated to a glass harmonica and organ recital in St. Mary's Church, with hymns, chorales, fugues, and varia- tions all of the chastest kind, as the concert-giver states.   On July 5, 1826, the church of the neighbouring town, Werdau, advertises *The Creation*, with a strong orchestra, and invites Zwickau. On October 25, 1826, on the occasion of the consecration of the town church, the cantor prepares the following programme : Naumann's *Our Father*, Lindpaintner's *Te Deum*, Sturz's *Praise of God*, and concluding chorus from *The Creation*. A great concert was held on February 24, 1830, in the more distant Nordhausen, with 350 performers under Fr. Schneider as conductor, and Spohr as solo violinist.

I shall not say much about the plenteous display of advertisements of the musical wares of the municipal and military bands, exhibited where the visitors of town and country places of amusement were likely to see them. Here are one or two specimens :

To all my patrons and friends of music I hereby make known that the Summer Concerts at the Hill Ice Cellars of the Himmelfahrt begin at once weekly, weather permitting, every Sunday and Wednesday. Schröder, Town Musician.

All honoured subscribers to the concerts that are given at Däumel's Rooms are hereby informed that on Sunday, February 11, the fifth will be held.

May 13, 1821. First concert at Neudörfel.

July 15, 1829. Fourteen daily concerts in the Shooting-house. Schröder.

The military bandmaster has advertisements, too, but fewer : one is of a mixed instrumental and vocal concert in the theatre ; a second is of a concert by the combined bands.

The most interesting part of my story is still to come— namely, the co-operating of mixed companies : on the one hand, the performers of pure tragedy and comedy, and on the other hand, of song-plays (*Singspiele*) and magic operas (*Zauberopern*). Of course, the different parts were not always equally well provided for ; the exponents of opera had often more talent than skill. Among the performances of musical works of very different merit we meet with masterpieces of the greatest genius, such as Mozart's *Don Giovanni* and *Seraglio*, Méhul's *Joseph and his Brethren*, Weber's *Freischütz* and *Preciosa*. Then there are Kauer and Wenzel Müller with their fertile naïvetés and lightnesses of the popular Viennese opera of their day, and their older successful colleague from Berlin, Himmel. Johann Adam Hiller takes us back to an earlier phase of German opera, when the composer was content to set the words of the nobility in aria form and those of the people in folk-song form.

The reader will be pleased to be reminded that Schumann may have heard some of these operas when he was about the age of twelve to eighteen.

(In the following list of song-plays [operettas] the first name mentioned is that of the manager : that in parentheses is the composer.)

1822, January. Liebl and Saul : *Fanchon, das Leiermädchen* (F. H. Himmel).

1823. Hermann's Company : For the inauguration of the new theatre in the Cloth Hall the first Zwickau performance of *Der Freischütz* was given (Weber).

1824, July. J. A. Hnadeck : *Der Wollmarkt, oder das Hôtel zu Wiburg* (Ferdinand Kauer).

1826, January. F. Michaelis : *Das Donauweibchen*, first and second parts (Kauer). *Die Alpenhütte, oder die Gefahren auf dem St. Gotthardtsberge* (?). *Die Zauberzither* (Perinett). *Die Teufelsmühle am Wienerberge* (Wenzel Müller). *Der Geisterseher* (Wenzel Müller). *Der Dorfbarbier* (Schenk). *Ehrlich währt am längsten* (?).

1827, February. Rosenthal : *Der steinerne Gast* [or *Don Giovanni*] (Mozart). *Der lustige Schuster* (J. A. Hiller). *Das Sternenmädchen im Meidlinger Walde* (Wenzel Müller).

1828, February. Sigismund Pitterlin : *Jacob und seine Söhne* [or *Joseph*] (Méhul). *Die Entführung aus dem Serail* (Mozart). *Die Mühle von St. Aldernon* (Melodrama by Schubarth). *Die Waise und der Mörder* (Melodrama by Ritter Seyfried). *Preciosa* (Weber). *Die Unsichtbare* (Eule).

CHAPTER IV

Influence on Robert Schumann of his father and mother respectively—
Family friends—Robert's early general and musical education and
achievements—Kuntzsch—Death of August Schumann.

ON the occasion of the birth of his son Robert we saw August
Schumann referred to as " a notable citizen." No doubt
this was merely a locally conventional way of speaking, and
no honest man of sense would understand the words differently.
But in this case the words coincided with reality. For
August Schumann was held in sincere esteem and admiration
by his fellow-citizens, who perceived in him a man out of the
common, recognizing not only his capacity for hard work, his
perseverance, wide information, and practical acquirements,
but also his infinite resourcefulness, bold speculation, shrewd
insight, uprightness, and reliability. Much indeed was
given him, but one thing he lacked : moderation. What he
willed, he willed passionately, vehemently. He could not
restrain, could not control the desires that spurred him on in
the pursuit of his cravings—capital for the development of
his business and means for the education and endowment of
his family. Far be it from me to suggest that in his transactions Schumann was never influenced by artistic and scientific
reasons ; but we cannot overlook the fact, which does not
necessarily carry any blame with it, that his eye was too much
on the main chance in the choice of his publications, both
literary and commercial. For instance, the publication,
already mentioned, of portraits of military and political
celebrities of the time was said to be a shrewd speculation that
laid the foundation of Schumann's prosperity. And who
could blame him for taking advantage of such favourable
time and circumstances if the work was otherwise well done ?

The project, also already mentioned, of combining Heinse's work on Napoleon with a lottery was finally and fortunately rejected, for that would not appear to be legitimate bookseller's speculation. But enough of this criticism. Let us now see what were the disastrous results of August Schumann's overstrenuous efforts at literary production.

At Leipzig in 1792 during his University studies he passed days and nights at the writing-table making and finishing sketches. Afterwards at home for eighteen months he indulged in a veritable orgy of literary creation to earn the means to start in life and marry. This bout of sitting injured his health, bringing on an abdominal complaint which increased every year. Soon after, at Ronneburg, he was stricken with a prevalent malignant type of dysentery from which only the utmost care of doctor and wife rescued him, and ever after constant sickliness was his lot, although it never quite overcame his ardent spirit. Then came the fresh stimulus of Byron's poetry, the enthusiasm and excitement of the translating of which markedly enfeebled his health until it failed completely with *Beppo*. Visits to watering-places in the hope of alleviation were almost more than his weakened body could sustain. Finally, he suffered from frequent giddiness, making occupation impossible for days together; and often in terrible throes of gout he continued to work, disregarding the entreaties of family and friends to desist, with the result that no treatment procured him relief.

August Schumann's bad health had become chronic, one may say, before his marriage, and grew increasingly worse as time went on. It is, therefore, not surprising to find that his children had no long span of life: Eduard, 42; Carl, 48; Julius, 28; Emilie, 19; Robert, 46. I shall not attempt guesswork, and nothing shall be said here about Eduard and Carl. Julius, who appears to have been a young man of great amiability and charm, but of delicate constitution, died prematurely. The main facts of the sad history of Emilie as related by C. E. Richter are as follows. The lively, intelligent and beautiful girl, the joy and favourite of her father, was attacked by a mysterious skin disease, the terrible result of which was a lasting mental affection showing at times symptoms of melancholia. " One can imagine the sorrow of the father at the sight of the beloved child cut off by her condition from most of the pleasures of life. For this very reason he loved her all the more, and she repaid his love with the greatest childlike devotion and most careful attention to all his wishes, tending him most faithfully when illness and weakness confined him to his room or bed." F. G. Jansen relates in *Die Davidsbündler* that in the end Emilie fell sick of typhus fever and drowned herself during a fever paroxysm. As we shall see, Robert Schumann was visited as early as November, 1833, by serious mental disturbances which he himself describes most distinctly, leaving us in no doubt as to the instability of his mental constitution.

What are we to think of the mental condition of Robert Schumann's mother? Her son refers to it in many of his letters to her, often gently remonstrating. June 29, 1828:

You have indeed written me some lines, but great as my longing is every post-day, I wished nevertheless that they had not been written by you; they were so gloomy that I could only come to gloomy conclusions as to your state of mind and body.

October 24, 1828:

If only you had sometimes been more cheerful I know of nothing else that could have completed my happiness; the everlasting sitting in the grandfather or grandmother chair on the step at the corner window compels my imagination to picture and think of you so and only so, as you were when you settled yourself down at the window. . . . Be cheerful; do not in sadness throw away unenjoyed the gifts of life bestowed by God.

July 17, 1829:

So write me lots of news, but more cheerful than in the last letter, which left a dreadful discord behind in my soul. . . . Farewell, then, dear mother, do not overlook that life has its sunny sides as well as its shadows.

December 4, 1829:

Oh, mother, again you can't tear yourself away from the grandfather chair, you have been sitting there for two everlasting hours, saying not a word, singing a dead old song, stroking up and down the window with your hand. . . .

A man who, like August Schumann, was so anxious a learner cannot have been otherwise than a zealous educator. He would have something to say on the subject. As early as his sixth year Robert was sent to the private school (*Sammelschule*) founded in 1816 by *Archidiaconus* Döhner, which under his direction enjoyed an excellent reputation, and flourished as an institution under a man so able, active, and enlightened could not fail to do. There appears to have been, however, yet another earlier teacher, a senior pupil from a Latin school, who attended at the house of the parents for about two years, receiving in exchange free board, a very common arrangement in those days. Inquiries on the spot showed that the available information is scanty and uncertain. Among the names mentioned I met with that of Vollert ; but the uncertainty need not trouble us. It is, however, noteworthy that this young man is credited with having imparted the first notions of music to the pupil. Robert entered the *Quarta* of the Zwickau Lyceum as a pupil at Easter, 1820, and went regularly through this and all the higher classes till at Easter, 1828, he obtained the leaving certificate with the creditable note, *eximie dignus*. He himself tells us that he was two years in *Quarta* (4th class), one year in *Tertia* (3rd class), three years in *Secunda* (2nd class), and two years in *Prima* (1st class). Herzog's *History of the Zwickau Gymnasium* mentions that in 1827 the pupils of the Lyceum *Prima* numbered 27, in 1828, 23 ; altogether in the six classes there were 182 ; in other years considerably over 200.

Among the men that formed the staff of the Lyceum were some of the most active citizens of Zwickau and no doubt friends of August Schumann. One of these was *Magister* C. F. Klopfer, subsequently appointed to the Gymnasium of Celle (1823), and professor at the *Ritterakademie* of Lüneburg (1825), among the first of the rectors to pay attention to the special study of the German language (1817–23), not only teaching literary history but also instituting regular declamatory and musical performances by the pupils, at fixed charges. He was gratefully remembered in later years by Zwickau, and his successor, Rector Hertel, remained faithful to the tradition. Friedemann, who in 1816 founded the school library, was no doubt a congenial colleague. *Archidiaconus* Döhner was another of those always ready when called upon to take up any burden.

August Schumann knew *Magister* Richter in his scholastic and early ecclesiastical stage, *i.e.* even as elementary mathematical master and as *Conrector ;* and knowing how ingenious and enterprising he was, would to some extent be able to guess and foresee how he would develop in after years. After the scholastic and ecclesiastical came the editorial and political stage (*Die Biene,* 1827–33, suppressed, later unsuccessfully resuscitated). The various enterprises of Richter comprise the establishment, with a partner of the same name, of a business consisting of a bookshop, newspaper reading-room and music library (1830). Takes part in the furtherance of several clubs and a choral society. Communal representative (1830). Paid town councillor (1832). Representative in Constitutional Diet (1833). Emigrated to America (1835), then to Switzerland. Returned to Zwickau (1849). Died April 8, 1863. But this is long after the days of August Schumann and even of the Zwickau days of his son.

Of the greatest friend of the founder of the house of Schumann I have not yet spoken, and I ought to say at once that his name cannot be mentioned in the same breath with the rest. This was Dr. Friedrich von Kurrer, a pharmaceutical chemist. The two men were not mere acquaintances, but real, intimate friends. They were choice spirits, affinities, one heart and one soul. The biographer Richter said of the two friends : " Both were lively men, enthusiasts for everything great and noble, both ardent admirers of Napoleon, both also warm admirers of science and art. Thus at last he [Aug. Schumann] found in him a kindred soul that gave him not only many-sided intellectual enjoyment, but also cheering comfort in all the troubles that befell him in business and at home." To their mutual regret the friends had to part when the Kurrers removed to Augsburg, not meeting again until the last days of August Schumann's life. He was then a wreck of his former self and died during Kurrer's visit to Zwickau.

Another friend of a cast very different from Kurrer and the schoolmasters was the wealthy shopkeeper Gottlob Rudel, a successful cloth and iron merchant. His merits were highly valued by August Schumann, for in spite of a quarrel his appointment as Robert's guardian remained undisturbed, fortunately for the ward, although the latter may have thought differently. A Zwickau acquaintance described him to me as a stiff business man who looked as if he had swallowed a ruler.

What provision did August Schumann make for the musical instruction of his son ? The teacher chosen was Johann Gottfried Kuntzsch, who, in 1797, at the age of 22, was called as schoolmaster to the Garrison at Zwickau, where before long he found a more satisfactory and permanent post. Born in the village of Wilschdorf near Dresden on December 20, 1775, he was educated at the Dresden Friedrichstadter *Seminar* (Training College) for schoolmasters under the direction of the famous pedagogue, Dinter. In 1802 (May 17) he was inducted as master of the sixth and lowest class of the Zwickau Lyceum (a secondary school) with the title of *Baccalaureus*, and on May 22 he played on trial on the organ of the principal church, St. Mary's, and is said to have done so in a praiseworthy manner. This seems to be the only record left of Kuntzsch as a musical performer. As a conductor his activity seems to have been almost equally modest, to judge from the advertisements of his festivals, which announce his responsibility as manager, but are silent as to his conductorship. But even at this early stage he was endeavouring to stir up the musical life of his new surroundings. On October 16, 1801, he combined the Town Musician and his men with the military band and a number of amateur vocalists for a first subscription concert; and on March 11, 1802, he realized the more ambitious scheme of a first performance of Haydn's *Creation*. When, near the end of his life, the people of Zwickau remembered their obligations by conferring on him the freedom of the city and presenting him with a medal for distinguished services, they had in mind less the ordinary labours of organist and schoolmaster than recollections of his meritorious endeavours and exertions for music generally. The Jubilee celebration took place on July 7, 1852, but the organistship he kept till his death, March 12, 1855. There was a change from the Lyceum to the Bürgerschule in 1833 or '35; in 1837 he retired from the schoolmastership entirely, owing to age. Up to the very last Kuntzsch was busy with music. When his landlady returned one night from the theatre she found him at his writing-desk fallen asleep, as she thought, his right hand hanging down, the ink still wet on his pen. His manners were old-fashioned and formal. For the benefit of the school children he gave the interest on 500 thalers (1842), then on 200 more, finally leaving another 100 thalers. Of Kuntzsch's accomplishments as an organist and a pianist, and the extent of his general musical knowledge, nothing is known. Did he pick up some scanty scraps of music at the *Seminar*, or make the most of fortunate opportunities later in life? Nobody supposes him to have had a regular musical education. His teaching of Robert Schumann seems to have begun when he noted down having lent the seven-year-old boy some music. Indeed, music study with Kuntzsch may have consisted in little more than his telling the pupil what to practise and the first elementary rules of fingering; his teaching being what teaching so often is but should not be—prescription without exemplification, happy-go-lucky chance without purposeful system. The dearth of information has, I am afraid, misled W. J. von Wasielewski, in his *Schumanniana* (Bonn, Emil Strauss, 1883), into being taken in by the vainglorious story of Schumann's *soi-disant* fellow-pupil, Friedrich Piltzing, the bandmaster's son, whose account of the relationship between Kuntzsch and Schumann is unconvincing, lacking in psychological verisimilitude. We must remember that Kuntzsch regarded his pupil with admiration, and that Robert was the gentle offspring of highly respected parents. According to Piltzing, the master let them play pieces, giving instruction as to fingering and expression. The pupils could never be sure of escaping a box on the ear, and on one occasion Robert's bad timekeeping was even corrected by a stout blackthorn. And what are we to think of the statement that when they were asked to play on the small organ chorales with improvised interludes, Schumann was rarely successful ? How strange !   Poor Robert !

If Kuntzsch taught Schumann so little, how was it that Schumann had all his life so good an opinion of him ?   Here is part of the letter that gives the explanation (July 27, 1832) :

> You will hardly believe, my most honoured teacher and friend, how often and how gladly I think of you.   You were the only one who recognized the predominating musical talent in me and indicated betimes the path along which, sooner or later, my good genius was to guide me. For the encouragement and for the instruction you gave the boy, the youth can offer you nothing in return but a new question, whether he might dedicate a composition to you, and the petition that you would permit it.

This is the important part, and it shows us distinctly what the obligations were.   Schumann's words are confirmed by a letter of Kuntzsch's addressed to his pupil on learning from the mother of Robert's abandoning law for music with her consent (Wasielewski's *Robert Schumann*, p. 16) :

> . . . When I think . . . of your splendid musical talent, your lively imagination, your ardent love for the art which showed itself so strongly in earliest youth, and the seriousness, zeal, and steadfast perseverance with which you pursue your aim, there can be no doubt that with such a happy concurrence of outward and inward resources only the best results are to be expected, that in you the world will number one more of the greatest artists, and your art will bring you much honour and immortality.   This, honoured friend, is my firm conviction.

There are other letters which show the nature of the intercourse and the affection between master and pupil.   They had to do specially with the loan of operatic scores, the old gentleman's jubilee, and such-like amenities.   The collection of operatic scores is really noteworthy.   Interested as I was, I wrote to ask Madame Schumann if she could tell me something more particular about her husband's pupilage with Kuntzsch. She wrote, May 28, 1889 :

> I saw Kuntzsch only once, but I know that my husband thought a great deal of him.   He was certainly not distinguished enough to be my husband's teacher, the pupil was superior to the master.

In education the relations of teacher and pupil are infinitely various, both in nature and in extent. Nothing could be more mistaken than to think of the pupil's share in the outcome resulting from the combined efforts as purely passive. The Schumann-Kuntzsch case affords a most striking exemplification of this. Here obviously the pupil's share shows itself preponderatingly active, initiative, nay, creative. But this anticipatory element—Schumann is always anticipating—is more than mere guessing. With him it is a presentiment, a revelation of a pre-established harmony, the immediate comprehension of the mysteries inherent in the art. This explains the self-confidence and obstinacy of the pupil face to face with the master, and his assumption of leadership whenever he collaborates with his fellow-tyros. It is related that Kuntzsch was displeased by his pupil's display of independence; and because he was not consulted with regard to his public performances and his private music-makings at home, he declared that Robert did not need his instruction any longer, that he could shift for himself. In fact, the youth's doings apart from his master cannot but have a special significance.

Here we have first to speak of his experiments in ensemble music. Four-hand pianoforte music presented itself most readily. The above-mentioned Piltzing, who had come to Zwickau at the age of fourteen, was one of the comrades with whom he exercised himself in this kind of music, noting, among the compositions which he remembers them to have played, arrangements of Haydn's, Mozart's, and Beethoven's symphonies and overtures—Beethoven at first of course more rarely and in cautious selection; and the original *à quatre mains* compositions of Hummel, Weber, Czerny, etc. Robert's father was always ready to supply his son with any music he wanted, pieces for two or four hands. But the young enthusiast did not stop here: imagination, speculation, and ambition called for more. Chance helped. One day, for example, he discovered among the contents of his father's shop the orchestral parts of Righini's overture to *Tigrane*, which in some mysterious way had got there. To increase the repertory recourse would have to be had to purchases

D

and to arrangements, and even to compositions by the young
maestro. The usual proceeding was to place the regular
printed or MS. parts before the respective players, leaving
the rest to be filled up on the pianoforte by Robert and by
supplementary instruments for which special parts were prepared by him. The father was generally the only auditor, and
showed his sympathy by buying a good Streicher grand
pianoforte, and desks for the convenience of the performers.

With Schumann's wonderful musical gifts it is not surprising to hear that his earliest attempts at composition date
from his seventh or eighth year; indeed, we should be quite
prepared for an even earlier date. Little dances, we may be
sure, were the first-fruits of the young pianist, and song
melodies cannot have left him long untempted. But our
maestro is not likely to have been always so humble and un-
ambitious. Among his bolder ventures we are informed of a
setting of the 150th Psalm for voices and instruments, etc.,
etc. Be it frankly confessed, however, we know very little
about these adventures which the boy undertook without
instruction. His improvising is not likely to have begun later
than his composing.

The scarcity of facts induced Wasielewski to make the
most of a brief and partly unauthenticated sketch, which is to
be found in an obscure and out-of-the-way place. The 50th
volume, 1848, of the famous *Allgemeine Musikalische Zeitung*
(Leipzig), then under the editorship of J. C. Lobe, brought
the first series of the paper to an end with No. 52, December
27, 1848, and for the next fifteen years it ceased to appear.
But in April, 1850, the publishers, Breitkopf and Härtel,
issued a supplement (*Beiblatt*, of four quarto pages, eight
columns) containing three biographical sketches of Robert
Schumann, Clara Schumann, and Adolph Bernhard Marx.
The first of these is little more than two pages long, and
although as a short sketch quite a fair piece of writing, it is not
the valuable biographical contribution to Schumann's boyhood
and youth that Wasielewski would apparently have us believe
it to be. In fact, the only part of it that has a semblance of
originality is the short passage about improvisation: " It is

related that even as a boy Schumann had a special inclination and gift for painting feelings and characteristics in tones; indeed, it is said that he was able by certain figures and passages to depict on the pianoforte so exactly and comically the various personalities of the comrades standing beside him that they broke out into loud laughter at the resemblance of the portraits." The later-known aptitudes and successes of the composer may have acted suggestively on the writer of the sketch.

Robert Schumann also took part in public musical performances. First I must mention one of Kuntzsch's grand vocal and orchestral festivals in St. Mary's, Zwickau, in the autumn of 1821, to which Schumann refers in vol. i, p. 266 of the *Gesammelte Schriften*—an article from the *Neue Zeitschrift für Musik*, July 28, 1837:

. . . Many years lie between to-day and the time when the present writer accompanied, *standing* at the pianoforte, a performance of the *Last Judgment* in the same church, where, amidst the confusion of the instruments, he had no time to investigate how the music sounded in this building. . . .

Next we must speak of his appearance at the declamatory and musical entertainments given by the Lyceum pupils. The advertisements are variously signed, mostly by Rector Klopfer or *Baccalaureus* Kuntzsch. Robert Schumann takes part both as reciter and as pianist. In the latter capacity he displayed his ability in Moscheles's Alexander March variations (named after the Russian Emperor, the most popular monarch of the Holy Alliance), the climax of the virtuoso's first, superficially brilliant, period; Henri Herz's variations on Méhul's famous air from *Joseph* (*À peine au sortir de l'enfance*); and Bernhard Anselm Weber's melodrama for Schiller's *Gang nach dem Eisenhammer*. If we looked for them, we should no doubt find in the later years of the youth's career instances of public appearances in Zwickau and the neighbouring towns, such as Schneeberg.

Of far more importance for his artistic development are certain friendly connections. The manufacturer and merchant Carl Erdmann Carus (not J. F. Carus, as Schumann has it) was born at Bautzen in 1774 and died in 1842 at

Zwickau, " a worthy man, a true devotee to art, and a warm friend of artists." His fine house at Bautzen and afterwards at Zwickau was open to every artist, whether musician, actor, reciter, or singer, etc. Among his musician friends may be named the Leipzig *Concertmeister* Matthäi, and the Dresden 'cellists Dotzauer and Kummer. Carus himself was a good violinist and also fond of the guitar and the bassoon. He had a quick eye for talent in the young, and a ready hand where help was needed. The foregoing quotation from the obituary notice by Schumann in his paper for January 23, 1843, may be continued, for the reason that the dearest recollections of his youth were associated with the deceased.

. . . It was in his house that the names Mozart, Haydn, Beethoven were among those talked of daily with enthusiasm ; in his house that I first got to know the rarer works of these masters, especially quartets, hardly ever to be heard in small towns, and was sometimes allowed to take part on the pianoforte—the Carus house, well known to most artists of the fatherland, where they received the greatest hospitality, where all was joy, serenity, and music. . . .

In 1827 there came to Zwickau a lady, an amateur musician, but well schooled, and endowed with genuine artistic qualities. Schumann felt at once that here was a kindred spirit. This was Agnes, the wife of Dr. Ernst August Carus, a nephew of the aforesaid Carl Erdmann Carus, who from 1824–28 practised medicine at Colditz, a small town not far from Zwickau. The two musicians-by-the-grace-of-God very soon found and recognized one another. They were constantly engaged in making music together—songs of all sorts, but especially those of Schubert, and at other times four-hand pianoforte music, also largely by Schubert. The friendship thus formed was continued and included the husband, who was also musical. And so it came about that much of Robert's holiday time was spent in the house of the new Colditz friends, a paradise always resounding with the most delightful music. There Robert went by the pet name of Fridolin, the sweet and gentle character in Schiller's ballad, *Der Gang nach dem Eisenhammer*, which, with B. A. Weber's melodrama music, he may at the time have been in the habit of performing.

One important means of improvement has still to be mentioned—the encountering in the flesh of a great virtuoso to be admired, imitated, and emulated in every way—in short, an ideal. This was realized when Robert accompanied his father to Carlsbad in the summer of 1819. Moscheles, one of the most brilliant stars of the time, if not the most brilliant, gave that year two concerts, on August 4 and 7. At one of them our two visitors were present and the nine-year-old enthusiast was completely dazzled. More than thirty years later, when thanking Moscheles for the dedication of his Sonata Op. 121, in E major, for pianoforte and violoncello, Schumann told him that he had kept for a long time as a relic the programme touched by the hands of the virtuoso. " At that time I never dreamed," he adds, " that I should ever be honoured in this way by so celebrated a master." The impression must, indeed, have been deep on so sensitive a nature.

I wish we could complete the review of what Zwickau did for the musical outfit of her talented son. But as to concerts and theatrical performances I could do no more than point out possibilities and probabilities. It would have been interesting to be able to indicate with certainty what symphonies and overtures he heard, and what famous stage performances such as Weber's *Freischütz* and *Preciosa*, Méhul's *Joseph*, Mozart's *Don Giovanni*, etc., came within his ken. I must leave this, however, to the reader's ingenuity to find out, and must content myself with having provided him with some of the raw material.

Robert's father was by no means unmindful of his son's needs. In the latter part of his life he was in communication with Weber with the object of inducing him to undertake the musical education of Robert. The answer is said to have been favourable but for the time indefinite. Its nature may be guessed at. It is a great pity that nothing remains of the correspondence. Weber, from February, 1821, to July, 1824, had Julius Benedict, the son of a Stuttgart banker, as a pupil, so there might have been room for a subsequent pupil. But the circumstances were now different : Weber's work had become heavier (*Euryanthe*, 1823, and *Oberon*, 1826), his health grew more and more wretched, and things were at their worst when he set out in spring, 1826, for London.

August Schumann watched the development of his son Robert with great care. Him alone among his sons he had destined for literature, art, or science. Although his own work did not allow him much leisure, yet his occasional conversations with his son on literature and kindred subjects must have greatly benefited the boy, who in after years kept his father in admiring and reverential memory. Robert Schumann speaks in his letters to his mother and others of " the great mind of my good father, who understood me early and destined me for art or music." The portraits in gilt frames of his father, Jean Paul Richter, and Napoleon, hang above his writing-desk at Leipzig. He recalls his father's urgent advice to apply himself to modern languages. The father's talk on literature and his references to the bookshop and the treasures of his private library would be infinitely instructive and fascinating, especially if intermixed with recollections of living authors, such as Matthisson and others. Robert had also his father's help and encouragement in his pursuit of coin collecting. But of unique value was the practical introduction he got at home into the making of literature. He was, for example, induced by his father to contribute, at the age of fourteen, to the publication on which the firm was engaged, *Portraits of the Most Celebrated Men and Peoples of All Times* ; subsequently he took part in the proof-reading of the new edition of Forcellini's famous Latin dictionary which his brothers had in hand.

The reader will remember our account of August Schumann's long sufferings and the hard blow caused by the death of his beloved daughter Emilie. The end came at last prematurely while his wife was at Carlsbad for the cure. In the local paper we read :

Died on the 10th August [1826] Herr August Schumann, distinguished Citizen, Merchant, and Bookseller here. Fifty-three years and five months old. (Whole School.)

The school attendance mentioned at the end of the announcement speaks of the general esteem in which he was held. It was a great loss—to the town and country at large, to book publishing and printing, to the Schumann family, who continued the business till 1840, and most of all to Robert Schumann, now left as a youth of sixteen, at a most critical period, without a father's guidance.

Piltzing, the youth who was so much in the Schumanns' house, describes the father as quiet, serious, and reserved ; the mother, on the other hand, as easily flaring up and violent, but generally good to the boys. Wasielewski, in summarizing what he had discovered, describes her as a woman of natural understanding, provincial manners, and limited education, with a certain *aplomb* in her bearing ; an inclination to a visionary sentimental exaltation combined with sudden passionate outbursts and a propensity to singularity, showing themselves later in life. Old Frau Clementine Wieck (eighty-four when I saw her at Dresden in 1889) had seen Robert's mother only once, and remembered her as a portly lady not otherwise remarkable. These and other pronouncements leave us unsatisfied, and we naturally turn to Robert's numerous letters to his mother to interpret her. But without hers to supplement them the endeavour is hopeless. According to him, his mother is a poetess and a wit, and a moral and intellectual paragon, whose letters he reads to admiring friends. I am afraid that a portrait deserving the name of likeness cannot be extracted from the letters. We must certainly discount a great deal, for, in the first place, Robert was well aware that his mother had often to be humoured ; and, in the second place, his own strong filial affection and his poetic gift of expression led him, consciously or unconsciously, to exaggerate. Two points have, however, to be made clear : that, unlike the father, the mother opposed an artistic career for Robert ; and that in other respects she indulged his desires in every way and on all occasions—in short, she thoroughly spoiled him. " Robert," she used to say, " is my bright spot " (*Lichtpunkt*).

CHAPTER V

Robert Schumann finishes his studies at the Lyceum—Survey of his educational equipment—Rudderless.

On March 17, 1828, we find the youth meditating as follows :

School is now done with and the world lies before me. I could hardly refrain from tears on coming out of school for the last time; but the joy was greater than the pain. Now the inner, true man must come forth and show what he is : thrust out into existence, flung into the world's night, without guide, teacher, and father—here I stand, and yet the whole world never appeared to me in a lovelier light than now as I confront it and, rejoicing and free, smile at its storms.

Whether the young man quite realized the seriousness of the situation of being without a guide, teacher, and father may be doubted. The " lovely light " bewitched him, and the storms did not frighten him. Death, which within the last two years had deprived him of his father, had not so far let him feel the loss at its acutest. Till he got the Lyceum leaving-certificate Robert's education was cut out for him. Thenceforth paternal guidance would become more and more needful. Owing to his strenuous business engagements and ill-health the father may not have been as watchful over his son as he otherwise would have been. With so fond and ever-compliant a mother, a father's firmness and foresight were all the more needed. The dangers of university student-life are obvious enough—greater command over money, free choice of company, free disposal of time, allurements of inexperience, lack of the safeguard of home-life, etc., etc. A father's acquaintance with a son's wants and temptations will often enable him to step in wisely and energetically where a credulous and inexperienced mother would easily be duped.

In spite of his unmistakable talents and graces, sympathetic observers of Robert Schumann at this time must have thought of his future with great anxiety, nay, even despair. There could be no doubt that he was a thoroughly spoilt child, self-indulgent in every respect. Had it not been for his native genius and nobility of character, nothing could have saved him. Without these he would have been lost in unrestrained amateurishness and selfish pleasures. It was these that gave his personality as a man and an artist its well-known and generally-recognized characteristics. For him *noblesse oblige* and *génie oblige* were equally true. And note this throughout his life : he might neglect the teaching of his masters, but his genius would afterwards make good the neglect by redoubled industry and strictness.

There can be no more appropriate time for taking stock of Robert Schumann's educational equipment than between the completion of his school studies and the commencement of those at the University. It is often said that as boy and youth he did not especially distinguish himself at school ; but I am sure that such a bright and intelligent lad as Robert could not have failed to outshine the average schoolboy. Having regard to the natural influence of the *milieu* he grew up in—paternal authorship and the whole world of books and book production and distribution—too much must not be made of his childish dramatic and other literary activities ; they furnish no proof of unmistakable merit. Nor are proofs of extraordinary musical merit forthcoming. It seems surprising that Schumann should not have preserved those of his early attempts at composition which he did-not mean to publish, yet nothing in his letters and conversations shows that he attached much, if any, value to them. As might be expected, such of his school essays and other sketches as have come down to us are more remarkable for their linguistic expression than for the underlying thought. Here we are confronted with what I cannot but call a most significant fact.

On December 12, 1825, a German Literary Society was

founded by a number of the Zwickau Lyceum pupils, of whom Robert Schumann, then fifteen years old, was the life and soul. As editor of the statutes he declared " that it is the duty of every man of culture to know the literature of his country." Robert, for one, remained true to this principle, the society continuing until shortly before his departure from the Lyceum and Zwickau, when the thirtieth and last meeting took place (February, 1828). The proceedings were businesslike, the following programme being aimed at if not always carried out :

1. Reading of some verse or prose masterpiece.
2. Reading of the biography of a celebrated author, and opinions thereon.
3. Explanations of obscurities.
4. Reading of original poems by members, and criticism by the audience.

Schiller's dramas were read with distributed parts. Why Goethe never appears on the agenda we shall learn presently. More surprising is the lateness of Jean Paul Richter's appearance. As a rule the minor schools of poets receive more attention than the great classics. The most remarkable thing about the part Schumann plays in connection with the society is his stirring, energetic activity. He showed that he was already capable of organization, management, clearness and conciseness of statement—in short, of businesslike conduct.

This leads me to speak of a matter which throws light on characteristics of Schumann's nature not at all or little known. At this time, March, 1828, his brothers, the printers, were busy with a new edition of Egidio Forcellini's *Totius latinitatis Lexicon* (first edition, 1771, Padua, 5 vols., etc.). That this piece of work should issue from the Zwickau and Schneeberg press is surprising. But so it was, and the house of Schumann made a great effort to turn out something to its credit— scholars in great numbers, and not a few of outstanding fame, being secured as contributors. Robert Schumann, too, was called in to assist as a proof-reader. To Flechsig, March 17, 1828, he writes :

I am hard at work on Forcellini, assisting with correcting, excerpting, consulting books, reading through the Gruter inscriptions; the work is interesting : one learns a great deal from it, and many an extra copper flows into one's pocket. I get a thaler for every proof-sheet. Moreover, all the most eminent philologists are at work on it—Passow, Beyer, Hermann, Beik, Matthiä, Kärcher, Lünemann, Frotscher, Lindemann, Weber, Lenz, Hand, Niebuhr, Orelli, Zumpt, Ramshorn, Wunder, Weichert, Kiessling, Jakobs, Wüstemann. Our rector [Hertel] perspires over it day and night, and is hardly equal to the task. I have just had to rummage through the whole library, and have found many MS. *collectanea* by Gronow, Gräv, Scaliger, Heinsius, Barth, Daum, etc.

We will leave Robert among the library dust, looking up the learning of the philologists; and while he is so usefully employed, we will inquire what the letters of 1827 and 1828 reveal of his acquirements and tastes in literature. He writes to Emil Flechsig, a fellow-pupil at the Lyceum, and a fellow-lodger as a student at Leipzig University. Most of the authors mentioned are the common Greek and Latin classics. As we have not yet heard of Schumann's classical studies, his remarks should be of interest, but I must say at once that, for the most part, these do not amount to much. They are often short and slight and, as a rule, are disfigured by would-be cleverness.

Of Homer he remarks, without comment, that he has taken up the *Iliad*, and intends to gallop through it by Easter. Equally without comment he states that, excepting *Philoctetes*, he has read through the whole of Sophocles. Elsewhere he writes of " the glowing south pole of Sophocles, towards which I am still bravely steering." " Lately I began Plato's *Crito*, but could acquire no taste for him, and did not always understand him "—an honourable confession that-does Schumann credit. And of course we agree with him that " Plato is food for men." The Latins bring up Schumann's pet aversion, Cicero, whom he cannot stand. " After all, he was nothing but a pettifogger, charlatan, and windbag. If he is to please one, his individuality must be ignored. This, however, I cannot do." At one time Schumann sees in Horace a libertine and nothing more. On another occasion

he calls him a fine rake—or shall we say " voluptuary " ?—
but not stopping there, saves himself by adding, " with real
seven-league poetic boots." He finds Horace's satires more
difficult than all Cicero's writings, " for while in those there
are difficulties of comprehension, in these there are only
linguistic difficulties ; the latter one can overcome, the former
can be solved only with maturity of years." Cæsar he holds
more difficult than Horace's *Odes*. Tacitus and Sallust
attract him very much. But who is the poet over whom
Schumann waxes most enthusiastic ? The " Polish Horace,"
Matthias Kasimir Sarbiewski—Latin Sarbievius—(1595–1640),
in whose new Latin *Odes* Schumann revelled as much as in
the writings of Jean Paul Richter, the German literary idol
of the day. Schumann not only passively admired, but
actively imitated Sarbiewski's muse, and tells his friend that
he had translated with all due fire some of the *Odes*, and
promises to read them at their next meeting.

The attention paid to the classical languages leaves him
little time for remarks on German authors. The star Jean
Paul does not seem to have risen for him till the year 1827—
he now quotes him and alludes to him incessantly. He
advises his friend to get from the nearest circulating library
Richter's famous romance, *Der Titan*, and is sure his friend
will thank him for the hint. Goethe, Schumann confesses,
he does not yet understand ; he often finds him more difficult
than Klopstock. As to Schiller, whom he esteemed as a
dramatist and writer of ballads, he had lately been very much
charmed by his elegy, *Der Spaziergang*. After a visit at
Teplitz to the grave of J. S. Seume, the author of the *Prome-
nade to Syracuse*, *My Summer*, and *My Life*, and *Poems*, not a
genius of the first rank, but an honest outspoken man, a
scholar, a soldier against his will in America and Europe, a
simple liver and traveller, a bold upholder of right and justice
such as appeals to the young, Schumann writes : " A wreath
of oak leaves which I cut from his grave adorns his portrait
which hangs before me."

The way in which Schumann gushes over Jean Paul
Richter is very characteristic of his immaturity at this stage

of his life. And still more characteristic is the way in which he imitates the moods, style, and mannerisms of the idol. Occasionally the specimens are poetical, oftener they are extravagant and even atrocious, and not seldom downright silly. The desire to be excessively witty or sentimental is always evident, and the lack of sincerity cannot but be sadly felt. The fact is the would-be romantic efforts tempt us not seldom to smile, indeed to laugh. In 1827–28 he writes to Flechsig:

Like a wide, wide evening landscape on which a rosy kiss of the setting sun still trembles faintly, my whole life lies before me. . . . Feelings, my friend, are stars that guide only when the sky is clear; but reason is a compass that guides the ship further when stars are hidden and shine no more.

This may seem somewhat pretentious in familiar correspondence between two schoolfellows still in their teens, but it may pass. On the other hand, our patience is tried by reading stuff like this:

I feel now for the first time the pure, the highest love, which does not for ever sip from the intoxicating cup of sensual pleasures, but finds its happiness only in tender contemplation and in reverence. Oh, friend! were I a Smile, I would hover round her eyes; were I Joy, I would skip softly through her pulses; were I a Tear, I would weep with her; and if she then smiled again, I would gladly die on her eyelash, and gladly—yes, gladly—be no more.

One more specimen, grotesque, and in the worst taste imaginable (to his mother, August 3, 1828):

Nature is the large outspread handkerchief of God, embroidered with His eternal name, on which man can dry all his tears of sorrow, but also his tears of joy, and where every tear drops away into a weeping rapture, and the heart is attuned silently and gently, but piously, to devotion.

But enough of books, authors, and Schumann's opinions concerning them. Let us now turn to the first two of the items of the famous triad of greatest joys lauded by some of the wisest, and applauded by the majority of mankind:

Who loves not wine, woman, and song,
Remains a fool his whole life long.

Or, to give the saying in the pretty Italian version :

Chi non ama il vino, la donna, e il canto,
Un pazzo egli sarà e mai un santo.

In 1827 Schumann had both a Liddy and a Nanni, and
the next years make it abundantly clear that he was far from
indifferent to the charms of the fair sex.   But at this time he
did not show to advantage.   He had been in love, and now
was out of it, but still ready to play with it.   The flames of
passion had changed into friendship, esteem, and Madonna-
veneration, and a pretty face had ceased to blind him to inner
hollowness.   It was the puppy stage—before youth has
developed the social virtues of discretion, sincerity, respect,
etc.—or describe it otherwise if you will.   Robert's talk
about his sweethearts is by no means edifying ; it has all the
assumed superiority, all the crudity, and, let us say the word,
all the silliness of these young dogs that have not yet come to
years of discretion.   Hence we can very well pass over his
amorous confidences until we encounter more serious adventures, such as have influence on the hearts and souls of those
affected.

Our next subject is Schumann's love of champagne, which
began in these early days and stuck to him all his life.   We
have here an example of his self-indulgence at any cost.   In
his letter to Flechsig (July, 1827) there are as many as three
allusions to champagne drinking.   The first indicates where
he got it, " at the Swiss Sepp's."   The following extracts
give the second and third :

To climb the many-fountained regions of sunny Pindus one must
have a friend, a sweetheart, and—a glass of champagne. . . . In the
absence of friend and sweetheart it is clear that I cannot drink champagne, the third requisite for the vigorous ascent of Parnassus; only in
the intimate circle of sympathetic friends does the blood of the grape
pass glowingly and inspiringly into our own.

A month later he writes :

Passions still surge up too mightily in me; I should like to drink champagne every day to stimulate me. I have to wrestle hard with myself. Passions are nearly always poetic liberties that moral liberty takes.

Here follows a further reflection which seems to show that the influence of one of his sweethearts was greater than I rated it:

Nanni was my guardian angel; vulgarity had already greatly soiled my youthful soul. This good girl appears to me as with a halo. I should like to kneel at her feet and adore her like a Madonna.

This last estimate, however, does not harmonize with other depreciatory remarks. After all, we have here only flirtings, only insincere play of the imagination.

But whereas Schumann's favourite drink was champagne, wines, beers, and spirits appealed to him in many forms. At Prague (August, 1827) Hungarian Tokay "made me merry." Later, in cold December at a country inn, he and two schoolfellows had each a big beer-glass of grog, which brought them warmth, elated spirits, and much jollity. Nor did he fail to appreciate beer, especially Bavarian beer. The reader, however, had better not jump to conclusions till he has considered the whole case with me. For there is a case, which resolves itself satisfactorily if thoroughly investigated.

One failing of Schumann's has yet to be mentioned. It may be considered by many the worst. He had no sense of the value of money. He found it impossible to square his allowance with his expenditure. With money in his pocket he could not resist any of his desires. If his funds had to be renewed, he was never at a loss for a remedy. There were the fond mother, the kind brothers and sisters-in-law, friends and business connections, and even the crusty guardian. You will believe me with difficulty when I tell you that Schumann is a master in the art of writing begging letters, nay, an unequalled virtuoso in all styles. He confesses his fault, blames himself, but does not repent. How he plays on his victims! How he cajoles the poor mother and appeals to her pity! How he tries in all modes and keys to enchant all and sundry, and with success! " Were I only not always such a poor, miserable Job in money matters! " To his mother, July 1, 1830:

That I am not a practical person I feel now and then, and really it is nobody's fault but heaven's itself, which has given me imagination to illuminate the dark places of the future.

To his mother, December 15, 1830:

This contempt for money and squandering of money is pitiful in me. You would hardly believe how careless I am, and often I obviously throw money out of the window. I always reproach myself and make good resolutions, but next moment I have forgotten them and again find myself giving a big tip. Foreign countries and travel have much to do with it, but most of all my confounded recklessness. I am afraid I am incorrigible.

Schumann's talent for spending money without thought of consequences manifested itself most strikingly on his Swiss and Italian journey in 1829. To Eduard's wife from Brescia, September 16:

Infinitely grateful though I must be to Eduard [his eldest brother] for having sent me so much money, yet I cannot conceal the fact that I have to do without a great many things, as on a closer inspection of my purse, I am confronted by the cursed thought that it will not suffice, and that I shall even have to pawn or sell my watch. If God would but let it rain ducats! Then all tears and letters to guardians and brothers would vanish.

The suggestion of the pawnshop is excellent.

Ah [he writes to his friend Theodor Töpken], you have not yet learnt how one feels when one has to ask the landlord's indulgence from fortnight to fortnight, and then again to come out with the request for prolongation—for you were always in funds.

The subtle casual hint of money-lenders in a letter to his guardian Rudel will be recognized as a stroke of genius. March 26, 1830:

How much you would oblige me, most honoured Herr Rudel, if you were to send me as soon as possible as much as possible! . . .

Believe me, a student never spends more than when he has not a penny in his pocket, especially in the small university towns, where he gets as much as he likes on credit. During the last seven weeks there was a fortnight when I had not a farthing, and I can tell you candidly that I have never spent so much as in these seven weeks. The innkeepers there write down with double chalk, and one has to pay with *Doppel-Kronenthaler* [double crown-pieces ; a *Kronenthaler* was about 4*s*. 6*d*.].

How Schumann must have enjoyed writing this epistle! And how the close-fisted grumpy guardian must have looked on his polite, sweet-spoken ward as a good-for-nothing spend-thrift to be kept at a distance! Well, I am sure that an Anthology of Begging Letters culled from Schumann's early correspondence would supply us with the best possible of the kind. Nowhere else would one find quite the same quantity and quality of elegance, ingeniousness, poetry, humour, and in fact, imagination. In the course of the biography brilliant examples for quotation will present themselves. To these opportunities I draw the interested reader's attention.

In connection with these letters one aspect has always appeared to me very strange. It is this, that Schumann's pride and delicacy of feeling—and he had both in high measure—seemed to find nothing humiliating, nothing galling in this. The solution of the riddle lies, I suppose, in his disregard for such trash as money.

What has been set forth in the preceding pages about young Schumann's tastes, inclinations, and habits must have given much anxiety to those interested in him. The outlook was indeed dark, seeming to foreshadow storm and disaster. But, as I pointed out early in the chapter, there was no real cause for fear—Schumann was saved by the nobility of his character and by his genius.

E

CHAPTER VI

Still rudderless—Trip with Rosen to Bayreuth, etc.—University life at Leipzig, Easter 1828 to Easter 1829—Friends and music—Wiedebein—Pianoforte lessons with Wieck.

ALTHOUGH both mother and guardian were perfectly aware of Robert's "eternal inner soul-struggle" between music and law, he left Zwickau with the distinct understanding that he would follow the advice and wishes of his elders, and prepare himself to embrace the latter profession. But there can be no doubt that this was not his real intention. He wanted only to postpone to a more convenient time a disagreeable discussion and final decision, living in the meantime free and undisturbed according to his own fancy. In this he would not blame himself for deceit, but would persuade himself that painful contentions could not be otherwise avoided.

His final Lyceum examination over (March 15, 1828), Schumann did not lose time in looking after some necessary preliminary business in connection with his joining Leipzig University. He wrote to Emil Flechsig, already there, that, leaving Zwickau on Sunday evening the 23rd of March, he expects to be with him early next day, Monday, and will stay with him; and he proposes to travel back again the following Thursday, accompanied by his friend. Of course the chronology did not turn out exactly so. One important piece of business which had to be attended to was matriculation as a student in the faculty of law, which took place on March 29, 1828. A second piece of business would no doubt be the choosing of lodgings. A third event of these days was the making of a new friend, Gisbert Rosen, who at once took possession of Schumann's fancy and heart. He was a law student on the point of migrating from Leipzig to Heidelberg. They met first at a tavern, where Moritz Semmel, another law student and brother of Eduard Schumann's wife, Therese, introduced them to one another. They were so quickly drawn to each other by their amiability and congenial tastes—one of these being their common enthusiasm for Jean Paul—that instead of separating at once they agreed to postpone it as long as possible. Schumann therefore invited his new friend to visit him at Zwickau, and offered to accompany him as far as Munich on his way to Heidelberg. How the lively romantic youths must have enjoyed the towns, historically so interesting, of Bayreuth, Nuremberg, Augsburg, and Munich, to which Schumann added Ratisbon (Regensburg) on the return journey home. But these places had other than purely historical interests. Bayreuth was remarkable not only as a characteristic example of a small, pretentious, princely capital with numerous " palace-like houses," a splendid theatre and other stately public buildings, parks, country pleasure-villas for the use of the Court, beautiful surroundings, and a great variety of lovely distant views ; it was memorable also as the home for a long period (1804–25) of Jean Paul Richter, after his death becoming a place of pilgrimage for innumerable worshippers of the poet, the traces of whose life, work, and death they piously followed. Schumann was certainly one of the most pious. He was very " blissfully living in the remembrance of Jean Paul." How thoroughly he did the thing is shown by the fact that he devoted fully two hours to an interview with Frau Rollwenzel, the landlady whose inn in the neighbourhood of Bayreuth served Jean Paul for so many years as a study and *pied-à-terre*. From Bayreuth he also sent home a portrait of Jean Paul given him by the poet's widow. In a wider sense and higher degree than Bayreuth, however, Nuremberg, Augsburg, Ratisbon, and Munich may be called historico-artistic picture-books, or museums, in which the ecclesiastical and civil buildings illustrate the different arts and styles of art. In Augsburg Schumann made the acquaintance of his father's best friend, Dr. von Kurrer, and his family; and thanks to a connection of theirs he was able in Munich to

present himself to Heinrich Heine with a letter of introduction. Heine had already become sensationally famous
since the appearance of the first two volumes of the prose
Reisebilder with occasional verse intermixtures (*Harzreise*,
etc., 1826–27), and the *Buch der Lieder* (1827). Whatever
weight the letter of introduction had with Heine, it certainly
procured the friends more attention than they had a right to
expect. Schumann had several hours of lively conversation
with the great man, and the visitors met him again later in
the afternoon at the Leuchtenberg Gallery. Thus they had
ample opportunity of becoming acquainted with Heine's
sarcasm and biting wit, for which hearsay had prepared them.
Heine himself described his outward man as "mad, wild,
cynical, repellent," in sharp contrast with the inward life.
Heine was at this time in business relation with the famous
publisher Cotta, the proprietor of influential daily and
periodical papers. His reception of Schumann would undoubtedly have been warmer if the poet could have had a
presentiment that the *homo ignotus* in his presence was
destined to become one of the most successful interpreters
of his lyrical muse.

At Munich the two sympathetic souls, Gisbert Rosen
and Robert Schumann, said farewell to each other, with what
deep regret may easily be imagined. The time must have
been delightful to them. I cannot help thinking that the
form of address adopted by Schumann in writing to this
friend, and to no other—" my agreeable [*angenehmer*] Rosen "
—has a real, and not a merely conventional, significance.
To his mother he writes, on April 28, 1828 : " Rosen is an
amiable fellow, and seasons our journey with interchange of
ideas and feelings." No wonder that after the parting much
of the jollity ceased, and the one left behind took to moralizing.

On returning to Zwickau Schumann stayed only long
enough to pick up the things he needed for Leipzig. In
spite of the entreaties of mother, brothers, and sisters-in-law,
full of questions about the experiences of his journey, three
hours later he was moving on his way, seated in a corner of
the post-chaise thinking sadly of what he left behind—kind

hearts, beautiful places, etc.—weeping quietly. On May 21, 1828, he writes his first letter to his mother from Leipzig:

I arrived here last Thursday quite well if in melancholy mood, and, with a sense of my academic dignity and citizenship, made my entry for the first time into the great, spreading city, into stirring life and the world at large. And now, having been here for some days, I feel quite well if not quite happy, and long with all my heart to be back in the greater peace of home, where I was born, and spent happy days with nature. Nature, where shall I find her here? Everything disfigured by art—not a valley, not a hill, not a wood where I can abandon myself to my thoughts—no place where I can be alone except my bolted room, with everlasting noise and racket below. This is what makes me dissatisfied.

Here you have Schumann's case in a nutshell, or at least you have part of it. The other part we shall see presently.

We saw that Zwickau, during Schumann's early lifetime (1810–28), was a small town, industrially and commercially little developed, whose population grew in that space of time from about 4,000 to 7,000. But what was Leipzig like in 1828, which Schumann describes in the above letter as " a great, spreading city " with " stirring life "? What he meant was a busy place with a population of about forty to fifty thousand inhabitants. Leipzig, as it developed during the second half of the nineteenth century, Schumann did not know at all. In the same way those who knew it at a later stage find it difficult to realize the older Leipzig of the first half of the century. The rate of increase was enormous— in 1860, 85,394; reaching in 1880, 149,081; in 1890, 357,122; in 1895, 399,963; and in 1900, 456,124. The ring of suburbs, the modernization of the older parts with the broad streets, spacious squares, parks, and magnificent public buildings—Museum, Theatre, University, New Gewandhaus Hall, Conservatorium, Post Office, Booksellers' Exchange, Imperial Law-Courts, are all of the post-Schumann-Mendelssohn period. Of the old landmarks only a very few are still standing—notably, the churches of St. Thomas and St. Nicholas, in which J. S. Bach officiated, and the sixteenth-century Town-hall in the market-place.

Grosse, the author of the *History of the Town of Leipzig* (1842), says of the Leipziger that he is—

well-mannered, has down to the lowest rank a certain polish, is civil and sociable, but not so obliging as the Dresdener, and especially in the higher or lowest ranks is fond of affecting a certain condescension when he meets citizens of small country towns. . . . Commercial life shows itself everywhere in this city of world-wide trade; the merchant-princes set the fashion because they have the money power.

Schumann's lamentation over the absence of Nature from the surroundings of Leipzig—no valley, hill, or wood—reminds one of Moritz Hauptmann's description of them as a wholly " *gegendlosen Gegend*," a landscapeless landscape, a featureless region, in short, a district without striking romantic characteristics. Things were, however, not really so bad as Schumann made them out to be, and by contradictory remarks he makes it clear that he exaggerated. At first he seemed as little inclined to take kindly to the town as to the country. The uncomplimentary epithets he applies to Leipzig include even " infamous nest," " disgusting," etc.; but this did not last beyond the first year, nay, he began to feel at home there in less than half a year.

Schumann's social intercourse in Leipzig was very limited. There were first his Colditz friends, Dr. Ernst August Carus and his wife, Agnes, now settled in Leipzig (Professor of Medicine till 1844, and thenceforth till 1854 at Dorpat). He found them still the same—" hearty, intimate, warm "—as before. This was at first the only family with whom he was on familiar visiting terms, and by whom, as heretofore, he was called by the *sobriquet* Fridolin. Frau Carus's singing became appreciated no less in public than in private, but, alas! she died as early as 1839. In the meantime the home music-making with Schumann was continued, and opportunities for meeting musical people, professional and others, were frequent. Among them was Friedrich Wieck, a personality of great importance and interest, who has soon to be introduced properly to the reader. Here I will note only the sequel from one of Schumann's letters (August 22, 1828):

I am very often at the house of Wieck, my pianoforte-master, and
have daily opportunities of getting to know the best Leipzig musicians.
I often play à *quatre mains* with Demoiselle Reichold, one of the best
pianists [pupil of Wieck's], and am to perform a concerto à *quatre mains*
with her at one of the Grand Concerts next winter.

This plan came to nothing.   Now, too, Schumann saw the
nine-year-old Clara Wieck, who a dozen years later, after a
tremendous struggle, became his wife.   It is not certain
when Robert and Clara met for the first time, though it is
just possible it was on the occasion of an evening party at the
Caruses' on March 31, 1828, where she played in Hummel's
Trio, Op. 96.   Schumann had come for a few days to Leipzig
about March 24.   We may at once note the fact that there
was a difference of nine years between the two :   Robert,
born June 8, 1810;   Clara, September 13, 1819.

The friends among Schumann's University fellow-students
were neither numerous nor very intimate.   There is first his
old school comrade and present fellow-lodger, Emil Flechsig,
not a perfect companion, but one easy to get on with, although
his unimaginative temper must have been trying in times
of low spirits.   In Moritz Semmel we have a friend by habit,
an acquaintance pure and simple, without community of
tastes and sympathy, one associate drifting beside another
from force of relationship and propinquity.   Besides these
two, Schumann names only Wilhelm Götte, a law student
from Brunswick, as one with whom he is on terms of friendship.   He calls him one of the noblest, and writes to him
as if he really regarded him as such.   Then there are two
students that became connected with Schumann through
their musical qualities, their usefulness in ensemble (trio)
playing :   Glock, first a theologian, then a medical student
(afterwards doctor at Ostheim);   and the philologist, Fr.
Täglichsbeck, a brother of the violin virtuoso, Thomas
Täglichsbeck, of Hechingen, who in 1828 made his début
at the Leipzig Gewandhaus concerts.   Schumann and Glock
were so intimate as to say " thou " to each other;   and on
one occasion Schumann writes to his mother that he would
come to her accompanied by his old friend Glock.   The trio

consisted of Schumann (pianoforte), Fr. Täglichsbeck (violin), and Glock (violoncello). When a viola was required, the Bavarian student Sörgel was called in.

I must reckon as a friend of Schumann's, Gottlob Wiedebein, of Brunswick, the composer of one, and only one, book of published songs, acquaintance with which Schumann made at the Caruses'. But there was only written communication between them—not a long double series of letters, merely two letters from the admiring untrained amateur who modestly submits some specimens of his own songs, and a single letter from the kindly-advising and warmly-encouraging older master. Wiedebein's words were words of a true friend, and must have done much good to the disciple, inspiring him with hope and strength. We shall hear more of him shortly.

Most of what we learn from Schumann about his University studies we have to gather from his letters to his mother, although some information may be culled from other letters and different sources. But to what extent can his statements be accepted as trustworthy? Only in a small degree, I am afraid. We meet asseverations like these sceptically : "I attend the meetings of the College classes regularly." " I attend the meetings of the College classes regularly and like a machine." The fact is, as I believe, that he soon attended them irregularly, and later on not at all. On July 4, 1828, he writes to his guardian Rudel :

I have definitely chosen jurisprudence as my professional study [*Brodstudium*], and will apply myself to it diligently, icy cold and dry though it is at the beginning.

This cannot be otherwise characterized than as a fib. Here we are again face to face with the eternal inner soul-struggle. Now compare the above words with the following honest confession to his mother (May 21, 1828) :

Cold jurisprudence, which crushes one with its icy-cold definitions at the very beginning, cannot please me. Medicine I will not, and theology I cannot study. I find myself in such an eternal conflict with myself, and seek in vain for a guide who could tell me what to do.

And yet—there is no other way. I must tackle jurisprudence; however cold, however dry it may be, I will conquer : if a man but wills, he can do everything. Philosophy and history, however, shall be part of my main studies too. So much for this. All will go well, and I won't look with anxious eyes into the future which can still be so happy if I do not falter.

I called the confession " honest," but Schumann is not so simple as the reader may think. We must always be on our guard, unlike the unsuspecting mother, against being taken in by the wily persuasiveness of the sweet-tongued youth. Schumann, so far from being artless and guileless, was capable of the subtlest and longest-spun-out manœuvres. He is a master of suggestions and indirect appeals. After writing early in the session about settling down to law, and his determination to be diligent and work hard, he makes it quite clear no later than August 3, 1828, that Leipzig, its professors and their teaching, do not occupy him at all, that his mind is full of Heidelberg, where he expects to be at Easter 1829, with the celebrated jurists Thibaut and Mittermayer, in all the best conditions imaginable for himself and everybody else, as he will demonstrate to his good mother without fail. As a matter of fact, instead of quoting from a letter of August 1828, I might have stated simply that Schumann had made up his mind to go to the University of Heidelberg at Easter 1829 even before he had entered Leipzig University at Easter 1828. The friendship with Rosen settled that question. And it was also settled by several other factors that swayed his imagination. Schumann was not yet a strong man. On the contrary, he pleased only himself, obeyed every fancy. I am afraid we shall often be inclined to call this amiable idealist a deceiver and a fraud, but often, no doubt—alas! not always—he is so unconsciously. This should be kept in mind in reading the following extracts (June 13, 1828) :

I go regularly to University lectures, practise two hours every day, read a few hours, or go for a walk—these are all my pleasures. In a neighbouring village, Zweynaundorf, in the loveliest part of all the surroundings of Leipzig. I have often been whole days alone, working and poetizing. So far I have had no close intercourse with a single student. I fence at the fencing school, am friendly to everybody while maintaining my own dignity; but I am most careful about making closer acquaintance—without being repellent one can assume a certain air with such people so that they keep at a distance and do not treat one as a freshman.

I spent my birthday lovingly with Flechsig in a lonely spot amidst the calm joys of nature. We thought fondly of home, sweet home, where we were wont to celebrate it if not more heartily, yet more happily in the circle of intimate relatives and friends.

The fine-feeling Schumann found nothing to please or attract him in the coarse ways of the students, with their drinking, swashbucklering, and unintellectual silliness. He writes to Rosen on June 5, 1828:

You are mightily mistaken if you believe that I am dissolute—not a bit of it—I am more proper than ever, but quite wretched here, and student life seems to me so low that I should not like to plunge into it. . . . Ah! what ideals I had formed of a *Bursche* [member of a students' club], and how miserable I found most of them.

Twice he joined one of these clubs for a short time, at Leipzig and Heidelberg, but he had too much contempt for them and their ways to feel at home among them. Moreover, he was influenced by his friend Semmel's small interest in the *Burschenschaften* (students' clubs) and his sarcasms on their nebulous patriotic notions.

His weakness for spending and borrowing money, and his total lack of responsibility in this respect, continue to be characteristics of Schumann's. Take the following requests from a letter to his mother (June 13, 1828):

My lodgings are excellent, but they also cost ninety thalers. I wish you could see them, so that you might be personally convinced of our patriarchal housekeeping—you would certainly be pleased. Moreover, I am much more orderly than you and even I had thought. The pianoforte which I have hired costs me a ducat a month; all the same, although this hired one is quite excellent, I should like to have my beloved old grand here at Michaelmas, for it is the most beautiful remembrance of my boyhood and youth, has felt with me all I have felt—all my tears and sighs, but all my joys as well. . . . If I had four hundred thalers to spare, and you and the guardian would allow it, I should at once buy myself a Stein instrument here. But the gods will probably refuse me this, and I comfort myself with the pleasing hope for the future. . . . I should also be glad if you would kindly remember your promise about the riding-lessons.

This lodging of Schumann's, on the Brühl, is described by Fr. Täglichsbeck as a more than usually elegant student's abode, consisting of two cheerful adjoining front rooms, one of which could really be called large, and was suitable for music-making, the furniture, inclusive of a very good grand pianoforte, showing a certain degree of opulence.   It was in these rooms that, when the trio players were ready to perform the work they had been enthusiastically practising—Schubert's Trio in B flat major, Op. 99—Schumann arranged a festivity to which he invited several other musical students, and as chief guest his redoubtable master, Friedrich Wieck. It was a great occasion.   Besides the music there was a brilliant supper, with champagne flowing in such abundance that, as Täglichsbeck reports, perhaps only the well-seasoned host could be said to be unaffected by over-indulgence.   In contrast to such occasions were the usual evenings spent in playing chess with his fellow-lodger Flechsig.

Visiting but seldom at the houses of friends, avoiding the common run of students, and not giving much time to beer-houses and the like public resorts, Schumann lived a very retired life at Leipzig.   So we do not wonder at his writing home for what remains of Jean Paul Richter, nor that he works a great deal in his rooms.   Indeed, except for walks alone or with congenial friends, he stays indoors playing, reading, musing.   To his mother, August 22, 1828 :

If only I had somebody here who understood me rightly and wholly, and did everything for my sake out of love for me ! I get on quite well with Flechsig, but he never cheers me up ; if I am sometimes melancholy, he ought not to be melancholy too, but should be humane enough to stir me up.   I do feel that I often need cheering up.

On the whole one is glad that he is not living by himself. The monotony and joylessness of human life with its trivi-alities often depressed him, and he still felt like an exile in

dull Leipzig.   He writes in summer, 1828: "Here in
Leipzig I fare badly, and am becoming quite soured;" and
two months or so later he confesses that for the first time
he feels really at home in Leipzig, hoping that winter will
make up for the painful hours of summer.   Of course we
must be careful to distinguish, in the case of such an easily
affected, sensitive individuality, between passing moods and
opinions on the one hand, and character and fundamental
principles on the other.   His varying judgments on his less
intimate friends—Flechsig, Semmel, etc.—cannot be depended
on.   And it is the same with his varying views on things at
different moments.   Let us remember, in connection with
Schumann's tendency to sombreness of temperament, his
remark that his is a lyrical nature; and then his pathetic
words to his mother (August 31, 1828): "I am too soft, I
feel it clearly; everyone who feels deeply must be unhappy."
This reminds me of an apt remark about Jean Paul which
we meet in one of Schumann's letters to Rosen (June 5,
1828):

If everybody read Jean Paul, they would assuredly be better but
unhappier.   He has often brought me near madness : but the rainbow
of peace gleams through all tears, uplifting and gently irradiating my
heart.

The only musical occupation of Schumann since his
arrival in Leipzig which we have so far discussed is his
practising of ensemble music, of trios and quartets.   Concerning this we have to note only that it was carried out with
the help of amateurs.   Allusion has also been made to those
excellent music-lovers, the Caruses.   What is strange is that
among all the available correspondence we come across only
one reference to the varied public musical life of Leipzig.
It is in a letter to Rosen: "The splendid Grand Concerts
complete my happiness."   This refers to the famous Gewandhaus concerts which go back as far as 1781, and J. Adam
Hiller; and which in 1828 were under the management of
twelve directors, chosen from the most esteemed citizens of
the town.   The main series of concerts numbered twenty-four,

not to mention extra concerts, and special concerts, such as concerts for the poor, etc. The orchestra was an excellent body of players employed at the concerts, at the theatre, and at two of the principal churches. From 1827 to 1835 Christian August Pohlenz acted as conductor of the Gewand-haus concerts, and Heinrich August Matthäi as leader of the orchestra (*Concertmeister*). Schumann, in his letters, says nothing of the happenings at the opera, nothing of the happenings at the churches, nothing, for instance, of the interesting function briefly called the *Motet*, sung by St. Thomas's choir, trained by the cantor of the church school. As I said, this is strange. But then, after all, Schumann was as yet an outsider, not one of the musical world.

However, two other events in Schumann's life at this time are of greater importance than the above—the correspondence with Wiedebein and the teaching of Wieck, for these we may look upon as the first serious, though still hesitating, endeavours after professional study of his art.

Gottlob Wiedebein (1779–1854) came of a thoroughly musical family, and was endowed with a specially enthusiastic musico-poetic nature. At the time of the Wiedebein-Schumann correspondence, Wiedebein was *Capellmeister* at Brunswick, enjoying a good reputation for musicianship among his contemporaries. Bad health obliged him to retire from his post in 1830. He was a composer, but not a very productive one. For this his modesty and diffidence on the one hand, and his excessive morbid fastidiousness on the other, may have been answerable. Among the works he was known to have composed was the one and only book of songs which he published about the middle of the third decade of the nineteenth century. It made a very different impression from similar single publications of other com-posers. The number of the better class of public professional singers and amateurs that it reached is really remarkable. That Schumann was not the only admirer we may gather, for instance, from the glowing words of a well-known singer who spoke of Wiedebein's "depth of feeling, soulfulness of melody, and rapturous melting moods." The story of a short acquaintance between Wiedebein and Beethoven is told by Jansen in *Die Davidsbündler*. Their intercourse by correspondence and conversation was very characteristic of both men. Each seemed to feel instinctively the sincerity of the other's nature, though they had regretfully to pass by on their respective ways.

Schumann, as already related, made the acquaintance of Wiedebein's one song *opus* at the Caruses', and his admiration did not let him keep silent; he was impelled to tell the master what he felt on hearing the songs, and also to ask his advice concerning his own attempts. His first letter to Wiedebein was written on July 15, 1828. I shall extract from it only the main and most characteristic points. Let me begin by saying that it is written in the right spirit of devotion, reverence, and modesty, proper from a youth of eighteen. For him the master's songs are sublime beyond all praise; they have procured him many a happy moment; they have unriddled the veiled words of Jean Paul's mystic spirit-tones, much as two negatives make one affirmation; the whole heaven of tones, those tears of joy of the soul, irradiating his every feeling. It was Kerner's poems, with that mysterious supernatural power often found in Goethe and Jean Paul, that first induced him to try his weak powers, because every word in them is, indeed, a tone of the spheres [allusion to music of the spheres] which the [musical] note alone can determine. In another part of the letter Schumann prays: "Be indulgent to the youth who, uninitiated in the mysteries of music, was himself fired to create with uncertain hand, and to lay before you these attempts for your kind but strictly impartial judgment." And Schumann signs his letter "*Studiosus juris,* living on the Brühl, No. 454, 1st floor." (For this correspondence see F. G. Jansen's *Die Davidsbündler,* pp. 118–21.)

Wiedebein's answer, written two weeks later (August 1, 1828), must be given almost in full:

DEAR SIR,
Your kind confidence has given me pleasure; here, then, is frankness in return for confidence. Your songs have many, sometimes very many, shortcomings; but I should call them sins, not so much

of the spirit [*Geist*] as of nature and youth, and these are excusable and pardonable when pure poetic feeling, genuine spirit [*Geist*], shines through. And it is precisely that which has pleased me so much.

If by these sins of nature and youth I mean the visible want of sureness in the elements as well as in the higher study of the art, I cherish the lively wish to make myself more clearly understood to you some years hence. Meantime you will not take unkindly, nor misinterpret, some other remarks.

During the moment of divine consecration we should abandon ourselves completely to the fine inspiration; but afterwards calm searching reason must have its due and with its bear's paws scratch out mercilessly any human imperfections that have crept in. What is wild may grow up wild; nobler fruits demand care, the vine needs not only most diligent cultivation, but pruning as well; and if both were carried out in beautiful Italy, the gift of the gods there would not turn sour with years.

Above all, look to truth. Truth of melody, of harmony, of expression—in a word, poetic truth. Where you do not find this, or where you find it even threatened, tear out, even should it be your dearest.

First examine—each singly—the declamation, the melody, the harmony, and then the expression and spirit which should make the whole divine; and if then all the parts harmonize, and it feels to you like the moment at which two stretched strings blend into one tone— then do not trouble about the world, you have lifted the veil. But if you find doubts, of whatsoever kind, believe me again, sin has crept in.

You have received much, a great deal, from nature; use it, and the respect of the world will not pass you by. . . .

This letter was reprinted by Schumann in the *Neue Zeitschrift für Musik*, April 3, 1838, without the name of the writer, and with the title: " Letter of an old Master to a young Artist," accompanied with the footnote:

The above letter seems to us to contain such golden words that we communicate it unchanged. The worthy writer has made himself famous especially by *one* book of songs, one of the most beautiful of modern times; also the young artist has since grown older, and his name is well known.

We agree with Schumann: " golden words " indeed. And we can well realize the joy of the young man in reading the wise and timely advice and the generous, prophetic encouragement. Four days later (August 5, 1828) Schumann posted his answer to his " sacred priest in the mysteries of the world of tones," and must have shown him how full his heart was of gratitude. His promises, however, were not immediately fulfilled; for instance, harmony, counterpoint, etc., were not studied till later. Here is the chief part of the letter with its interesting and instructive frank confession of his complete ignorance of technique—interesting and instructive, too, are the enthusiastic, significant æsthetic views, in spite of their awkward and uncouth form :

My warmest, warmest thanks for the letter, in which every word is dear and sacred to me. I had probably forgotten to tell you in my last letter that I know nothing of harmony, thoroughbass, etc., nor of counterpoint, but am a pure and simple disciple of guiding nature, following solely a blind, vain impulse that wished to shake off all fetters. But now the study of composition shall be taken in hand, and the knife of Reason shall mercilessly scratch out all that unruly Fancy—which to youth at least presents herself as ideal and life, and does not get on very willingly with her co-ruler Reason—would fain smuggle into his territory. Certainly, the hard lion-paws of Reason should not completely crush the tender hands of the lyrical Muse of tones who plays on the keys of our feelings; yet Reason, as with the Romans, should not be the maid who bears the train of Fancy, but should go before, with lighted torch leading her into the world of tones and lifting the veil. This last is the solution, and difficult because tones are indeed veiled flames of Venus, seen smiling through a veil too tenderly ethereal and unearthly for us to lift. Therefore music does not quiet the strife of the feelings, but rather stirs it up, leaving behind that confused, nameless something; then such a feeling of well-being takes possession of one as if a sweet, peaceful rainbow had appeared in the heavens after a thunderstorm. This, too, was my experience when I heard and played your songs.

And so with fresh courage I will mount the steps that lead to the Odeon of tones, and in which I see you as my sole and unsurpassable ideal. Allow me to give you an account of my poor endeavours at the end of a year.

The whole world lies open before my youth, and I will take courage and do what I can. . . .

Writing to Schumann's mother, who had asked for advice as to her son's taking up the career of a musician, Friedrich Wieck (August 9, 1830, Litzmann's *Clara Schumann*, i, 21–24) mentions incidentally and severely criticizes the lessons which the young man took from him at Leipzig in 1828–29. Schumann, as Wieck makes clear, was a most unsatisfactory pupil, and could not be otherwise to any strict teacher such as Wieck undoubtedly was.   But it must be admitted that, in spite of his irritating shortcomings, so highly gifted a scholar cannot but have profited much.   The master's first complaint was of Robert's erroneous view that " pianoforte playing consists entirely of sheer mechanism."   He held that Robert's chief difficulty was " the calm, cool, carefully-considered and persevering conquest of the mechanism as the primary raw material of all pianoforte playing."   And he complained that when, after hard struggles with, and much contradiction from his pupil, and unheard-of pranks which his unbridled fancy played on them both, he at last succeeded in convincing the recalcitrant student of the importance of " pure, precise, equal, clear, rhythmical, and, finally, elegant playing," this often bore little fruit at the next lesson ; and when Wieck returned to the subject, as he was in duty bound to do, the incorrigible disciple would absent himself, sending all kinds of excuses week after week.   Nor could Wieck induce him to adopt the special instruction in chord playing which it was the master's habit to inculcate upon all his pupils.   It was plain that he was an amateur, and was unlikely to become anything else.   He wished to be a dreamer and an idler.   But from what Schumann says about his play-ing in Heidelberg, and his comparison of his own playing with that of others, we see that against his will a good deal of Wieck's excellent teaching had filtered into him.   Wieck said that when Schumann left Leipzig for Heidelberg he knew more about pianoforte playing than he did afterwards. In short, my judgment is that he was improving, though not in a thorough way.

And here we will interrupt for a while the course of the general narrative, and dwell in a separate chapter on the personality of Friedrich Wieck, who in various ways plays an important part among the dramatis personæ.   After this episode we shall resume in Chapter VIII the narrative of Chapter VI.

F

CHAPTER VII

Friedrich Wieck (1785–1873)—Birth and education—Personality—Teaching method.

FRIEDRICH WIECK was born at Pretzsch, a townlet midway between Wittenberg and Torgau on the Elbe, on August 18, 1785, the second of five sons of a poor trader come down in the world. Thanks to a variety of supports, he was enabled to attend the Gymnasium of Torgau for four and a half years (1800) and the University of Wittenberg for three years and two months (1804), theology being the aim of his studies. The bread and butter sent him by his mother was at one time supplemented twice a week by plates of hot soup given him by kind people. It was a blissful time when somewhat later a family invited him to a complete dinner—roast mutton and green beans usually—the thought of which would make his mouth water all the week. The lessons in reading and music which he was engaged to give for a fee of about twopence a week were, of course, very helpful, especially when in the case of one family it amounted to sixteen groschen a month. The clothing, too, of the poor lad must have been very insufficient, for the same coat had to serve him for summer and winter alike. With regard to his music, " helpless and very poor, I had to rely solely on my self-education, and on the many chances of my destiny." In fact, his music studies were simply a picking up of the art in the society of amateurs and professional musicians he frequented—players on the pianoforte, harp, violin, bass, horn, etc. From joining the school choir he was unfortunately prevented by his weak chest and suspected tendency to consumption. However, he was not altogether without lessons. When *Oberförster* Herr von Loewen thought his wife and daughters would be

the better for some finishing lessons, he induced the famous
pianist and harpist Milchmayer (or Milchmeyer), then living
at Dresden, to visit them for some time at Torgau, and persuaded the great man to give Friedrich Wieck, too, the benefit
of some six or eight gratis lessons.

There is little that is not obscure in Milchmayer's life.
The early authorities give his baptismal name as " Johann
Peter." What determined Riemann to prefer " Philipp
Jacob " is not explained. Munich, Paris, Mayence, Dresden,
seem to have been the principal stages in the man's life. He
had the reputation of being a clever mechanician, but this
part of his capacity has left no trace unless it be in a description he gives of an instrument. It is different with his
capacity as pianist and harpist—in short, his executive
musicianship. His residence in Paris is said to have extended
from 1770 to 1780. His titles included that of Bavarian
Court Musician and Member of the Musical Academy. In
1797 he himself published at Dresden *Die Wahre Art das
Pianoforte zu spielen* (*The True Way of Playing the Pianoforte*) ;
and about the same time or soon after, before the end of the
century, he likewise published a Pianoforte-School in Parts,
a selection of pianoforte pieces of famous composers graded
as to difficulty, with fingering, expression, and ornaments.
He declared in 1787 that twenty-five years earlier he had
already begun to give instruction in pianoforte playing. A
criticism of the *Wahre Art* in the *Leipziger Musikalische
Zeitung* is very severe ; the writer remarks that the author
says only what he heard and saw in Paris and Lyons. At
Torgau Milchmayer was a paralytic, a mechanical contrivance
moving him from his bed to the pianoforte.

Friedrich Wieck passed all his examinations, theological as
well as others, satisfactorily, and at last a day was appointed
for the preaching of his trial sermon. Alas ! this was the
only sermon he ever preached. I do not know the inwardness
of this—was it dissatisfaction with himself or despair of his
prospects ? Perhaps he may have had no choice but that
between starving or accepting a tutorship. Thus nine years
had to be spent for the most part on the estate of an eccentric

nobleman, and the rest of the time in more normal and less trying conditions with a general's widow of good birth. In the former case he had as fellow-tutor the musician Bargiel—let us note the name, we shall hear of him again. Next, Wieck was attacked by a troublesome face complaint, which dragged him from doctor to doctor, and no cure was found until he consulted the celebrated homœopath Dr. Hahnemann of Leipzig. But at last the time had come when a definite career promising a livelihood had to be chosen. He decided to establish, as the dictionaries and biographies used to put it, a pianoforte manufactory combined with a circulating music library, at the same time taking in hand the teaching of the pianoforte. But there was in fact nothing like a real manufactory that supplied new instruments. The second Frau Wieck told me that her husband had a pianoforte manufactory for a short time only, but even that is perhaps saying too much, although I should on the whole rely on her authority rather than on that of any other contemporary. In the diaries and letters of Clara (Wieck) Schumann, we have the two business occupations of Father Wieck properly proportioned. He had a circulating music library and along with it [nebenbei] a small trade in pianofortes. If he sold new instruments he procured them from makers with whom he had a business connection, like Johann Andreas Streicher of Vienna, and others. For this, enterprise was not enough : capital, too, was needed ; but that, six thousand thalers, was supplied by a trusty friend who believed in the " stickit minister."

As to his pianoforte teaching, at first he considered it advisable to study Logier's system, which then enjoyed great favour. By and by, however, this did not give all the satisfaction it promised at first. Original ideas forced themselves more and more on Wieck, and he substituted more and more distinctly a method of his own.

Now that he thought he had excogitated a way of livelihood he thought, too, that this was the time to choose a wife and make a home for himself. His choice fell on Marianne Tromlitz, daughter of the Cantor of Plauen, a musical maiden of nineteen, a pupil of his own, and the marriage took place on May 23, 1816. But, as the result showed, the union was ill-advised, for—owing to incompatibility of temper—the young wife was so unhappy that she left her husband on May 12, 1824, and married again after a divorce. She must have been a person of much energy and spirit, for she bore her husband five children, gave many lessons, and played pianoforte solos three times at the Gewandhaus concerts, in 1821, 1822, and 1823. There were to begin with two girls, of whom the first died shortly before the birth of the second, this second girl being the famous Clara. Of the less important boys, I need mention the eldest only, Alwin (1821–85), who studied the violin under David, and began his career in Russia (Italian Opera Orchestra). Later on he returned to Germany and, following in his father's footsteps, taught the pianoforte and singing. After a short attempt to form a teaching connection in Leipzig, the first Frau Wieck, now Frau Bargiel, settled in Berlin, where husband and wife continued their profession as music teachers. One of her children of this marriage was the excellent composer and teacher of composition, Woldemar Bargiel (1828–97), who was consequently a step-brother of Clara Wieck. The reader will recognize in Bargiel *père* the fellow-tutor in music of Wieck during his first general tutorship.

Wieck was not in a hurry to marry again; he now took time for reflection—about four years. At last he thought he had found what was necessary for his own and his family's happiness. Clementine Fechner, born at Gross-Särchen, Lower Lusatia, on October 5, 1804, was a clergyman's daughter, and sister of the famous Professor of psychophysics, Gustav Theodor Fechner, and of another brother, Eduard, who successfully cultivated the art of the brush and pencil in Paris. As the first Frau Wieck took and kept the youngest child (Victor) of her first marriage, and had to give up Clara into her father's hands at the age of five, the second Frau Wieck had at her marriage three step-children—Clara, Alwin, and Gustav—and as time went on, three of her own : Marie, musically the most distinguished of the second Wieck family; the likewise musical Cäcilie, who performed in public at the age of twelve, but whose career was cut short by a mental disease; and Clemens, who died in 1833, not much more than three years old. Frau Wieck was devoted to her husband and the children. After forty-five years of married life with Wieck, and sixteen years of widowhood, at the age of eighty-four she volunteered to me the following rare praise of her husband : " He was amiable not only in company, but at home too." But excellent at heart though Wieck was as a man and as a husband, he was not an angel —nay, it may even have to be admitted that he had trying faults. I am sure that a wife, to get on with him, must have required a great deal of tact and managing ability, in which respects the old lady with the shrewd and watchful eyes seemed to me to have been well equipped all her life.

Wieck, with his confident belief in his own rightness derived from constant and acute observation and carefully-worked-out conclusions, was naturally critical, disputatious, pugnacious, and opinionative; and consequently, with his lively spirits and hot blood, he was easily excitable, and flared up into a passion without a moment's notice. There was a distinct tartness of thought and expression in him. Tartness was, indeed, a peculiar characteristic of Wieck's individuality. Rudeness and causticity not only came to him naturally, but he affected them purposely and cultivated them, as the sayings and dialogues in *Clavier und Gesang*, and his *Peasants' Adages* (*Musikalische Bauernsprüche*) prove. Honest man though he undoubtedly was and the possessor of excellent qualities, he could on occasion be harsh in his actions, even thoughtlessly cruel. Like other men of strong character, he had the defects of his qualities. He dearly loved to indulge in controversy, being sure he was the man to put everybody right; to meddle with things most people have nothing to do with; and to clothe his ideas in the most caustic and rude words he could think of. This people were apt to call impertinent and take offence at, and would have done so oftener had this caustic rudeness not been on the whole rather amusing. Schumann, who had a good opinion

of Wieck, wrote on one occasion to his mother : " You can
have no notion of his fire, his judgment, his attitude to art ;
but if he speaks in his own or Clara's interest, he becomes
quite savage " (December 15, 1830). Dorn, who knew him
well, appreciated his solid worth, while equally ready to laugh
at his weaknesses. " He had read, heard, and meditated so
much that, with his acute understanding but extremely
sanguine temperament, he was not disturbed by the fact
that he stood alone in his judgments." The following
anecdote told by the almost always sarcastic and sometimes
bitingly sarcastic Dorn is characteristic of Wieck's foible,
his well-known pride, his overweening vanity with regard to
his genius as a teacher, and his jubilations over his pupils—
more especially his daughters, and most especially his eldest
daughter, Clara, " my Clara," to whom this name was given
at baptism to indicate her destiny—the illustrious, the peerless,
the glorious one. " Yes, my dear friend," said Wieck to
Dorn, " but I said ten years ago to Liszt that if he had had
a proper teacher he would have become the first pianist in
the world."

Now, however, the moment has arrived when we have to
inquire into Wieck's method. To begin with, it has to be
stated that whereas it was universally admitted that Wieck
was an excellent teacher—one might even say a heaven-born
teacher—he was neither a virtuoso nor a composer, nor to
any great extent a notable writer on music. But he sometimes accompanied his pupils on the pianoforte ; and in his
younger days he had made attempts at composition, even
corresponding about them with Weber ; and now and then
he took pen in hand and expressed his thoughts more or less
effectively. A. v. Meichsner, in his booklet *Friedrich Wieck
and his Two Daughters*, says : " He himself did not play as a
virtuoso, but as one who had feeling in every finger-tip."
The manner in which he performed accompaniments he
regarded with pride and satisfaction. I never heard discussions on or even allusions to any solo pianoforte performances of Wieck's. What, however, is much more
extraordinary is that in spite of much inquiry I have never

yet succeeded in meeting a fairly adequate presentation of Wieck's method by himself, by his pupils, or by his critics. It is extraordinary, and yet one might say it is quite in the nature of things. A method, unless it is merely a concoction of a few tricks, is difficult to reduce to a system of rules. Thus, perhaps, after all, doubt in the existence of a Wieck method is not an unwise position to start from. My theory of the master's teaching is this. Wieck was an acute observer of the processes of pianoforte playing and the constructive and obstructive ways of pianoforte players. Next to seeing things as they were, his concern was to explain them in the clearest manner possible—simply and rationally. From this resulted a grand common-sense system of instruction in which the teacher appeals continually to the experience and reason of the pupil, and avoids all that does not conform with the most favourable conditions. Wieck's most important publication is *Pianoforte and Singing : Didactic and Polemic.* (*Clavier und Gesang. Didaktisches und Polemisches von Friedrich Wieck.* Leipzig, 1853. F. Whistling.) The reader will no doubt peruse it with interest, but he will be surprised to find how little his curiosity is satisfied. I am quite sure that when I questioned Madame Schumann—the most carefully, patiently, lovingly, and perfectly trained pupil that ever went through his hands—about her father's method she was taken aback and really puzzled. She said that her brother Alwin Wieck's *Materialen* (finger exercises) gave an idea of it. Of course they can do nothing of the kind. Then, trying as it were to seize the main features of the method, Madame Schumann remarked (conversation at Frankfurt on June 12, 1889):

> He aimed especially at equality of touch, and the cultivation of right feeling for the use of the soft pedal [*Verschiebungsgefühl*].

In trying to give an analysis of Wieck's method, we shall do best to gather it from what has come from his own lips and pen, here and there slightly supplementing it by additions from other sources. As far as possible his own words will be adhered to. In his *Clavier und Gesang*, his main contribution to the subject, Wieck disclaims the intention of writing a learned and systematic book. What alone he claimed — passionately claimed — are these three things : (1) the receptivity given him by nature for all that is good and beautiful ; (2) a right instinct and a passable understanding for avoiding the untrue and the ugly ; and (3) the impulse to higher knowledge which guided him to observe all he encountered on his life's path. In fact, he ventures to say without fear that he had striven according to his powers to fulfil his destiny on earth. Note carefully these three qualifications, these three possessions of his. Otherwise you will miss the secret of the man's success. Wieck asserts that he was never a pedant, never under the domination of formulas (*ein Chablonenmensch*), that on principle he avoided slavish obedience to a method. He was a teacher who lived wholly in his work ; his heart and soul were in his lessons. Hence he never gave too many lessons, so that he might be able to devote all his interest to his pupils. This was Fräulein Marie Wieck's explanation. Wieck, it is clear, was not one of the money-loving fashionable teachers who teach from early morning till late at night, and never seem to require a moment for planning and preparing their lessons. Daily he took counsel with himself about the education of his daughters and the others whom he formed to be artists ; and this we gladly allow him to have done, as he himself says, with some talent. Qualifications of a good master are, he considers, firmness, decision, energy, keen and subtle observation, skill in the art of saying not a word too much or too little, sureness of oneself and one's subject, and constant intentness on increasing, with considerate kindness, the courage and confidence of the pupils. What Wieck most emphatically insists on is that he never bored his pupils during the lessons ; as to whether he did so at other times he pretends to be no judge. But everyone, he says, had to admit that his pupils, without exception, always looked forward with pleasure to their lessons ; which must be so because progress was visible and gratifying, and everything developed naturally. To stimulate, tutor, inspirit, and form the talentless and languid, was nòt, he said, in his line—in fact he could not do it at all. Now we come to a fundamental point in his doctrine. A teacher of the pianoforte, whether he be a teacher of the elements or of the higher developments, must understand the art of singing. Wieck studied the art under the famous Dresden master Mieksch, who derived from the Italian school, of which Wieck, too, was a follower. When he speaks of singing, he means beautiful singing (*bel canto*), the basis of the finest and most perfect musical presentation, and also of the most beautiful possible touch on the pianoforte. The following saying testifies to Wieck's wide and conscientious views on art and artists : Even the most experienced artist always remains a pupil, and the teaching of the art is a daily learning.

After the reader has come so far he will probably exclaim, " This is all very excellent, but these generalities arouse a keen desire for particularities." But this is the way of Wieck, who left these things for *viva voce* communication at the lessons. It is, however, clear from the few hints we get here and there that in every case the master takes the way of nature. A few examples will show what is meant.

Some familiarity with the keyboard precedes the knowledge of notation ; acquaintance with the treble notes precedes that with the bass notes. Pupils should not have to grapple simultaneously with physical and mental difficulties. In advising playing without music at first, the master had in mind the acquirement of a good touch. For the production of a good *legato* tone Wieck recommended loose and quiet fingers and a docile and mobile wrist without assistance of the arm. In the early stages he gave only easy and short pieces, with no outstanding difficulties, as the correct and skilful performance of them could not but give the executants pleasure. The struggle with isolated passages embitters all joy, lames talent, and produces weariness and disgust. Wieck did not approve of too much practising. Fatigue has to be avoided. He never forced his daughters in any way, although he guided them up to the highest virtuosic development—a statement fully endorsed by the daughters. He had a wide knowledge of pianoforte literature which enabled him to choose what was best for his pupils. He made them play a good deal of superficial virtuosic music—Herz, Czerny, etc. The classics he recommended only for those of his pupils who were ripe for them, and as far as they were ripe for them. On the other hand, he was among the very first to introduce Chopin, Schumann, Henselt, etc. The use he made of the superficial virtuosic music was well considered —he wished to further ease, elegance, and brilliancy. Wieck tells us what he tried to teach Schumann, and no doubt his pupils generally—" pure, precise, equal, clear, rhythmical, and, finally, elegant playing."

Among the pupils of Wieck was Hans von Bülow, a paragraph in one of whose friendly letters to his master runs thus :

It was you who, first laying a firm foundation, taught my ear to hear, impressed right rules and logical order on my hand, led my talent out of the twilight of the unconscious up into the clear light of the conscious. He who fostered the invisible seed with such unusual conscientiousness, care, and love, may claim the real co-creator's share in the developed fruit.

And now I should like to conclude this chapter by attaching as motto to Wieck, always intent on the True, the Beautiful, and the Artistic, the enumeration of what he considered the three indispensable qualifications of a good pianoforte and singing master :

Finest taste,
Profoundest feeling,
Most delicate hearing.

CHAPTER VIII

By diligence from Leipzig to Frankfurt-on-the-Main : Stay of a few days at Frankfurt, a short tour on the Rhine, arrival at Heidelberg on May 21, 1829—Three terms at Heidelberg (summer 1829 to autumn 1830), with autumn holiday in Switzerland and Northern Italy, 1829—Thibaut—Paganini—Receives his mother's permission about August 1830 to exchange law for music—After a visit to the Lower Rhine, returns in autumn 1830 to Leipzig to devote himself entirely to music.

THE close of Schumann's first year in Leipzig was rather eventful. Early in the year his delicate brother, Julius, fell dangerously ill. The worst was feared, and old Frau Schumann appealed to Robert not to leave her alone should the worst befall her. By the end of April, however, the sick man was out of danger. It was about this time—to be exact, on April 30—that Schumann wrote to Rosen of a " brilliant concert at Zwickau," at which he played before an audience of 800–1000, one of a cluster of festivities including various kinds of balls—*bal paré*, *thé dansant*, and school ball—dinners and *déjeuners*, and a quartet entertainment at the elder Carus's, with *Concertmeister* Matthäi of Leipzig. An event of another kind made it terribly difficult for him to say farewell to Leipzig. The reader will easily understand. " The soul of a beautiful, bright, and good woman had captured mine ; it cost struggles, but now all is over." That is to say, one more illusion had gone the way of the many others. Would it be cynical to say : " Heaven be thanked ! " ? He announces his departure from Leipzig to Rosen for Monday, May 11 (1829), and thinks he will be hanging on his friend's neck in three weeks. But Robert was still the same impecunious old Robert, with many debts to pay before getting away from Leipzig, and counting on Rosen to help him out during the few lean weeks in Heidelberg.

Schumann did not travel straight from starting-point to destination, but in a roundabout and leisurely way, the later portion in particular being very decidedly for pleasure. Leaving Leipzig by diligence, after a day and night he reached Frankfurt-on-the-Main, where he sojourned a few days; he next took coach to Wiesbaden and the Rhine beyond; and lastly proceeded by land and water through the most lovely and picturesque region (*Rheingau*) of that romantic river with its castles, ruins, peaceful towns and villages, and vine-clad hills, down to Cologne, and up again to Mayence, further to Worms, Mannheim, and at last to Heidelberg, the final stages by coach and on foot. He had a glorious time. Leipzig to Frankfurt was like a " flight through hundreds of spring skies." But it was rather the spring within him than the spring without that made him what he then was—merry, talkative, even boisterous. Later on, between Wiesbaden and the Rhine, he himself exclaims : " How wild I was ! . . . How I entertained the whole company ! . . . I don't know when I have ever before been in such a joyous, divine mood ! " This was indeed literally true. Schumann had hardly ever been in such an elated frame of mind. On approaching the Rhine, full of expectation, he closed his eyes, and when he opened them again : " It lay before me—calm, still, grave, and proud, like an old German god, and with it the glorious, blossoming, green *Rheingau* with its hills and valleys and the whole paradise of vineyards. In six hours we passed through Hochheim, Erbach, Hattenheim, Markobrunnen, Geisenheim, etc." Well might he speak of the *magic Rheingau*. The names just mentioned (and Rüdesheim, Assmannshausen, and many more suggest themselves) were engraved on our traveller's mind. But I must recommend the reader not to neglect the letters in which Robert gave spirited and delightful reports of his journey to his mother. They are far superior to his earlier letters to her and his school-fellows, and show how much he has grown in observation and thoughtfulness, and how much he has outgrown his conceited silliness of so short a time before. What lively pictures the populations everywhere presented to him ! How, for instance, he was struck by the difference of the Catholicism of the Rhineland as compared with that of Bohemia and of Bavaria.   And the different character of the towns of Mayence, Coblenz, Cologne, Worms ! For the most part he sees merely the comic side of his fellow-travellers in the diligence ; they are for him so many dramatis personæ in a comedy—the Prussian secretary of legation singing the praises of his young wife at home and producing poems and miniatures to testify to her charms ; a matronly old lady, an ardent frequenter of the theatre at Gotha ; three commercial gentlemen, one German, the others French, the former discussing leather, the latter, intensively, the wine of the country.   But among the passengers there was one that interested Schumann more, and not merely for sport.   I mean Wilhelm Häring (the descendant of a French family, Hareng, immigrants in the time of Louis XIV), better known under the pseudonym Willibald Alexis, as a writer of verse and especially of prose.   In 1823, after some earlier attempts, he published a novel that caused a great sensation and was translated into several languages : *Walladmor*, " freely translated from the English of Sir Walter Scott with a preface by Willibald Alexis."   The origin is ascribed to a bet.   A writer in the *Encyclopædia Britannica* states that the German author imitated the style of the author of *Waverley* so closely as to deceive even Scott's admirers.   De Quincey contributed to the *London Magazine* of October, 1824, a laudatory analysis of *Walladmor*.   When, in 1825, he was pressed to furnish the promised translation, he seems to have been disinclined to give to the work the necessary time and application.   Professor David Masson says in his biography of De Quincey that his author " so cut and carved the original, and De Quinceyfied it by insertions and compressions," as to treat the affair as a practical joke.   In 1827 Alexis followed up *Walladmor* by a second novel published in the same way, entitled *Schloss Avalon*.   But he did not reach his full powers till a few years later, when he began the series of historico-patriotic Prussian novels, dealing with the Mark of Brandenburg and Frederick II (*Cabanis*, 1832, etc., etc.).   The novelist and the student soon became friends, and when at Frankfurt the other passengers parted, these two remained together for some time, both in the city and during part of the wanderings on the Rhine. Literature was, of course, the common interest, the first subjects of conversation Alexis's past and future, the enterprises of Schumann's father and brothers. Then Heine's name would come up, whom Alexis knew in Berlin, and whose acquaintance Schumann had made in Munich a year before. Whether Alexis and Schumann ever met again in later times is not known ; but Schumann thought of his fellow-traveller of these days when writing in 1832 to Ludwig Rellstab, the novelist, critic, etc., and asked to be particularly remembered to Wilhelm Häring, in whom he had a merry companion on a Rhine tour, and who spoke of Rellstab kindly and often.

Schumann " did " Frankfurt very thoroughly. He visited the house of Goethe's birth, Städel's museum, Dannecker's famous Ariadne in Bethmann's garden, a play at the theatre, the quays of the Main, the public promenades, the chief thoroughfares and squares, and especially the picturesque out-of-the-way corners, for which Alexis as well as Schumann had a passion. The new-found friends also paid their calls in duet form. At one house they met the beautiful English wife of Ferdinand Ries, the favourite pupil of Beethoven, who from 1814 to 1824 played a leading part in London as composer, pianist, and conductor, appearing in these capacities at the Philharmonic Concerts. Ries lived now in and near these parts, a shining light and the hero of the Rhenish and other festivals. His compositions are all one can desire, but, as Schumann remarked later, " it is as difficult to speak and there is as little to say about such works as about the blue sky that is shining through my window." Schumann had more to say about Frau Ries ; in fact, he was in ecstasies, the English type of feminine beauty being his ideal. " When she spoke English it sounded like the lisping of an angel."

I must not tarry over the details of the Rhine tour, but confine myself to the statement that throughout the journey from Leipzig to Heidelberg Schumann's mood was of the serenest, happiest, and most sociable. Unlike the retiring, dreamy, and melancholy Schumann we know best, we see him here striking up acquaintanceships with all sorts and conditions of men, not only with select individuals, but also with promiscuous companies, such as are brought together by the landlords of inns. What has become of the aristocrat Schumann ? What has become of his fastidiousness ? I am thinking of the tipsy dancing-master, and of the improvised musical academy at the hotel at Coblenz. Here Schumann said good-bye to Willibald Alexis, who turned westward on his way to Paris, he himself turning southward to Heidelberg. Next evening at Mainz he made a startling discovery : on counting his money he found that he had only three florins left. This obliged him to calculate ways and means carefully ; for one thing, he had to walk the last part of the journey, from Mannheim to Heidelberg. He reached his destination on Thursday, May 21, 1829, about nine o'clock in the evening, where, no doubt, the neck of Rosen was ready to receive his friend's arms, and the full pockets of the one would quickly correct the emptiness of the other's. Nothing could have harmonized more beautifully with the lovely sunset of which we hear and the mixed feelings of joy and melancholy that moved our hero. In fact, a complete Jean Paul Richter mood !

The Rhine and Neckar made a new man of Schumann. We no longer recognize in him the exclusive student of Leipzig. The joyous atmosphere of the land of the vine transformed the retiring dreamer and melancholic into a very different being. In the Rhine and its hills Schumann admired their virile beauty, in the Neckar valley its feminine charms. The natural features of Heidelberg are well known, many, and striking, and so are the architectural and romantic beauties of the castle ruins, the many lovely walks of the district, and the more distant excursions to Schwetzingen, a miniature château à la Versailles ; the town of Mannheim, aristocratic, if too regular and monotonous ; and other famous sights, ancient and modern, natural and artificial, including the hilly range of the Taunus.

Summer life in Heidelberg Schumann thought splendid : " I rise at four o'clock every morning, the sky is ravishingly blue. Until eight o'clock I am busy with pandects and

private law; from eight to ten I play the pianoforte; from ten
to twelve I attend the lectures of Thibaut and Mittermayer;
from twelve to two I have dinner and walk in the streets;
from two to four further lectures on law by Zachariä and
Johannsen; then to the castle, or to the Rhine or to my
beloved mountains." At first, at least, we hear nothing but
good accounts of his studies in law. He announces that he
greatly relishes the lectures of Thibaut and Mittermayer,
Heidelberg's legal luminaries, and declares that now for the
first time he feels the real dignity of jurisprudence which
furthers all the holiest interests of humanity. Comparing
Thibaut with his former dry-stick Leipzig professor, Schumann finds that though he is twice as old, he is overflowing
with life and spirit, and has hardly time and words enough to
express his ideas. Still, I am afraid it was not for much longer
that he could say, hand on heart, " I do not miss a single
lecture," as he did at the beginning of the term. Later in the
term he had to confess : " Of course I am not famous for the
regularity of my attendance." No, the leopard had not
changed his spots.

As Thibaut was not only a great legal light but also a
musical celebrity he has to be considered in both respects.
We need not doubt which was the more effectual influence
in the case of Schumann. The musical fame of Anton
Friedrich Justus Thibaut dates from 1825, when he published
the first edition of his *Purity in Musical Art*—a pamphlet of
125 small octavo pages without the author's name (Heidelberg: J. C. B. Mohr). It created a sensation, but discordant
voices were likewise heard, chief among them that of Hans
Georg Nägeli. Of the several later editions, only the second
need be mentioned—that of Heidelberg, January, 1826,
improved and greatly enlarged by the author, with four new
chapters. In the preface to the first edition the author states
that some years previously he had visited a South German
convent famous for its church music. At the request of the
Mother Superior he wrote down the observations now forming
Chapter I, *On Genuine Church Music*, to which later, in order
to let his views be more widely known, he added the rest.

G

In his *Musical Rules for Home and Life* (1851) Schumann immortalizes Thibaut's work by the following judgment: " A beautiful book on music is Thibaut's *Purity in Musical Art*. Read it often when you are older." This, however, is neither criticism nor truth. If the booklet is to be characterized it ought to be said that it is full of doubtful statements with some really good sentiments—the outcome of ill-regulated enthusiasm. It is the work of an out and out amateur without the slightest tincture of musical craftsmanship and book-learning.

In autumn, 1827, Mendelssohn (aged eighteen) happened to be in the neighbourhood, and was reminded by his family not to forget Thibaut while in Heidelberg. But there was no danger of this, as Mendelssohn wished to borrow one of Thibaut's beloved old Italian possessions, and before the arrival of the home instructions Mendelssohn, duly arrayed in dress-coat after the German fashion, had called at the great man's house. Being taken for a student he was shown into the study unannounced, and it was not until next day during a second visit that Thibaut asked his visitor's name. The reader will see that the young man had good powers of observation. In a letter to his mother (September 20, 1827) Mendelssohn says :

. . . It is strange, the man knows little about music, even about its history ; he is guided mostly by pure instinct, I understand more about it than he does—yet I have learnt ever so much from him and owe him a great deal. For he has enlightened me about the old Italian music, he has warmed me towards it at his fiery stream. What an enthusiasm and glow when he talks—I call that flowery speech ! I have just come from taking leave, and as I told him much about Seb. Bach and had said that the head and greatest of all was still unknown to him, for in Sebastian all was summed up, he said at parting : " Farewell, and let us link our friendship in Luis de Vittoria and Sebastian Bach, just as two lovers promise to look at the full moon and in so doing believe themselves not far apart."

If we compare Mendelssohn's impressions of Thibaut with Schumann's various utterances, not solely with his extravagant laudation of the great lawyer's inroad into musical æsthetics, we shall find that their opinions differ less than we may at first have thought. Both, while aware of his utter amateurishness, were charmed by his unassuming modesty and the enthusiasm of his personality. The friends of Schumann knew that he always spoke of Thibaut with tenderness and fond admiration of his eloquent genius. Franz Brendel, for instance, remembered especially one occasion when Schumann recalled his old professor sitting at the pianoforte with a Handel score before him and tears in his eyes. We find this more fully expressed in a letter to his mother (February 24, 1830):

Thibaut is a splendid, divine man, my most enjoyable hours are spent with him. When he has a Handel oratorio sung at his house (every Thursday more than seventy singers present) and accompanies enthusiastically on the pianoforte, two big tears roll down from the fine, large eyes beneath the beautiful silver-white hair, and then he comes to me so delighted and serene, and presses my hand and is silent from sheer emotion. I often don't know how a poor beggar like myself has the honour to be admitted to listen in such a holy house. You can have no idea of his wit, acuteness, feeling, pure artistic sense, amiability, powerful eloquence, and wide outlook.

But that Schumann could be critical with regard to him we may gather from the following passage in a letter to Wieck:

An opposition to Thibaut has been formed in which I, too, figure. You will hardly believe what splendid, pure, noble hours I have spent with him, and how painful is his onesidedness and truly pedantic view of music along with his infinite manysidedness in jurisprudence and his animating, enkindling, and, at the same time, *crushing* mind.

We can guess the meaning of the opposition referred to from a sentence in another part of the letter: " Thibaut with his Handelian operatic airs must under the table."

Dr. E. Baumstark, afterwards professor at Greifswald, was during thirteen years (1825–38) a faithful follower in law and music of Thibaut at Heidelberg. The Reminiscences concerning his adored master which he published do not contain much of interest, nor have they any literary flavour, but they enable us to gather a few plain facts about Thibaut's nonprofessional occupations. He formed a musical society consisting of students and others, men and women, for the cultivation of old art-music and folk-songs. Two evenings a week were devoted to the practice of the single choral parts, a third evening to the simultaneous practice of all the parts, and twice every term Thibaut allowed approved friends to be present as hearers. The most valuable part of Dr. Baumstark's information is the chronological list he gives of the performances brought to a hearing in the music-room of the professor from November 10, 1825, to March 28, 1833, embracing works by Palestrina, Lasso, Vittoria, Carpentras, Durante, Leo, Pergolesi, Lotti, Marcello, Caldara, Galuppi, Handel, Bach, and Cherubini.

Zuccalmaglio (Waldbrühl), one of Schumann's favourite contributors to his paper, the *Neue Zeitschrift für Musik*, wrote in the first two numbers of the year 1841 an essay on Thibaut, whose acquaintance he had made not long before while at Heidelberg University. (Thibaut died in March, 1840.) The editor was pleased with the likeness of the portrait, but corrected his contributor when he blamed the professor for his piecemeal performance of Handel's oratorios, stating in a footnote : " Yet in 1829 I heard many a whole oratorio." Repetitions of favourite works and parts of works were common enough at these private performances, and the programmes did not by any means exhaust the available store of music. The family ultimately sold Thibaut's rich and valuable library to the Library at Munich.

Unsatisfactory and unauthoritative as Thibaut must have been as an expounder of the history of music, more especially from the point of view of craftsmanship but also from that of reasoned artistic appreciation, yet his eloquence, enthusiasm, and ardent feeling for the beautiful could not but make a deep and lasting impression on so eminently sensitive a mind as that of the poetic Schumann, where the beauties and perfections thus revealed would germinate and blossom in the course of time. Other impressions were, no doubt, more immediate and intense, for example, that made by the unique violin virtuoso, Paganini. At the age of forty-six (1828) Nicolò Paganini left his own country, and visited

Vienna, Germany, Paris (1831) and London (1831–32), and made Europe stare open-mouthed at him as the greatest miracle of his day.   All the world greeted him with one voice, the voice of infinite wonder and admiration.   And not only the distinguished many, but the distinguished few, the geniuses, felt inspired by his originality.   And his power did not end with his dizzy skill—there was undoubtedly something demonic in his personality.   The historian Macaulay, who heard him at a musical party in London (May 28, 1831), writes :

> The man seems to be a miracle.   The newspapers say that long streamy flakes of music fall from his string, interspersed with luminous points of sound which ascend the air and appear like stars.

Some people thought they saw the devil himself guiding the uncanny player's bow.   The raptures of the musicians are equally astonishing.   The sober Moscheles regretted the impossibility of finding adequate expressions to describe Paganini's achievements at his concerts.   He admired among these the long-drawn tone penetrating to the innermost heart.

As will be seen presently, Schumann heard Paganini on Easter Sunday, 1830, at Frankfurt, whither he went with three fellow-students.   The virtuoso seems to have stayed, resting for the most part, for about a year at the Free Town on the Main.   Jansen, in *Die Davidsbündler* (p. 220, note 31), states that Schumann heard Paganini with Aloys Schmitt in Frankfurt in 1829, and that in 1836 he wrote as follows (note the interesting comparison and characterization) :

> One can hardly imagine greater extremes.   Aloys Schmitt is undoubtedly a masterly pianist, but the man of the *étude* peeps through everywhere, while in Paganini's hand the driest exercise formulas flame up like Pythian pronouncements.

(Schumann envied Wieck because he had heard Paganini at no fewer than four concerts in Leipzig (1829, October 5, 9, 12, and 16), and, moreover, had had some intercourse with him and asked him for information.)   The results of Schumann's experience are his Op. 3, Six Studies arranged for

the Pianoforte after [24] Caprices by Paganini (Op. 1); and
Op. 10, VI Études de Concert composed after the [24]
Caprices by Paganini (Op. 1).

Let us throw a glance at Schumann's rich and varied
human Heidelberg intercourse. In Semmel and Rosen he
discovered every day more tender and beautiful sides and new
charms of their lovable characters. Rosen he regarded as a
mediator between—

> my world of feeling and Semmel's world of reasoning; we form a very
> harmonious trefoil. . . . My friendship with Semmel was one thing,
> that with Rosen another; with the first it was more manly, firmer,
> more rational; with Rosen, more chatty, girlish, more full of feeling;
> but with both equally open, equally noble. . . . With Rosen, who is
> one of the best known and best liked students here, I live in intimacy
> and brotherliness.

Besides Rosen, Schumann has found another who, he says,
understands him entirely and knows how to treat and appreciate him—an Italian belonging to Trieste, Weber by name,
son of the Austrian Consul-General.

> We revel right royally in Petrarch and Ariosto, not to mention the
> fact that he sings like a god, and loves the world nobly. He is an
> Italian who has become calm and clear and resplendent like a profound,
> quietly billowing sea; moreover, he is the least egotistic man I have ever
> known, the first in whom I have noticed an equal balance of the spiritual
> powers, so that he seems always to feel with his head and think with his
> heart. If I were to read this praise to him, sheer modesty would
> prevent him from loving me a whit more.

These are the good friends of Schumann. But he mentions
also less intimate ones—some East-Prussians, some Englishmen, and a Greek Count M. And then there must have been
closer companions such as (Albert) Theodor Töpken, of
Bremen, a musical amateur and doctor-of-law-to-be, whose
future correspondence with his whilom Heidelberg fellow-
student proves him to have been a sympathetic friend and
agreeable associate, who, moreover, had never experienced the
discomfort of being without money and in debt to his landlord.
How strangely friends come and disappear in the lives of men,
we see in certain words quoted by Schumann from his diary

and communicated to Töpken three years later (1833): "Of
Weber, with whom and yourself and Hille I made the excursion
in a one-horse carriage to Frankfurt to hear Paganini, well, I
have never heard of Weber again." Sad, after the foregoing
raptures! But the friendship reappears later.

Schumann tells us that besides those already enumerated
he has perhaps a hundred acquaintances—that is, about a
hundred people to whom he bows and with whom he converses
conventionally. In fact, he boasts to his brother that he has
no idea how much he is liked in Heidelberg, that he goes by
the name of "favourite of the Heidelberg public." This, of
course, was the result of time, and especially after his successful
performance at a concert. But what he writes to his brother
in February, 1830, about his social engagements is truly
astonishing. He tells him that almost every evening he is at
parties and balls—every Friday at Thibaut's (his celebrated
historico-musical performances), every Tuesday at Professor
Mittermayer's, every Thursday at a brilliant gathering of
English ladies, every Monday at the musical society, and every
Saturday at the house of the widowed Grand Duchess Stephanie
(usually residing at Mannheim), who invited the young man
very pressingly by word of mouth. Among families he
visited notwithstanding his disinclination, we hear of Dr.
Wüstenfeld (with a beautiful daughter and a clever governess);
Professor Morstadt, another legal light; Dr. Lauter, an
influential courtier; Monsieur Dammance, his French
master (homely people and good-looking, insignificant
daughters), and others; but Rosen was his only friend and
confidant. We are surprised to find him connected with a
students' club, "Saxo-Borussia," and taking part in their
festivities. Schumann is, of course, known as a dancing man.
He stands up for the ladies of Zwickau, who as dancers are
superior to those of Heidelberg. He seems to have been to
the fore on all festive occasions—at carriage and sledge parties,
at carnival masquerades, etc. In a club sledging-masquerade
representing a peasants' wedding, he personated the bride's
mother, and "according to the Heidelberg ladies, I looked
the part very well."

The Heidelberg University summer term had scarcely begun when it was ended, lasting only about six weeks. Professors and students were hurried by a visit to Heidelberg of a Natural History Congress. During the last weeks Schumann worked hard at French and Italian, and was fairly satisfied with his progress. Towards the end of August, 1829, he set out, but without any of his travelling companions, for his longed-for Switzerland and Northern Italy. In the former country he touched Bâle, Zürich, Zug, Interlaken, Lucerne, Thun, and Berne, ascended the Rigi, crossed the Gemmi and other beautiful passes—in short, gained a good idea of some of the most characteristic mountain and lake scenery of Switzerland, and did so partly on foot. On August 31 he was in Berne, intending to enter Italy next day by the Gemmi. There his first object is the Lago Maggiore, and in five or six days he expects to be at Milan. What was to be a sojourn of two days was extended almost unawares into six (September 9–15, 1829). On September 16 we find him at Brescia, where he tells his correspondent that he'll proceed the day after to-morrow to Verona, and later on to Vicenza, Padua, and Venice. We know he was in Venice, but the times of his arrival and departure are not certain. We may, however, take it as certain that he was for the second time in Milan on October 4, 1829.

Although Schumann saw much of the country and the people that was characteristic and interesting, his experiences in Italy were largely unpleasant. At Venice he had a short, sharp illness of a few days and thought himself fleeced by his doctor ; in his capacity of confiding greenhorn he fell victim to a designing railway acquaintance ; cheating shopkeepers were, of course, waylaying innocent foreigners, and the foreigner in question was constitutionally incapable of keeping hold of his money. The consequence was that long before his return home he was penniless, and had to turn over in his mind thoughts of borrowing money and pawning a gold watch, the gift of his mother. In this predicament he bethought himself of the kind hotel-keeper in Milan, Reichmann of the Belvedere, who on their first meeting had made him offers of credit without inquiry as to security, and now, on their meeting again, was ready to fulfil his promise, and granted a loan of sixteen gold napoleons free of interest.

Schumann showed by his letters from Switzerland that he had a lively appreciation of the beauties of Nature. But the letters from Italy show no trace of appreciation of art. I cannot imagine that he was dead to architecture, sculpture, and painting. Yet, strange to say, we read here no comments on his impressions of the fine examples of art in Milan, Verona, Padua, Venice. He cannot have thought his family and friend Rosen incapable of sharing his enthusiasm. Art, moreover, is not purely a matter of theoretical study, but also of natural appreciation. We could have dispensed with the love romances which Schumann is so fond of spinning out— about a beautiful English lady, a fascinating French widow, another beautiful English lady who had fallen in love with his pianoforte playing; thus space would have been found for a subject of more interest.

Returning through Switzerland to Germany, the last places he visited were Chur and Lindau on Lake Constance. Then he paid a visit to his friends the Kurrers, at Augsburg, where the first thing he did was to borrow money from the old man. By Stuttgart he proceeded next to Heidelberg, where he arrived on October 20, 1829, after about seven weeks' absence —" again as poor as a beggar."

A passage from a letter of Schumann's to his master Wieck (November 6, 1829) sums up what the musician Schumann learned in Italy. All who have been in Italy themselves will concur in the statement :

A fortnight ago I returned from travels in Switzerland and Italy the poorer by some napoleons, but so much the richer in knowledge of the world, and my heart full of high and sacred memories. You have no notion of Italian music, which has to be heard under the sky that has evoked it, the sky of Italy. How often I thought of you in the Scala Theatre in Milan ! And how enraptured I was by Rossini—or, rather, Pasta, to whose name I add no qualifying word, from reverence, indeed from adoration. In the Leipzig Concert Hall I have sometimes thrilled with rapture and awe in the presence of the genius of music ; but in Italy I learned to love it ; and there is just one evening in my life when it seemed to me as if God stood before me and let me look openly and hushed upon His face—that was in Milan when I heard Pasta and Rossini. Do not smile, honoured sir, for it is true. But this was the only musical enjoyment I had in Italy. Otherwise music in Italy is hardly to be tolerated; you have no idea of the slovenliness and, at the same time, the spirit with which they fiddle through everything.

In another letter he writes :

You can as little form an idea of the fire with which the Italian music is played as of the slovenliness and small amount of elegance and precision. Naturally, however, there are exceptions, as, for instance, La Scala at Milan.

When he first came to Heidelberg, Schumann found the state of music in the town very low. Much love for music there undoubtedly was, but little talent and less active genius, with now and then, of course, some old-fashioned art criticism. Schumann himself confesses to his mother at that time that he had been neglecting his pianoforte playing, but hopes to make up for it in winter, as one generally prefers to improvise in summer and to study in winter. And so it really came to pass, as the subsequent correspondence shows. In his report to Wieck after his return from Italy (November 6, 1829), he says :

I have, as I believe, neither greatly retrogressed nor progressed, which, no doubt, is tantamount to standing still; but I feel that my touch in *forte* has become much richer, and in *piano* much freer and more *schwungvoll* [swingful, to employ an un-English but suggestive literal translation]; I may, however, have lost in facility and precision. Without over-estimating myself in the least I am truly and modestly conscious of my superiority over all the Heidelberg pianists. It is impossible to imagine the slovenliness and roughness of the performances. . . .

Schumann handed on to his new friend Töpken what he had learned during the preceding winter from Wieck, with whom he had then studied Hummel's A minor Concerto. But he tells us also that he is studying the last movement of Hummel's F sharp minor Sonata, Op. 81, which he regards as a truly great titanesque epic work, " the picture of a pro-digious, struggling, resigned spirit," and that he means to play this, and this alone, to his master when he sees him at Easter.

Of his diligent practising we get an idea from his account of the Heidelberg concert at which he played Moscheles's brilliantly virtuosic Op. 32, the Alexander Variations (*La Marche d'Alexandre* for pianoforte solo with orchestra, or string quartet, or second pianoforte *à deux mains* or *à quatre mains*). The enthusiastic audience kept calling "Bravo" and "Da capo," the triumphant virtuoso noting significantly that the Grand Duchess applauded most heartily. What, however, pleased him more was that he could say : "But I had studied it for eight weeks and played it really well, and felt I had." This initial success brought Schumann many invitations from neighbouring towns to take part in public concerts, which, however, he declined.

We have seen that Schumann entered Leipzig University as a law student in May, 1828, and pursued these studies at Heidelberg in 1829 and 1830. But all this time law was more or less of a pretence, even when he assured his mother of the contrary and professed belief in his brilliant professors. Quite at the end of his studies he seems to have made a last desperate endeavour to retrieve the failure of his career, for he attended a law *repetitorium* to make up for lost time. At last, however, the time was near when shilly-shallying would no longer do. A definite resolution had to be made, and a decisive word had to be spoken.

. . . You speak of music and my pianoforte playing. Ah ! Mother, this has almost come to an end, and I play rarely and very badly—the torch of the beautiful genius of music is flickering faintly out, and all my musical doings seem to me like a splendid dream that existed once, and of which I can only remember dimly that it did exist. And yet, believe me, if I ever achieved anything in the world it was in music. I have always felt a powerful impulse towards music, and, without over-estimating myself, perhaps also the creative spirit. But—bread-and-butter-study ! Jurisprudence so ossifies and freezes me that no flower of my imagination will ever again long for the world's spring.

These were hard pulls at the mother's heart-strings, on

which he knew how to play cunningly.   He was fond, too, of appealing by word of mouth and in writing, to " the great spirit of our good father," and of reminding his mother that he understood his son, and early destined him for the art. He was sure that these appeals would tell.

Well, the critical time has now come : Heidelberg, July 30, 1830, at 5 p.m.   The precision of the moment marks its importance.   The persons involved in the series of fateful letters were Robert Schumann, his mother, and Friedrich Wieck.   They are important for the decisions taken and the confessions made.   My quotations shall be brief but emphatic. Writing to his mother, Robert first sums up the history of his life.   He says that it has been a twenty-years struggle between poetry and prose, between music and law ; that in practical life he had as high an ideal as in art—namely, practical activity and the hope of having a wide sphere for his endeavours ; but that for a lawyer in Saxony the chances are poor unless he is of noble birth, or has high patronage and means.

In Leipzig I lived carelessly without a plan of life.   I dreamed and loafed, and, strictly speaking, accomplished nothing.   *Here* [Heidelberg] I have worked more, but, both there and here, have become more and more closely attached to art.   Now I stand at the crossways, and am startled at the question—whither ?   If I follow my genius it directs me to art—I believe, the right way.   But in truth—do not take it amiss, I say it only lovingly and gently—it always seemed to me as if you obstructed my way.   You had, of course, your good, motherly reasons, which I understand very well, and which you and I called " precarious future and uncertain bread."   What next ?   There can be no more tormenting thought for a man than an unhappy, lifeless, empty future of his own preparing.

He reminds his mother that his imagination is still youthful and can be cultivated and ennobled by art ; he has no doubt that, with diligence and patience and a good teacher, six years will enable him to rival any pianist ; that he has some imagination, too, and perhaps creative talent as well ; that if only he makes right and proper plans, with quietude and determination he is bound to win through to his object ; that in this battle he is keener than ever, sometimes madly bold and relying on his strength and will, sometimes anxious when he thinks of the long road which he might have travelled already, but which is still before him. He begs her to consult Thibaut, who had long ago directed him towards art and away from law.

But his final request to his mother is that she should write to Wieck, in whom he had complete confidence.

He knows me and can judge of my powers, and would then have to train me further ; later, I should have to go for a year to Vienna, and, if at all possible, to Moscheles. . . . Write yourself to Wieck in Leipzig, and ask straightforwardly what he thinks of me and my life's plan. Ask for a *speedy* answer and decision, so that I can hasten my departure from here, difficult though it will be to leave behind so many good folk, such splendid dreams, and a perfect paradise of nature.

We thoroughly agree with Schumann that this letter was the most important he had ever written, or ever would write.

On August 7, 1830, Frau Schumann did as her son desired, stating the case plainly, and enclosing Robert's own statement. It is rather a good letter, considering her depression of mind, fear, and trembling. She emphasizes that her son's views are not her own. He had studied for nearly three years, had spent a great deal of money, and now, just when she thought he was about to reach his aim, he wants to begin anew, and before the new aim can be reached, the whole of his modest means will be exhausted, and he will still be dependent on others. Her three other sons are displeased, and insist on her withholding her consent ; but she does not wish to force him. Robert is young and inexperienced, lives in the clouds and not among the practicalities of life. And she beseeches Wieck as husband, as father, and as the friend of her son, to act honestly, and give her his straightforward opinion as to what Robert has to fear, or to hope. Wasielewski gives the letter in full (pp. 60–61).

Wieck's answer is dated two days later : Leipzig, August 9, 1830. The letter is longer and more desultory than that of the " soul-sick " lady. The master is more anxious about his old pupil's character than about his talent. He pledges himself without hesitation to make Robert, with his talent and his imagination, within three years, one of the greatest living pianists, who is to play more warmly and spiritually than Moscheles, and more grandly than Hummel.

But—what about his unbridled fantasy combined with his wavering disposition? Will Robert be more sober-minded, firmer, stronger, than he used to be, and, if it may be said, colder and more manly? Can Robert make up his mind to study dry theory for two years under Weinlig? It was not so in the past. Wieck proposes that Robert should submit himself to a six months' test, after which the master is to pronounce the final judgment, yes or no! The other matters discussed in the document we may pass over: the necessity of the virtuoso's giving lessons, the limitation of Wieck's time, what with his trade concerns in several towns and his travels with his daughter Clara. (This is the interesting letter, given in Litzmann's *Clara Schumann*, already referred to on p. 64.)

I say nothing about Schumann's communications with his guardian Rudel, for they contribute nothing that is really new and important. We go on, therefore, to his letter from Heidelberg, August 21, 1830, to Wieck (Wasielewski, p. 62), which may be regarded as the concluding document in this affair. Since the arrival of the letters from Wieck and his mother, he had been, he says, in a state of great excitement. Now he is calming down. After self-examination, he agrees to everything and promises everything. The letter has, perhaps, too much of Schumann's enthusiasm. We could have liked at this moment something more sober. After all, as Wieck said, Robert has to show that he can really *will* something.

We may be sure that after this happy decision Schumann did not trouble himself any more about law. He could not do better than follow Wieck's advice: " Quit warm, hilly Heidelberg, where your imagination only becomes more heated, and return to our cold, flat Leipzig." But on September 18, 1830, he was still there, writing to his guardian for money. " I am the only student here, in lanes and woods I wander solitary, abandoned, poor as a beggar, with debts into the bargain." At last, on September 24, he sets out on a pleasure trip down the Rhine, further than he had gone before. On the same day he arrives at Mayence, and is at Cologne on the 25th, and at Wesel, Dutch in character, " cheerful and clean," on the 27th ; then, turning eastward, he goes by Münster to Detmold for one or two days to friend Rosen and his family, and lastly, by Cassel to Leipzig, where he arrives in the latter part of October.   He does not seem to have been in a hurry to get to work.   His first letter, to his mother, is dated October 25, 1830.   He complains that a fortnight's homelessness has brought with it a discontent, disquietude, laziness, and wretchedness, that make him incapable of thought. Alas ! this is a bad beginning.   What has become of the vigour, spirit, and resolutions of a few weeks ago ?

CHAPTER IX

Schumann's constitutional weakness in money management—The first serious music studies after abandonment of law : Pianoforte playing under Friedrich Wieck and its premature and disastrous interruption, ending with the laming of the right hand : Composition under Heinrich Dorn with its likewise regrettable abrupt conclusion—His musical and literary companions, acquaintances, friends, and the Leipzig musical *milieu* generally.

AT the end of Chapter V a summary was given of Schumann's unfortunate constitutional weakness in the management of money. It would be highly amusing were it not so tragically demoralizing. There have been frequent allusions to the subject in the foregoing chapters, as there will be in the following ones until he finds a guardian (or a wife) to keep him in check, and to protect him against himself and his tendencies. Thus far the habit was on the increase—all through the Heidelberg time and the early years after his return to Leipzig, we may describe his life as a continuous economic crisis. He suffers most acutely from impecuniosity when travelling. Change of place regularly brings on a hopeless state of indebtedness. The reader will remember how in Milan he borrowed sixteen gold napoleons of an hotelkeeper, how, soon after, at Augsburg, he confessed himself a poor, ragged pilgrim to generous old Dr. Kurrer, presently returning to Heidelberg an avowed penniless beggar. Now there are no long intervals to bridge here ; yet on his return to Leipzig in October, 1830, he again describes his condition as that of absolute destitution. At Heidelberg he is in constant need of money, and bombards every relative and connection, in every tone, tune, time, and dynamic variety, with urgent requests to supply him, the man at the end of his resources, for pity's sake. The letters to his guardian, Rudel, become more and more numerous, and now and then furnish interesting details of his expenditure (for example, those in Erler's collection): house rent, hire of grand pianoforte, University fees, dinner, supper, and breakfast, to say nothing of shoeblack and attendant for half a year, shoemaker, washerwoman, a bottle of beer a day, books, and matriculation. This, however, does not include the lesser and greater supplementary expenses, such as an occasional half-bottle of wine; and Sunday excursions to beautiful neighbouring towns—Mannheim, Darmstadt, Spires, Worms, Carlsruhe, Baden, etc., which the humane guardian will grant his ward. The figures given would amount to two hundred and twenty thalers half-yearly, which, as he gets from Rudel only one hundred and eighty thalers, leaves him forty thalers short half-yearly. It will not be out of place to warn the reader here that Schumann's frequent financial statements cannot be trusted—indeed, they are mostly influenced by factors other than arithmetical. The demands, trying in their amount and frequency, now and then embitter the life of the Schumann family, generally so loving and so mutually appreciative, and lead to interruptions of the letters and disturbance of the usual sweet concord. The silence is felt very sorely, but the unreasonable and inconsiderate calls on their charity—or, rather, generosity—stir up their impatience. Schumann writes to his mother from Heidelberg, July, 1829: " The last letter left a terrible discord behind "; and there are other passages of similar import. Let me refer to but one more. It is a soul-revealing confession, which, alas! cannot be accepted as an excuse. Leipzig, February 18, 1831 :

I should be embarrassed, dear Mother, if you were to ask me why I have not written for so long. It is all the more inexplicable since I have so much reason for gratitude and also for a request, both of which I have put off from week to week.

If I could indicate, even obscurely, what I feel, it would be something of this kind : that your last letters neither praised nor blamed properly, were neither cold nor warm, neither motherly nor stepmotherly. A long-suppressed discord between two human hearts is

H

much more wounding and dangerous than an open, straight reproach—that is, perhaps, why the real answer has been so long delayed, although against my wish, for I have begun at least six letters. To be frank, I have often wished that you would all neglect me thoroughly for once, so that my debt of obligation and thanks might be less. But you all go on heaping comforting and encouraging letters and tokens of love upon me, so that I would fain, and must, go with downcast look. . . .

Often the demands are not trifles, but a matter of a hundred thalers or more. Sometimes they border on the dishonest. Thus he writes to a brother to send him a bill of exchange, " but don't tell Mother." And to his mother he writes not to tell his brothers of his application to her. Worse are his requests to her to raise money for him to tide over the time until his coming of age. As I said, his statements as to his real expenditure cannot be trusted—for instance, the amounts of University fees, payments for language lessons, tradesmen's bills, etc. By the way, our proud young gentleman failed to pay his fees to the University, and was threatened with imprisonment and fine. How is this dishonourable conduct of Schumann's to be reconciled with his indubitable gentlemanliness and nobility of character? He himself knew that this contempt for money, this throwing of it away, was a pitiable trait in him. He admitted the carelessness that made him throw his money out of the window. But his self-reproaches and good resolutions never had any result—they were forgotten as soon as uttered. Let us see how Schumann philosophized about this weakness, how he justifies it.

. . . The only thing against a longer stay at Heidelberg would be that everlasting odious money, as it would cost twice as much. But I don't know—I am in my best youth, am not quite poor, can hope for exquisite moments of refined pleasure here ; I have splendid friendships and my friends are excellent men—why should I relinquish a happy present and future for a couple of hundred florins ? . . .

This is not the philosophy of a mature, wise man : as that of an immature, giddy youth, it may pass well enough—indeed, is likely to enjoy popularity.

When Schumann returned to Leipzig near the end of

October (his first letter from there is of the 25th), 1830, he was financially unprovided for and got quickly into endless difficulties. He considered it was not his fault—that if he had had money at the beginning he would not have been penniless at the end of six weeks, but free from debt and in order. So he asks his mother to oblige him—if it is not too much trouble—by sending him a hundred thalers, and thus rescue him from this disagreeable and disorderly way of life. In the course of a heart-rending report he tells her that for the last fortnight he has not tasted meat, roasted or boiled, more than twice, only plain potatoes, and although he likes these, it is rather too absurd ; his restaurant landlord treats him with scant courtesy because he owes him for three months ; he lacks money for postage, to get his pianoforte tuned, to get his hair cut, to get smart dress-clothes, those he has being too *nachlässig genial* [in a state of neglect, after the manner of geniuses] ; is at his last candle ; can't even shoot himself for want of means to buy a pistol ; has had to pawn the gold watch his mother gave him, and his books wander one after another to the secondhand shops. The desperation and courage of Schumann can be gauged by his daring to attack his redoubtable master Wieck, whom, after one or more smaller loans (the first of one thaler), he left his creditor for twenty thalers. We now come across new names, too, among the friends and victims of Schumann's persuasive charm. J. A. Barth, the music-seller, who by and by became the second publisher (1835) of the *Neue Zeitschrift für Musik*, Schumann regarded with some timidity. He was shy of asking Barth for a loan ; moreover, ten or twenty thalers would, he says, be of little use to him, as he already owes money to von der Lühe, who is really hard-up. Of this friend, a writer, we hear occasionally in Robert's later letters as being faithful and helpful, but too conventional in his views of life for close intimacy.

Wonderful are the characteristic moral reflections to which Schumann now and then gives vent.

Poverty may be the most terrible thing, for it excludes wholly from human society. I now realize it, and regret many things. Want of money cannot reduce me to sadness or even to desperation because

I respect it too little, and in its possession I am neither happier nor unhappier. But it is depressing and inconvenient.

With regard to the *vita nuova*, that is, the life the musician Schumann was to begin in Leipzig, he says that he must now shut himself up and turn himself into a chrysalis. This would no doubt have taken place had he not been the man he was: a man of moods—one moment one thing, next moment the opposite. We saw how he speaks of the discontent, restlessness, inertia, of the idleness and wretchedness of the early days after his return to Leipzig. But about the same time he writes of his industry and splendid progress, of his three and four years' studies, and his equalling Moscheles (December 15, 1830). His optimism becomes really delightful when he boasts of his patience and persistence and his ability to do much if he wills it. There's the rub. As Wieck said in his advisory letter: " Can Robert really *will* something ? " Alas! his disposition is very variable. He is as a rule ready to compete with any pianist, but he also admits lacking self-confidence before the world, although inwardly he can be very proud and hopes to remain strong, modest, solid, and sober. On the whole the following bulletin can be applied to his studies under Wieck. You see he is not in the least pessimistic. " I am so fresh in spirit and soul that life gushes and bubbles around me in a thousand springs—the doing of divine fantasy with her magic wand." That Schumann understood his failings may be gathered from the following reflections on himself, in which you have the besetting sins of our music student:

If only my talent for poetry and music were concentrated on one point the light would not be so much broken up. . . . I cannot reconcile myself to the thought of dying a Philistine. . . . As for me, I am lounging around. It is a fault of all lively young souls that they would like to be a great many things all at once, thus work becomes more complicated, the mind more restless; but a more sedate age will arrange and smooth everything. I can aim at being four things only— conductor, music teacher, virtuoso, and composer.

Nature and Destiny simplified matters for him by leaving him finally composition alone.

We do not know when Schumann resumed his pianoforte studies after the Heidelberg interval. Nor do we know much about the work done by either master or pupil. We do not even know when the studies came to an end. To begin with, Schumann was not in a hurry to return to Leipzig or to resume his lessons. Master Wieck with his other engagements, especially the travels with his daughter Clara, must have been very irregular. The accident to the pupil's right hand, too, leaves us uncertain when his studies under Wieck came definitely to an end. The only things known are a few sayings of the master, and the faithful devotion of the pupil. One of the master's sayings was that it would be better for Schumann not to possess a penny, for then one could be sure that something would come of him. Many sayings of Schumann's in his correspondence prove that as long as the lessons lasted, and subsequently too, the good understanding between master and pupil remained undisturbed. But the mentality of the two was different, and it could not be expected that their lives would be an everlasting unison. Moreover, there was the irritant that the pupil thought his progress was not quick enough. He liked to experiment, and in spite of his promises, he liked to do so without his master's advice. Let us note one point: his promise in August, 1830, to stick to Wieck's teaching for three years, and on December 12, 1830, his writing to his mother that next Michaelmas he was going to put himself under the tutorship of Hummel at Weimar. When he mentioned the matter *en passant* to Wieck, the latter, of course, flared up. Schumann said that his only object was to have the advantage of Hummel's name, and the mention of him as a desirable pianoforte teacher keeps coming up for some time. Wieck did not cease to appreciate Schumann's pianistic talent, or to take a lively interest in his musical and poetic talent generally. Schumann does not leave us in doubt about his own sentiments regarding his master: " He seems so sympathetic towards me now, I did not believe it before ; he gives way or quarrels when he thinks right, and encourages and stimulates me."

Now we come to the disaster which happened to the right hand of Schumann, and, after all the years of hoping and despairing, definitely brought his great virtuoso expectations to an end. The matter is first indirectly alluded to in a letter to his mother of June 14, 1832: " . . . . the strange misfortune that has befallen me."

It is fortunate that we have Wieck's own report of the finger accident, for had that been wanting there would have been nothing to put in its stead. It is to be found in his *Clavier und Gesang* (1853, with the author's signature to the preface, 1852). He mentions disapprovingly various kinds of apparatus used with finger-boards to assist the development of the fingers, saying that he uses nothing of the kind. And then he goes on: " nor the ' finger-tormentor ' excogitated by a famous pupil of mine, which he invented contrary to my wish and used behind my back to the righteous dismay of his third and fourth fingers."

Madame Clara Schumann had forgotten what really passed (she was at the time only thirteen years old). On my asking her she replied that her husband lamed his finger by practising on a very stiff dumb *Claviatur* (keyboard), and did not make use of any other apparatus. She distinctly stated it was the second finger of the right hand—although she did not seem sure about any of the circumstances. (Interview at Frankfurt, June 12, 1889.) That memory of these early days must have failed her is proved by the foregoing testimony of her father and the subsequent testimonies of her husband's letters and biographers' inquiries.

Before going further in the history of the finger-laming I should remind the reader of the two systems of naming the fingers of the hand: that of the anatomists, in which the hand has a thumb and four fingers, and that of the musical pedagogues, in which the thumb is included in the five fingers. If this is forgotten, statements are likely to appear ambiguous. Those of Friedrich Wieck and Clara Schumann are examples, and those of Wasielewski, F. G. Jansen, and others, may also be instanced.

The first we hear of the event from Schumann himself is

an allusion, already touched on, to a message which his elder brother Eduard is to give their mother. June 14, 1832 :

> Eduard will inform you of the strange misfortune that has befallen me. This is the reason of a journey to Dresden which I am going to take with Wieck next Monday. Although I undertake it on the advice of my doctor and also for distraction I must do a great deal of work as well there.

To his mother, Leipzig, August 9, 1832 :

> My whole house is a chemist's shop. After all, I was growing anxious about the hand, and purposely put off asking an anatomist about it because I was afraid of the sword-stroke, *i. e.* I believed he would say that the damage was irreparable. I had already made all kinds of plans for the future, had almost resolved to study theology (not law) and adorned my parsonage with living pictures—yours and others. At last I went to Professor Kühl, and asked him on his conscience whether it would get better. After some shaking of the head he opined it would, but not quickly, that is, not under half a year. As soon as I had his " yes " the weight fell from my heart and I joyfully did all he required. It was certainly enough—to take animal baths (get Schurig to explain to you), to bathe the hand all day with brandy, and at night to have the arm in a bandage of herbs, and to play the pianoforte as little as possible. The cure is not of the most charming, and I am much afraid that something of the nature of the cattle may pass into my nature ; but it is very strengthening, and my whole body so strong and fit that I feel greatly inclined—to give somebody a good thrashing. . . .

To his mother, Leipzig, November 6, 1832 :

> . . . As to the hand, the doctor keeps reassuring me ; I for my part am completely resigned and regard it as beyond recovery. In Zwickau I will take up the violoncello again (for which the left hand only is needed), which, besides, is very useful to me for symphonic composition. Meantime the right hand is resting, and rest is the right doctor. . . .

F. G. Jansen, in *Die Davidsbündler*, mentions Dr. Otto of Schneeberg as one of the medical advisers who treated Schumann with electricity.

To Th. Töpken, Leipzig, April 5, 1833 :

> I am still playing the pianoforte very little ; don't be alarmed I

am resigned and regard it as a dispensation—one finger of the right
hand is lamed and broken : owing to an injury in itself unimportant
but neglected, the trouble has become so great that I can hardly play
with the hand at all. . . .

To his mother, Leipzig, June 28, 1833 :

. . . My hand trouble is now being homœopathically treated.   Dr.
Hauptmann said laughingly that no allopath could cure it ; in a quarter
of a year it should be healed ; he produced a tiny, tiny powder, ordered
strict diet, little beer, no wine nor coffee.   The electricity I was using
before had perhaps rather done harm in this case, since the diseased
part is liable to be deadened by over-irritation.   Visionary as homœo-
pathy seems to me, still I was pleased by the confidence the doctor
showed—and that is something. . . .

To his mother, Leipzig, March 19, 1834 :

. . . Don't be uneasy about the finger.   I can compose without it,
and I should hardly be happier as a travelling virtuoso—I was spoilt
for that from the first.   It does not interfere with my improvising ;
it has, indeed, revived my old courage in improvising before people,
as I did lately at the house of Barth, who had invited me to dinner. . . .

In most cases (and especially in the less intimate ones)
Schumann makes light of the trouble, saying that it won't
prevent him from composing, which would have been a
more serious matter.   In considering the consequences of
the mishap it has generally not occurred to people that the
master's idealistic nature was not suitable for the career of
an executive artist, many of the conditions of which would
have been distasteful to him.   Now and then he became
conscious of these unsuitabilities.   The career of a virtuoso
might have duties and temptations not in harmony with that
of a composer.

To Simonin de Sire [of Dinant, Belgium], Vienna, March
15, 1839 :

I myself have been robbed by an unfortunate fate of the full use
of my right hand, and do not play my things as I have composed them.
The hand trouble is nothing more than that some fingers (probably
from too much writing and playing in earlier times) have become
quite weak, so that I can hardly use them.   This has often perturbed

me; however, heaven now and then sends me a good idea instead, and so I think no more about the matter. . . .

To Clara Wieck, Vienna, December 3, 1838 :

. . . I sometimes feel unhappy, and especially in that I have a maimed hand. And I will tell you that it grows steadily worse. I have often complained of it to heaven and asked God why He has brought this of all things upon me. It would have been of the greatest possible use to me here—all my music is so ready and alive within me that I should be able to breathe it out; now I have the greatest difficulty in bringing it out, one finger stumbling over the other. It is dreadful, and has already caused me a great deal of pain. . . .

The Belgian Simonin de Sire was a great admirer of Schumann, who, we may be sure, was exceedingly sympathetic towards him, and anxious to give a true picture of his feelings and ideas. But Clara Wieck, now soon to be Clara Schumann, was of course a more intimate being. To her he had to reveal his inmost self—his hopes, despairs, regrets, etc. To no other person does Schumann give so true a picture of his mind in this matter.

Coming to the biographers, we need mention only the general statements of Spitta and Wasielewski, passing by those of Jansen in *Die Davidsbündler*. Spitta's account, in his *Ein Lebensbild Robert Schumanns* * (Breitkopf & Härtel), is as follows—note what he says about the fingers involved :

. . . Schumann had excogitated an apparatus which was to give a short cut to the attainment of a comprehensive technique. By means of this apparatus the fourth finger was drawn up and held while the other fingers were exercised. In this way the tendons of the fourth finger were strained, the finger went lame, indeed for a time the whole right hand was maimed. This most serious condition was certainly improved by medical treatment; Schumann regained the use of his hand, and could at need use it for pianoforte playing. But the fourth finger remained lame, and thus the career of a virtuoso was closed to him for ever. . . .

* Spitta's *Schumann* was written originally for Grove's *Dictionary of Music and Musicians*. There the lamed finger is called the third—in accordance with English nomenclature, in which the hand has a thumb and four fingers.

I do not know to what extent we can believe Wasielewski in the ins and outs of his narrative of the finger-laming. For instance, he mentions that Töpken, while a fellow-student of Schumann's at Heidelberg, assisted him in elaborating manipulations. But in the first place, this is going beyond Töpken's own statement; and secondly, Schumann's letter to Töpken about his misfortune makes no reference to anything of the kind. Further, the statement as to Schumann's uncommunicative conversations with Julius Knorr is unconvincing. But the main points of the discovery seem to have been that—

Schumann, by means of a mechanism invented by himself, held up the third finger [dendritten Finger] of the right hand, then practised continuously with the other four fingers in order to attain the greatest possible independence.

To this I may add that the cumulative result of my traditional knowledge from the Düsseldorf time and the much later Leipzig time (Wenzel and Dörffel) agrees with Wasielewski's main points.

Various problems are raised by Schumann's misfortune to his hand. First the less important point of the influence on his pianoforte playing generally; and secondly and more especially the influence on the style of his future compositions for the pianoforte. The limited powers of the fingers affected not only the fingers themselves, but also the extent of the use of the pedal. Certain characteristics of his style are undoubtedly to be accounted for by his physical disabilities. The want of clearness is largely to be attributed to this cause. Schumann did not always feel the disability in the same way, he seems to have been able to forget it altogether at times. Interesting reports of his playing, and considerations of his qualities of style we shall discuss later on.

This brings us to the end of Schumann's pianoforte studies. Now let us see what he really did for the development of his powers as a composer.

When Schumann returned from Heidelberg to Leipzig in

1830, he found the twenty-six-year-old Heinrich (Ludwig Egmont) Dorn already established as Music Director of the Leipzig opera. Schumann, five years junior to Dorn, is said to have been introduced to him by his friend, von der Lühe, his purse-holder for the time being. There was at least one parallelism in the careers of the two musicians—both attended the University as law students, Dorn at Königsberg, Schumann at Leipzig and Heidelberg; but there was this difference, that Dorn's parents were content to let him choose music for his profession. Dorn's father, who died young, was, it may be mentioned, a well-to-do merchant anxious to give his son a liberal education by schooling and travel; and the mother's second husband was also well-to-do. Among the relatives there was an uncle, a musician, who took an interest in the music studies of his nephew. At first Königsberg did its best to provide Dorn with music masters. Afterwards Berlin most handsomely took this duty upon itself. Ludwig Berger, the pupil of Clementi and master of Mendelssohn, and a highly esteemed composer, took charge of his pianoforte studies: for composition he had two masters. One was Carl Friedrich Zelter (1758–1832), at first a builder (master-builder 1780) and later a pupil of C. F. Christian Fasch and his successor as conductor of the *Singakademie*, a notable figure in the history of the German *Lied* and a prized composer generally, the friend and correspondent of Goethe, and the outspoken adviser and master of Mendelssohn; the other was Bernhard Klein of Cologne, subsequently of Berlin, known by his instrumental and vocal music (mostly for the church—masses, hymns, motets, cantatas, and oratorios—*Jephtha*, *Job*, etc.), a composer of little originality but great if short-lived authority and fame. Dorn had some teaching and conducting experience before he went to Leipzig, having acted as music director of his native town since 1828. He spent a long and busy life as a director and *Capellmeister* of high usefulness and wide fame; composed much, especially for the stage, but did not reach the highest degrees of success. To those who may feel inclined to relegate his music to the category of " *Capellmeister* music " (technically perfect though uninspired music) it might be suggested that sometimes it is also a shade or two too good. After three years at Leipzig Dorn turned to Hamburg, Riga (theatre and church), Cologne (theatre, private music school, church, municipal music school, and municipal music director), and lastly to Berlin as conductor of the Court opera.

The reader will remember that Wieck recommended Cantor Weinlig for his pupil's master in theory. We know also that, shortly before, Wieck put his daughter Clara and some of his other pupils under him. Why was it that Schumann did not take Wieck's advice? The young man so recently come to Leipzig, two of whose works, the ballet *Amors Macht*, and the short opera *Abu-Kara* (1830–31), had been performed on the Leipzig stage, who had also made himself known by the earlier operas *Die Rolandsknappen* (1826, Berlin) and *Die Bettlerin* (1828, Königsberg), and, further, was heard as pianist in Leipzig in compositions of his own and others, for instance, works by Hummel (1830, 1831, and 1832), must have struck Schumann as more go-ahead than a cantor. This, at any rate, is very likely, and we need not look further for a cause. And Wieck, in the course of time, entrusted his daughter to the care of Dorn, whose counterpoint lessons she enjoyed from the end of May, 1832. It would, however, have been interesting if both those difficult pupils, Robert Schumann and Richard Wagner, had chosen the same master. Would Weinlig have been as successful with Schumann as with Wagner? The answer is of course incalculable. Let us see, then, first, what we can gather from Schumann's communications. At first it seemed as if the characters of master and pupil were irreconcilable, but this was not so. In fact, they soon became excellent friends, for the rest of their lives remaining correspondents on the best terms.

To Wieck and his daughter he writes from Leipzig to Frankfurt, January 11, 1832:

. . . I shall never be able to amalgamate with Dorn; he wishes to get me to believe that music is fugue—heavens! how different men are. All the same I feel that the theoretical studies have had a good influence on me. If formerly everything was inspiration of the moment, I now reflect more on the play of my enthusiasm, sometimes stop in the middle of it to take stock of where I am. Well, perhaps you have had a similar chiaroscuro in your life. Many never reach that point, like Mozart; others pull through, like Hummel; others stick fast in it, like Schubert; others even laugh at it, like Beethoven—of course this is mere opinion. . . . K[norr] played Chopin's Variations lately . . . they met with little approval; indeed, my neighbour at the concert whispered softly in my ear : " The composition seems to be miserable." I nodded approval, for, sir, if one were to argue about such things with every born idiot, one would oneself be one. Dorn, who was near me, was uncommonly pleased with my neighbour's judgment, and said in the room : " Well, I, too, can find nothing more in the Variations than Herz raised to the *nth* power." This time, again, I answered not a word, but perhaps my looks spoke all the more plainly, for next day Dorn said : " Have I offended you ? I understand that just as well as you do," etc. The next piece at the concert was a psalm by Romberg; the fugue began, I nudged Dorn and drew his attention to the audience —they were all talking and coughing; he understood me and was silent. . . . I have got as far as three-part fugue with Dorn, and have finished besides a sonata in B minor, and a book of *Papillons*, which latter will appear in print within a fortnight. Dorn gives a concert in four weeks. . . .

The following extracts are taken from Schumann's note-book, and tell us of the end of Dorn's lessons—how this came about and how he appreciated them. Their chief value is in the light they throw on the composer's mind, which was by no means so volatile and superficial as the reader may imagine, but, on the contrary, had a great deal of steadfastness about it. As I said before, he knew what was good for him and followed it with pertinacity : his genius and nobility of character were his guides and protectors.

To Dorn, Leipzig, April 25, 1832 :

Honoured Herr Director,—

What can have caused you to break off our intercourse so suddenly ? No doubt I begged so long for indulgence and forbearance that you got tired of it. But I could hardly have believed that the guide could desert me so near the goal; for only now, after having helped two acquaintances as far as ligatures, have I come to understand your thorough and sure method. . . . Do not believe that I have stood still or been lazy since your desertion. But it seems as if my whole nature resisted every external stimulus and as if I myself had first to attack the thing to work at it and put it in its right place. I therefore continued cautiously (after Marpurg) from where we stopped; but I don't give up the hope (I confess to you) of studying canon with you again, and I realize the out and out usefulness of theory, for the wrong and the harmful arise only from exaggeration or wrong application. I missed your help greatly in an arrangement of Paganini Caprices for the pianoforte, as the basses were often doubtful, but I extricated myself by simplicity. Also, I have ready, and should like to show you, six Intermezzi with *alternativi*, and a prelude with concluding fugue on three subjects (think of it!) in the old style. If I ask myself why this letter has been written, I must again answer, " for my own sake." Is that not egotism?

To his mother, Leipzig, May 8, 1832 :

. . . Dorn, my theory teacher, had advanced me inwardly a great deal. By dint of persevering study, I gained that beautiful clearness of which, indeed, I early had some idea, but which I often lacked. From now onwards my life becomes different; I am independent. I gave the manuscript out of my hands almost with hesitation : now it is printed. . . . Otherwise I am with Dorn and Herlosssohn [a literary man], but mostly with myself or with the future. . . .

To Kuntzsch at Zwickau, Leipzig, July 27, 1832 :

. . . The theoretical course with Dorn I completed some months ago as far as canon, which I have studied by myself according to Marpurg. Marpurg is a much-to-be-respected theorist. Otherwise Sebastian Bach's *Wohltemperirtes Klavier* is my grammar and, moreover, the best. The fugues in their order I have analyzed down to the smallest details; this is of great use and, as it were, of morally strengthening effect on one's whole being, for Bach was a man—out and out; with him nothing is half done, morbid, everything is written as if for eternity. Now I must take up score reading and instrumentation. I wonder if you possess old scores, say, of old Italian church music. . . .

To Dorn, Leipzig, September 14, 1836 :

Just as I had received and was about to answer your letter the day before yesterday, who should come in but Chopin! That was a great pleasure. We spent a delightful day, and yesterday I held an after-celebration. But to-day I am firmly resolved to pay off my old debt, as far as that is possible in so little space. So, firstly, I think of you almost every day, often sadly, because I studied so negligently; always gratefully, for I learned more than you believe. How much has happened and changed between then and now you know partly. The rest I reserve until we meet, which will, I doubt not, come to pass, however distant the time may be. . . . Thanks for the many marks of your sympathy with our effort. Much still remains to be done, but we are young, and the best comes with years. And special thanks for speaking about the paper and gaining friends for it [*Neue Zeitschrift für Musik*, begun April 1834]. . . . Secondly, of course, I look forward with pleasure to the *Phantasie*. If I could be of any use to you it goes without saying. I have come to know Haslinger as a very decent man. I will await a favourable hour and write the rest to you promptly. Moreover, you can readily believe that if the publishers were not afraid of the editor the world would learn little about me, perhaps so much the better for the world; meanwhile the black, firmly printed heads please one all too well. Let me draw your attention to my Sonata in F sharp minor, but still more to a concerto without orchestra which has just been published by Haslinger. I should be glad to learn what you think of it. . . . [Dresden, January 7, 1846.] . . . Perhaps you will find my Pedal Studies [Op. 56] not quite unworthy of your teaching. . . .

In his old age Dorn was not much inclined to rehearse his recollections of his famous pupil. Perhaps the ruler in high places thought he would be lowering himself by playing the part of a mere witness in illustrating the life of another musician. Before calling on him I made the acquaintance of Erler, the diligent author of the valuable *Robert Schumann's Life from his Letters*, and learned from his experience that Dorn might not be the loquacious veteran I expected. I have still a lively recollection of the retired *Herr Hof-Capell-meister* sitting beside me in his dressing-gown, on a sofa covered with American cloth in a scantily-furnished small room, as it were a study without books or music, but with plenty of smoke. He was still entertaining, and still preserved a good deal of the old humour, wit, and sarcasm of literary utterance. But enough, although I had a pleasant time with Dorn, my knowledge of Schumann did not profit much by the interview. The two personalities, however, became clearer in their action and reaction. Schumann's attachment to Dorn may no doubt be ascribed to the older man's thorough musicianship, and—what is more than musicianship—his personality; thus, with his *esprit* and his many interests, he was a congenial companion on walks and at other times.

The studies under Wieck and Dorn make us inquire if there are further instances of direct formal teaching to report. In Wasielewski's first (also third) edition of the biography, he mentions Music Director Kupsch, for some time a resident of Leipzig, as having been Schumann's teacher in theory for a short while. Why there were only a few lessons was not known. In after years Wasielewski heard from Dorn of the death of Kupsch; but no other information about him has reached us. Madame Schumann remembered nothing of Kupsch—knew nothing of his name or existence either through her husband or anybody else. He may have been a wandering theatrical bird—to-day here, to-morrow elsewhere.

It is different with Gottlieb Christian Müller, the violinist of the Gewandhaus orchestra (1826–38), conductor of the Euterpe concerts (1831–38), and later on music director at Altenburg in Saxony. He composed symphonies, overtures, concertinos, etc., heard at the Gewandhaus concerts, some of which were discussed by Schumann. In Schumann's notebook is the sketch of a letter to him, date and all. What became of it, whether there was any answer or result, we do not know. Nor is anything known of a personal acquaintance between the two. The letter runs thus:

To Music Director G. W. [no doubt should be G. C.] Müller, here; Leipzig, November 2, 1832. The undersigned takes the liberty of asking whether you would be inclined to give him instruction in instrumentation, humbly requesting that to this end you would go through with him a symphony movement by himself, shortly to be played at Altenburg. It is impossible to say how greatly you would oblige me by this, as I have worked almost entirely according to my own ideas without guidance, and am, moreover, rather distrustful of my talent for symphonic work. All other conditions I leave for your kind decision. May I beg you further to let me know, if possible by return, when I should find you at home to discuss the matter and to arrange about beginning. . . .

The letter was doubtless dispatched: the date and contents speak in favour of this. But was the proposition entertained?

Note that the request was not for regular teaching of instrumentation. Müller had had experience before of the ways of geniuses. I am reminded that on a previous occasion Richard Wagner approached Müller with the proposal to study harmony under him, with no satisfactory result to the pupil and still less to the master. The latter had not even the minimum satisfaction of finding that his pupil thought the labourer worthy of his hire. We may be sure that Schumann would have improved upon the methods of his fellow-genius in the way of fee paying.

If we take a general view of the friends of Schumann in the years 1830–34 we notice that the majority of them were men of letters and executive musicians (mostly the latter). Gradually the composing musicians gained the greater influence over him. At the beginning Wieck, without doubt—the correspondence proves it—had the greatest influence over him, and it was a good influence, the influence of a man of common sense, in whose judgment he had the greatest confidence. In the autumn of 1831 Schumann ceased to be a fellow-lodger in Wieck's house, where he had lived for about a year, but his intimate intercourse with the family continued. (In a letter to his mother of October 14, 1831, he writes of being already settled in a new lodging.)

Schumann was a great deal with the Wiecks. The second Frau Wieck remembered him and his ways very well. When there were visitors, she told me, he generally sat quietly in a corner swinging one foot. Alwin, the eldest boy, imitated his way of walking up and down the room with hands folded behind his back, saying, " This is how Schumann does." Schumann made a great deal of fun with the boys, but the greatest thing was when he told stories to both boys and girls —ghost stories, robber stories, etc. Once when Clara was on her travels Schumann reminded her in a letter (February 1, 1832) of the story-telling :

. . . I know you have a thinking head and understand your old, moonstruck inventor of charades—so, dear Clara, I often think of you, not as a brother thinks of a sister, or one friend of another, but rather as a pilgrim thinks of a distant altarpiece. During your absence I

I

visited Arabia to get all kinds of stories that would please you—six new *Doppelgänger* stories, one hundred and one charades, eight amusing riddles, and then the frightfully lovely robber stories, and those about the white ghost—whoo-oo-oo, how I shudder ! . . .

He made the boys perform all sorts of tricks, rewarding them by the lavish expenditure of pennies. What he says about the boys and their dress and ways must have interested their sister Clara very much :

. . . Alwin has become a very nice boy ; his new blue coat, and the leather cap like mine, suit him uncommonly well ; of Gustav there is little astonishing to be said ; he has, however, grown so astonishingly that you will be surprised . . . and Clemens is the most droll, amiable, headstrong boy, speaks in musical notes, and has a very sonorous voice ; he, too, has grown very much ; but one of these days the violin will run away with Alwin. To report on cousin Pfundt,* there is nobody in Leipzig (except myself) who longs so much for Frankfurt as he. . . .

Clara would be still more amused by Robert's questions :

How do the apples taste in Frankfurt ? And how is the thrice-marked F [otherwise F in alt] in Chopin's skipping variation [Op. 2, Var. 4] ? My paper comes to an end—everything comes to an end, only not friendship, with which I am Fräulein C. W.'s warmest worshipper.—R. Schumann.

When Clara and her father returned to Leipzig the friendly intercourse between the Wieck family and Schumann continued, not only at Wieck's house and here and there, but also in excursions to the Rosenthal and Connewitz, and occasional restaurants. The relationship between Robert and Clara, the youth of twenty-two and the girl of thirteen, the reader will consider most interesting and curious. He is mostly respectful and rarely uses words of endearment, while full of admira-

* A timpanist of world-wide fame. Beginning as a theologian, he became a student of music under his uncle, Wieck, and for a time taught music and led the Leipzig theatre chorus. In 1835, Mendelssohn engaged him as timpanist of the Gewandhaus orchestra, which post he held till his death in 1871. He is the author of a kettledrum Method.

tion for her musical achievements. But I think that owing to her early public appearances the womanhood in her was prematurely developed. The motherly instinct is very apparent in her watchfulness over him when on country excursions she pulls his coat tails to call his attention to a stone in his way, which his upward look, then habitual, prevented his noticing. His ideas of her artistic perfections were great and had no limits, but they seemed to be solely the admiration of a colleague, not of a lover. In addressing her he uses the polite *Sie*, not the intimate or familiar *Du*.

When Dorn left Leipzig in 1832 he was succeeded as conductor at the theatre by Ferdinand Stegmayer, who had already become known in this capacity and appreciated by Ferdinand David and Mendelssohn at the Berlin Königstädter theatre (1825). He was a very popular personality, but terribly impossible, because of the irregularities of his life. He was the son of the Vienna Court actor and poet, the author of the famous farce, *Rochus Pumpernickel*. We can easily form an idea of him from Schumann's remarks when introducing him to his correspondent, C. von Bruyck: "He is an old acquaintance of mine, a very experienced musician, whom I had to thank in earlier times for many a practical hint." "A splendid musical individuality, to whom I owe a great deal, but so wild and dissolute that it is impossible to get on with him. He wrote a petition to the Diet (which I signed) to be allowed to sleep by day and work all night."

Julius Knorr (1807–61), originally a theological student, turned afterwards to the teaching of music. After some appearances as a pianist at the Gewandhaus, he gave himself entirely to the art of pedagogy (school editions, guides for teachers, etc.). Later in life he distinguished himself more by his billiard than by his pianoforte playing. He was one of the initiators of the *Neue Zeitschrift für Musik*, at first its editor, afterwards a contributor. We can understand Schumann's intercourse with and friendship for a man of ideas like Knorr.

It is more difficult to understand the friendship for the music teacher, Carl Friedrich Günther, called by Jansen in

Die Davidsbündler " the good-natured but rather homely [*hausbacken*] pianist," with whom Schumann lived in 1833 and 1834 at the corner of Burgstrasse and Sporergässchen. When during Schumann's absence Zuccalmaglio was in Leipzig, Schumann writes to him : " . . . However, you will have found a faithful companion in good old Günther." But it would seem that good-natured Günther was something of a butt. Schumann writes to Clara : " . . . Do you sometimes think of Günther (preferably called the ' *genialische* ' [the genius]) ? "

Ernst Ferdinand Wenzel (1808–80) remained throughout a devoted and appreciated friend and fellow-contributor. How he was regarded in the latter character may be gathered from a letter of Schumann's from Vienna to his editorial *remplaçant*, O. Lorenz : " Has Wenzel shown himself active ? He has such a good head that it would be a pity if he remained idle. Greet him from me." I remember Wenzel well as a clever, lively, old man with whom I discussed Schumann with curiosity. He began his University studies with philosophy, and continued his music studies under Wieck.

Dr. Reuter (1802–53) was a characteristic figure among Schumann's friends, a figure such as one finds in humorous novels. He had studied medicine, but lived content without a doctor's vocation and without a doctor's practice. Nor do we hear that he had any musical qualities. But we do hear of his willingness to make himself generally useful—for instance, to look after Schumann's neglected laundry transactions, for which neither mother nor sisters-in-law were then available.

But the literary friends have at this time quite an unusual significance and importance. They brought him into actual contact with the inner working of the daily and periodical press of the time. Leipzig was, of course, then a centre of the book trade. And Ortlepp and Herlosssohn, the friends in question, knew all the intrigues and scandals of the Leipzig counterpart of Grub Street, for they had drunk of literature to its lowest dregs. In fact, their lives must have been full of the saddest experiences. We do not know the degree of their intimacy with Schumann, but it is clear that he enjoyed their company on his walks. Then he contributed to their publications, and when in 1834 the *Neue Zeitschrift für Musik* came into being, they contributed to it. Herlosssohn, as editor of various periodical publications, had it in his power occasionally to play the part of patron to his friend, doing him the useful service that an editorially connected *littérateur* can confer naturally and without much trouble. Both men were poets, dramatists, and novelists. Dr. Ernst Ortlepp (a Saxon, 1800–64) made his name known by *Songs of the Poles* (1831); Laudatory and Satirical Poems ; *The Cid* and *Gustav Adolf* (dramas); and *Friedemann Bach,* etc. (novels). Owing to his political obnoxiousness he had to leave Leipzig in 1836, and in 1864 his moral failings, intemperance among the rest, led to suicide by drowning. Georg Carl Herlosssohn (Prague, 1804; Vienna; and Leipzig, where he died in hospital, 1849) became especially known at one time by his editorship of *Der Komet* (1830–48), a critico-literary and humoristic periodical of good repute. Why Herlosssohn interrupted his editorship from 1840–44 I do not know, nor do I know why the paper ceased altogether in 1848. Among the periodicals which he edited alone or with others were also a *Theatrical Lexicon,* and a *Damen Conversations Lexikon* (Leipzig in the 'thirties). In the preface to the latter the editor speaks as follows: " To make a feature of mythology and music seems to us necessary. Feminine fancy likes to dwell in the land of riddles and chiaroscuro, of miracles and legends, likes to abandon itself to the magic of music, and often chooses her as faithful companion in a dull life." Schumann is the principal musical contributor to the first and second volumes of this periodical ; the chief contributor to the third and fourth volumes is " E. O." (Ernst Ortlepp ?). Schumann signs his articles " R. S." The signatures of other writers I shall not endeavour to trace ; one of them is Carl Banck, whom we shall know better by and by. Schumann contributed sixty-three more or less brief articles, of which that on J. S. Bach is one of the most interesting, considering how he then thought of him, The chief original works of Herlosssohn are the poems, the *Book of Love* ; historical novels dealing mostly with the Thirty Years' War, etc.

Of other publications to which Schumann contributed we may mention the *Leipziger Tageblatt* (1832–35); Fink's *Allgemeine Musikalische Zeitung* (1831); and Brockhaus's *Deutsche Allgemeine Zeitung* (1840–41).

It is possible to perceive an increase of seriousness in the first years after Schumann's return to Leipzig. The studies in composition led him to more earnest considerations and more weighty endeavours. His self-criticism became more severe, and the tasks put on himself more difficult. He is not so ready to pooh-pooh the advice of the older and experienced men. He often labours in silence and without rest ; and sets himself tasks that can only be mastered with enormous effort—as he did in the *Riesenwerk*, a sonata which he intended to dedicate to Moscheles in London. But it is not solely the artist, but also the man, who seems to have undergone the change. Whereas in the past he thought of his brothers only as people to be borrowed from, we see him now offering them, Eduard and Carl, his financial help in the most generous way. Schumann had in the meantime come of age, and the free disposal of his money reminded him of his responsibilities.

My money is in good keeping, lent out on good security. I shall never touch the capital.

Let us hope that he did not indulge in self-deception. I must confess that there are suspicious passages in the letters. For instance, in a letter to his mother we read :

. . . You will easily see that my interest does not cover my expenses ; I believe for certain that I must add two hundred thalers a year for five years, also, that by that time my finances will balance, what with honorariums, etc., etc. If you can meantime give me a help, do not omit it. I shall certainly repay you later.

I am afraid my fears are not allayed by the following determination :

If you have any influence with Carl and Rosalie [brother and wife], beg them to send me no more money than my legal interest. Otherwise there will be a dreadful muddle.

Schumann's moods, as we saw before, were very varied, but, as a musician, mostly happy. Describing his domestic life pictorially to his mother (May 8, 1832), he says it might be called Italian in the morning and Dutch in the evening. His dwelling is decent, roomy, and comfortable, in garden scenery. Early, about five o'clock, he leaps out of bed like a roe-deer; accounts, diary, and correspondence claim his first attention; till eleven he studies and composes and reads a little; at eleven o'clock every day comes his friend Lühe, who is a model of order and regularity; at midday, dinner; he then reads French or the newspapers; from three to six he regularly takes a walk, as a rule alone; if he is home by six, he improvises till about eight; then generally to a restaurant for supper, and so home. Such was the plan of his less full days, not of those others when the composer never left his house and chair.

And now a confession has to be made, made by himself to his mother (May 8, 1832), and reported to her also by friends and well-wishers:

You have yourself asked Rascher whether I really do drink so much. I believe he defended me; I should not have done so, for there was truth in the story. But as the drinking of Bavarian beer was a prosaic habit rather than a poetic passion, it was not easy to give it up, for it is infinitely easier to give up a passion than an old habit. But if you ask if it is given up, I say with a firm voice, yes.

There can be no doubt as to the truth of this confession; the cure, however, was not so sudden as is here made out. But although Schumann indulged in this weakness, and did so for a time, causing anxiety to his family and friends, including Clara, it must not be supposed that he was at any time a sot; and he recovered himself in the course of time. Beer was not the sole temptation he had to contend with— the second weakness had a firmer hold on him—namely, strong cigars. He writes to his family on April 28, 1832:

. . . I am very well; I am industrious, and have *almost* entirely given up cigars and beer; now I'm making progress. . . .

In 1831 and the following year cholera found its way from

Russia to Germany. The fear was general, and of no one did it get a firmer hold than of Schumann. He himself described it as " a distressful, almost childish fear." He made his will, and thought of refuges in Germany and Italy, the latter country occupying his thoughts for a long time. At first he wanted to apply for advice from his relatives, then to take flight and write for permission afterwards. The thought of visiting Italy again had at first a great charm for him ; and the old *Reiselust* came over him. But by May 5, 1832, that was already a thing of the past, and, he writes, " people are no longer thinking about cholera."

About the end of November, 1832, a great event took place in Schumann's life, an event which cannot be passed over in the life of any musician—the first public performance of his first symphony, or part of it. This took place in his native town, Zwickau. Friedrich Wieck had formed the plan of giving a concert there with Clara, and having heard of his pupil's achievement, gave him the opportunity of producing his work on that occasion. Schumann writes to his mother about the ravishing piece of news a fortnight previously at two o'clock in the morning (but he writes of one movement only). And on November 14, 1832, the following advertisement appeared in the Zwickau newspaper :

CLARA WIECK,

The celebrated thirteen-year-old pianoforte virtuosa will give with her father, Herr Wieck, a great pianoforte concert in the hall of the [Zwickau] Gewandhaus, with the co-operation of the Choral Society. Herr Schumann will at the same time produce some movements of his first Symphony. Price of admission, six groschen per person.

The thanks expressed by Wieck to the performers on November 21 do not include Schumann. For, alas ! it has to be admitted that the composition was not a success. On January 10, 1833, Schumann writes to Wieck in great haste from Zwickau :

. . . Great concert at Schneeberg [the neighbouring town, under the conductor Thierfelder]—Thierfelder has written asking for the Symphony—I am up to the ears in work—complete upheaval of the first movement—rewriting of the parts and score—adding the other movements. . . .

A letter to his mother, of June 28, 1833, contains a more favourable account.

. . . My Symphony * which was played here [Leipzig] shortly before Eduard's arrival has made me many friends among the greatest connoisseurs, such as Stegmayer, Pohlenz, Hauser. When I introduced myself to Matthäi, the leader of the orchestra, the following absurd incident happened. I distractedly said : " My name is Matthäi ! "

* Not published.

CHAPTER X

IN speaking of Schumann it is impossible for the writer on music to remain long silent on Jean Paulism. But to speak of it is very difficult if the remarks are to be adequately helpful and not too lengthy. The chief obstacles are the voluminousness of the poet's works and their almost complete neglect by the public of to-day—a neglect sufficiently accounted for by the vices of the author's style. Richter began with the writing of mediocre satires, and when success came he appealed to the public mainly by two kinds of composition—idylls of humble life in the world of pastors and schoolmasters, and romances of character development with the most extraordinary plots, fantastic personages, and meditations, observations, and flashes of wit and humour, full of the sensibilities of youth and all it dreams of. There was a time when I thought that nothing less than an analysis of all Richter's works could be considered a sufficient introduction to the works of Schumann. But as one grows older one's demands become more moderate and one's views as to the influence of the poet and the musician on each other change. Was Jean Paul's influence on Schumann as great as the latter supposed ? And did it not vary at different times of his life ? Nay, had Jean Paul at any time a predominating and exclusive influence on Schumann ? Another powerful influence was that of Goethe. When did it come in, and to what extent did it become a substitute for Jean Paul's ? Then, what were the influences of the romantic German lyricists, and the foreigners Moore and Byron ? It is an interesting task to pursue the inquiry where, when, and in what degree the poets moulded the style (subject and manner) of Schumann. It has seemed to me for a long time that his style has often very little in common with that of Jean Paul, and a great deal with that of Goethe and of the lesser German lights. Think only of the youthful pianoforte compositions, the songs and some of the maturer works in the larger forms. The epistolary and literary styles of Schumann teach us a great deal about his relation to his poet compeers, and incline us to treat Jean Paul's influence as negligible.

Of the literary historians that have written about Jean Paul, A. F. C. Vilmar has, in my opinion, characterized his style in the happiest way. What can be more true than his statement that Jean Paul was the author of undeveloped youth with its blissful dreams and fantastic questionings, its idyllic contentment and far-reaching projects, its trivial play and great thoughts ; that, indeed, certain periods of youth have something akin to Jean Paul's mental conditions, which never grew from youthfulness to the maturity of manhood ? Thus it is that youth at these periods still feels attracted by Jean Paul ; and those to whom it is either natural or who find it pleasant to retain throughout life the standpoint of poetic receptivity belonging to their twentieth year still feel drawn to him. Those, on the other hand, whose capacity for enjoyment develops from youth to maturity, invariably become indifferent to him later on, or even, having praised him, come to find fault with him ; and while there are many who have changed from admirers into opponents, there is not a single one who has changed from opponent into admirer.

A few more specially significant words have to be added in order to enable us to comprehend the strange mixture of qualities that go to make up Jean Paulism and Romanticism, which, of course, do not wholly correspond, the latter being naturally more comprehensive and varied. Here are the words : the obscure ; the foreboding ; the incomprehensible ; simultaneous laughter and tears ; yearning ; melancholy ; the deeply felt ; gleams of light, meteors, lightnings—in short, the varied fireworks of a summer night : we find sense impressions, feelings, reflections, rather than actions ; isolated beautiful passages, rather than a unified whole.

Schumann must have felt Jean Paul's shortcomings when he wrote the following words to his Clara in March, 1838 :

... I am very glad that you are reading the *Flegeljahre*. At the first reading do not stop too long over special passages that may not be clear to you. Try to get a general view of the whole at first, then begin again at the beginning. It is a book in its own way like the Bible ; you will come to the place : ' Listen, Walt, I do love you more than you love me.' ' No,' screamed Walt, ' I love you best.' Then think of me. Let me have a nice word to tell me how you like the book. . . .

Die Flegeljahre is one of Jean Paul's masterworks. Walt and Vult are the representatives of the poet's personality, just as Eusebius and Florestan were afterwards used by Schumann to symbolize two aspects of his own personality. But Schumann was not of those who lost their loyalty to the poet : on the contrary, he remained a lifelong admirer and extolled the poet's writings to all his friends. Indeed his case was that he loved Jean Paul not wisely, but too well. He was apt to regard as his personal enemies all whose admiration of Jean Paul fell short of his own. A characteristic occurrence, the truth of which is vouchsafed for by Hanslick, took place in 1850, when the musicians of Hamburg gave a banquet in honour of Schumann and his wife. After the toast of the guests, the silent Schumann rose, amid breathless silence, to make a speech—*mirabile dictu !*—and began by remarking the happy coincidence of the day of the festivity, March 21, with the birthday of two of the greatest geniuses of Germany —Sebastian Bach and Jean Paul, the immortal rulers of music and poetry. The toast was enthusiastically drunk, when up rose Grädener, director of the Hamburg *Singakademie*, who protested against the mention in the same breath of Jean Paul and Sebastian Bach at a gathering of German musicians. Before the speaker had elaborated his thought Schumann rose and left the hall in dudgeon, and it was not till next day that Grädener was able to effect a reconciliation.

On May 5, 1843, Schumann writes to his contributor Kossmaly :

. . . Here you have my confessions. You know without my telling you that Bach and Jean Paul exercised the greatest influence on me in earlier times. But now I am more independent. . . .

Richter and Bach he often couples together, but Bach's name is not the only one that he couples with Richter's. Schumann writes to Wieck on November 6, 1829 (note the early date):

. . . Schubert is still " my only Schubert," especially as he has every-thing in common with my " only Jean Paul." When I play Schubert I feel as if I were reading a romance of Jean Paul's set to music. . . .

But I think that Schumann had really forgotten a great many of his earlier impressions of Jean Paul, and unconsciously avoided what better models taught him to avoid. For an admirer it is strange that Schumann is so little of an imitator. In the early winter of 1833 there came to Leipzig the pianist-composer Ludwig Schunke, a young man of twenty-three, only a few months older than Schumann. The friend-ship that sprang from their meeting was unique, unlike any of Schumann's earlier and later friendships in its suddenness, intimacy, and artistic and musical kinship. When the new-comer died a little more than a year after (December 7, 1834), the friend left behind wrote of him: " . . . He was a man, an artist, a friend without an equal." He was, in fact, an ideal friend, companion, and colleague. Ludwig Schunke came of a large musical family, originally bakers by trade, his father being one of seven brothers, five of whom played the horn, for which they had great gifts and obtained great honours. Ludwig's father, Gottfried Schunke, found a post in the orchestra of the brother of Napoleon I, Jerome, King of Westphalia, and when the kingdom came to an end Schunke found a vacancy in the establishment of Stuttgart. The little son was born at Cassel, on September 21, 1810. No time was lost in commencing the child's musical instruction—his father began it at six, and took him on artistic tours at the age of eleven and fourteen. When eighteen Ludwig went to Paris, where an uncle of his was settled, and there Reicha was his teacher of composition, and the pianists Kalkbrenner and Henri Herz showed him the way on his chief instrument. Next he joined his father at Stuttgart, and after a time at Vienna he removed to Leipzig.

Schumann and Schunke lodged in the same (corner) house (Burgstrasse No. 21 and Sporergässchen), and often walked and skated together. Robert writes in the highest terms of Schunke to his mother (March 19, 1834): "He is an excellent man and friend, ever zealously striving after all that is finest and best. One patch of blue in the sky often gives one more joy than a whole expanse of blue. I could do without all other friends for this one alone." Schunke was not a commonplace man, not a Philistine. He reminded Schumann of the Apostle John, of a Roman emperor, and of Thorwaldsen's statue of Schiller, although he was even more Schilleresque than the original. Moreover, Schunke was not a long-suffering man, for he wanted to fight a duel with Nicolai (the composer-to-be of the *Merry Wives of Windsor*), but as Schumann was to be Nicolai's second the interests of peace prevailed. The merchant and music-lover, Carl Voigt, made the acquaintance of Schunke at Wieck's, and thus Schunke became intimate with one of the most musical households of Leipzig. And Schunke could not rest till his new friends got to know his *fidus Achates*, but knowing his shyness he induced Carl Voigt to make Schumann's acquaintance at Kintschi's coffee-house in the Rosenthal. At last Schumann became as intimate with the Voigts as Schunke, who not only grew to be a friend of the house but was devotedly nursed by them during his last illness. Henriette Voigt had been a faithful pupil of Ludwig Berger's, who in his turn was a pupil of Clementi. The greatest musicians of the time went in and out of the Voigts' house : Mendelssohn, Chopin, Löwe, Hauptmann, and others. Carl Voigt made a name for himself by giving an endowment for performances of Beethoven's Ninth Symphony at the Gewandhaus concerts.

Schunke was one of the founders of the *Neue Zeitschrift für Musik*, but his hand had less cunning in wielding the pen than in playing the pianoforte. Schumann's correcting pen was the main thing in Schunke's contributions.   But his health, already very poor, became much worse; the doctor held out no hope, spoke of one more winter only.   It was a matter of exhaustion; consumption was the trouble.   " May heaven give me strength to lose him," wrote Schumann.   But unable to bear the sight of his friend's growing weakness, Schumann had strength only to go home to Zwickau, from where he wrote to Henriette Voigt : ". . . How can I bear the thought of giving him up ?   If he dies, for heaven's sake do not write it to me, or let someone else write. . . ."

Dörffel notes down three Gewandhaus concerts at which Schunke played.   At the first he played the E flat Beethoven Concerto and three compositions of his own, a *Fantaisie brillante* with orchestra, a *Rondeau brillant*, etc.; and at another *Variations and Finale* for pianoforte.   The catalogue of Schunke's compositions comprises upwards of fifteen works, some of which are as follows : *Scherzo capriccioso p. Piano* (Paris); *Sonate* in G minor, dedicated to R. Schumann (*Leipzig*); *Allegro passionato* in A minor (Vienna); 2me *Caprice* (C minor), dedicated to Fr. Chopin (Leipzig); *Variations de Concert sur la Valse fun. de Schubert av. Accomp. d'Orchestre* (A flat), dedicated to Madame Henriette Voigt (Leipzig).

The preparations for the *Neue Zeitschrift für Musik* were begun in the latter part of June, 1833.   In a letter of June 28 Schumann writes to his mother :

. . . A number of young, well-educated people, mostly students of music, have drawn a circle round me which I, again, have drawn round Wieck's house.   We are chiefly possessed by the thought of a grand new music journal which Hofmeister is publishing, and of which a prospectus and advertisement will appear next month.   The tone and colour of the whole are to be fresher and more varied than in the others ; in particular we shall block up the old worn-out ways, although I have little prospect of ever bringing Wieck (who, however, is more and more friendly with me every day) into agreement with my views of art. Many heads, many opinions, even though there should be controversy. The directors are Ortlepp, Wieck, myself, and two others, music teachers —mostly executive musicians (my nine-fingered self excepted), which at once gives the thing an air, as the other music papers are edited by amateurs. Among the other collaborators may be mentioned Lühe, Hofrat Wendt, deaf Lyser, Reissiger and Krägen in Dresden, Franz Otto in London [singer and composer of songs].

Perhaps I shall gain from this enterprise something for which my nature (averse as it is from everything disorderly) longs, with many another artist : a more stable (bourgeois) background, which serves as a frame round the picture or as a vessel containing the spreading mass. Not to speak of the pecuniary advantages. . . .

Writing on July 31, 1833, to the publisher Hofmeister to ask him for Ortlepp's prospectus of the paper, the first number of which was to appear in April, 1834, Schumann confesses to having missed the authors' meeting (Ortlepp, Wieck, Schunke, Knorr, etc.) by being asleep at the time. The book-seller C. H. F. Hartmann, however, and not Hofmeister, became the first publisher of the *Neue Zeitschrift für Musik*. Among possible publishers, Schumann's brother Eduard was also indicated, but he was reluctant, pleading occupation with publications that took up his whole time. Wieck did not seem quite to trust Schumann's working capacity as editor. In fact, he promised his assistance only if he could count on his whilom pupil's sticking to his business. But he wronged him, for Schumann was bent on business and really stood in need of support and not of threats. Not only he but other contributors as well are ready to make sacrifices. If the enterprise does not succeed, Knorr, Ortlepp, and Schumann himself, as well as Wieck, undertake to forgo payment. Schumann was also to have 150 thalers as editor, and this, too, he renounces if the worst should come to the worst. To what length he was prepared to go may be gathered from his offer to lend Hofmeister 1,400 thalers if necessary. On March 19, 1834, Schumann mentions as directors of the paper : Stegmayer (*Capellmeister*), Wieck, Schunke, Knorr, and himself. It seems that his daily companions were his con-tributors Herlosssohn, Wieck, Stegmayer, Schunke, Stelle (*sic*), Ortlepp, Lyser, Berger, Bürck, and Pohlenz. It is strange that Schumann's name is never mentioned in connection with the early editing. Is this modesty or policy ? Knorr was at last appointed editor, and nominally remained so for the first

year.   But during his illness of many weeks the editorship
was in Schumann's hands, and the impression one gets is that
it always had been so.   And afterwards there was no question
as to his editorship.

The new music paper made its appearance under the title
Neue Leipziger Zeitschrift für Musik, " edited by a combination of artists and amateurs."   The publisher for the first
year was C. H. F. Hartmann, from No. 1, April 3, to No. 78,
December 29, 1834, the parts appearing twice a week, and each
part consisting of two quarto sheets—that is, four pages of
two columns each.   The yearly subscription was three
reichsthaler eight groschen (roughly, about ten shillings).
Among the twenty-two contributors mentioned are the following musicians : Carl Banck (song composer); C. F. Becker
(organist and antiquarian); Ludwig Böhner (a migrating
composer); Julius Knorr (musical pedagogue); J. C. Lobe
(flautist, composer, and writer); J. Mainzer (of *Singing for the
Million* fame, *Mainzer's Musical Times*, etc.); H. Panofka
(violinist and singing master, Paris); Ludwig Schunke
(pianoforte virtuoso and composer); Dr. F. Stöpel (teacher
of Logier's system, Paris); and Fr. Wieck (pianoforte and
singing teacher).   The following amateurs are also mentioned : C. Alexander; A. Bürck; Dr. Glock; Dr. Heinroth;
Ritter A. Kretzschmer; J. P. Lyser (novelist, etc.); Gustav
Nauenburg (theologian and afterwards singing master); Dr.
C. Seidel; Dr. K. Stein (Keferstein, pastor); and lastly, the
" Davidsbündler," of whom more presently.

It will be enough to say that the publisher Hartmann
resigned his undertaking, and by the editors' desire handed
over the publication to J. A. Barth at the end of 1834.   We
need not inquire what were the ins and outs of the affair—
the explanations are partly not of interest to us and partly not
forthcoming.

In the second volume of the journal (beginning with
January, 1835) the editorship of Robert Schumann was for
the first time openly declared.   Schumann might all his life
have been a publicist, gifted as he was with the publicist's
ready persuasive wit.   It may be said that among the con-

K

tributors he supplied all the genius, all the inspiration and even all the persevering patience. The artist-editor's sacrifice in the latter respect cannot be too highly appreciated. In the succeeding years of the *Neue Zeitschrift* Schumann names the following professional and amateur contributors besides those already mentioned: Heinrich Dorn; Ignaz von Seyfried (*Capellmeister* and author, Vienna); Richard Wagner; Carl Kossmaly (*Capellmeister* and composer, Königsberg); August Gathy (musical author, Hamburg and Paris); J. F. E. Sobolewski (pseudonym, J. Feski, composer and musical author, Königsberg); F. H. Truhn (composer and author); H. Hirschbach (composer and author); John Thomson (Reid Professor of Music and composer, Edinburgh); Dr. A. J. Becher (revolutionary, composer, and author); A. B. Marx (theorist); E. A. Mangold (composer and author); Oswald Lorenz (music teacher and author, and during Schumann's Vienna time and at other times his substitute as editor); Dr. A. Kahlert (æsthetician); Dr. E. Krüger (æsthetician); Theodor Töpken (correspondent); A. W. F. von Zuccalmaglio ("Waldbrühl," novelist, poet, folklorist, etc.); and others.

The prospectus of "The Editors," with which the publication begins, sets forth their intentions, which, however, were only partly realized. There were to be theoretical and historical essays; æsthetical, grammatical, biographical, pedagogic, acoustic matters; sketches of celebrated artists and of artists in the workshop; chronicles, criticisms of all kinds and specially of pianoforte compositions; a special feature was to be musical tales, humorous matter, anecdotes, extracts from great writers, etc., etc.

But the editors' prospectus of the year 1834 interests us less than the thoughts and happenings that were recalled to Schumann when, twenty years after, he wrote the introduction to his *Gesammelte Schriften über Musik und Musiker* (*Collected Writings on Music and Musicians*, selections from his contributions to the *Neue Zeitschrift für Musik*), which appeared for the first time in 1854. I am sure the reader will agree with me that his retrospect is too interesting to be summarized, and must be quoted in full:

At the end of the year 1833 there met in Leipzig every evening and as if by chance a number of musicians, mostly young, in the first place for social intercourse, but also for exchange of ideas about the art that was the meat and drink of their life—music. It cannot be said that musical conditions in Germany at that time were very pleasing. Rossini ruled the stage, Herz and Hünten almost exclusively the pianoforte. Yet only a few years had passed since Beethoven, C. M. von Weber, and Franz Schubert had lived among us. True, Mendelssohn's star was in the ascendant, and wonderful things were being heard of a Pole, one Chopin, but it was not till later that these exercised a more lasting influence. Then one day the thought flashed across the young hot-heads : let us not look on idly, let us be up and doing to improve matters, let us set about restoring the poetry of art to its place of honour. So there appeared the first pages of a new music periodical. But this youthful energetic band were not to enjoy their solidarity for long. Death claimed the sacrifice of one of the most precious among them, Ludwig Schunke. Some of the others at times completely severed their connection with Leipzig. The enterprise was on the point of being abandoned. Then one of them, the musical dreamer of the party, whose life had hitherto been dreamed away at the pianoforte rather than among books, resolved to take the editing in hand himself, and carried it on for about ten years till the year 1844. The result was a series of essays many of which are contained in this collection. Most of the opinions therein expressed he still holds to-day. What he wrote in hope and fear about many an art phenomenon has been confirmed in the course of time.

And another association may be mentioned here, which was more than a secret one, for it existed only in the head of its founder—the " Davidsbündler " [League of David, Davidites, etc.]. It seemed not unfitting, in order to express different points of view on art problems, to invent contrasting artist characters, of which Florestan and Eusebius were the chief, with Master Raro as intermediary. This " Davids-bündler " idea ran like a red thread through the paper, uniting " *Wahrheit* " and " *Dichtung* " in humorous fashion. Later these companions, not unpleasing to the readers of the time, vanished entirely from the paper, and since a Peri lured them to distant zones nothing more has been heard of their work as authors.

That Schumann has often been misunderstood without reason must be clear to everyone who remembers his love of mystification, fanciful playfulness without the least element of serious truth in it. But there are men who think that they must materialize everything, whatever may be the personality they have to deal with, whatever the humour, the general cast of mind. Schumann does not leave us in doubt what his meaning is, as will be seen from the following passage from a letter to Dorn (September 14, 1836):

> The " Davidsbund " is only a spiritual, romantic one, as you will have noticed long ago. Mozart was just as great a " Bündler " as is Berlioz now, as you are, without exactly being created so by diploma. Florestan and Eusebius are my double nature which, like Master Raro, I should like to fuse into a man. . . . The other veiled ones are *partly* persons, and much of the life of the " Davidsbündler " is also taken from reality. . . .

Schumann when discussing the League always lays stress on its imaginary existence:

> An association existing only in the imagination, whose members are recognizable less by outward signs than by an inward resemblance. It will be their endeavour by word and by deed to dam up the tide of mediocrity. . . .
> Mounting the grand pianoforte, Florestan spoke as follows : " Assembled ' Davidsbündler,' that is to say, youths and men who are to kill the Philistines, musical and otherwise, especially the tallest . . .

The " Davidsbündler " are, as we have already heard Schumann declare, partly taken from reality ; they are also of uncertain number, some persons (real or imaginary) being only casually enrolled. We know how Schumann gave two of his own aspects the names of Florestan and Eusebius, striving to combine their characteristics by help of a third, Master Raro. Florestan represented the fiery enthusiast ; Eusebius the gentle dreamer. Sometimes the Walt and Vult aspects of Jean Paul play a part ; Wina, too, occurs. Among others there was a favourite character with all the qualities required by Schumann, especially humour—an essential ingredient of contributors to the *Neue Zeitschrift*. This was Stephen Heller, then living privately with a family at Augsburg, later settled in Paris as the friend of Berlioz and other colleagues. Heller is veiled by the name of Jeanquirit. Another congenial " Davidsbündler " was A. W. F. von Zuccalmaglio, appearing as " St. Diamond." " F. Meritis " is Felix Mendelssohn ; " Chiara," " Chiarina," and " Zilia " stand for Clara ; and other names are to be met with.

CHAPTER XI

IN considering the productivity of Schumann, we cannot overlook his tendency at first to produce his compositions in groups.

Thus from 1830–39 we have exclusively pianoforte works, Opp. 1–23, Op. 26, Op. 28, and Op. 32.

Next, he devoted himself almost exclusively to songs: Opp. 24 and 25; Op. 27; Opp. 29, 30, 31; Opp. 33–37; Opp. 39 and 40; Opp. 42 and 43; Op. 45; Opp. 48 and 49; Opp. 51 and 53 (1840–42).

Then there are the remarkable groups of chamber music: three string quartets, Op. 41; the quintet for pianoforte and strings, Op. 44; and the quartet for pianoforte and strings, Op. 47 (1842).

The four symphonies and other important orchestral works come within a period of ten years, 1841–1851; but the tendency to grouping gradually disappears and Schumann produces, especially in the last years of the 'forties, a remarkable variety of instrumental, vocal, and mixed instrumental and vocal works great and small.

Of the four symphonies, two were composed in 1841— B flat major, Op. 38, and D minor (newly instrumentated in 1851 and thereafter known as the fourth), Op. 120; C major, Op. 61, 1845 and 1846; E flat major, Op. 97, 1850; *Overture, Scherzo, and Finale*, Op. 52, 1841; the Pianoforte Concerto, Op. 54, 1841 and 1845; the less inspired *Concertstücke*, Op. 92, 1849, and Op. 134, 1853; the *Phantasie Stücke* for pianoforte, violin, and violoncello,

Op. 88, 1842. In 1843 came the *Andante and Variations* for two pianofortes, Op. 46, and *Paradise and the Peri*, Op. 50; in 1844, the *Epilogue to Goethe's "Faust"*; in 1845, besides the C major symphony, the contrapuntal group for pedal-pianoforte, etc., Opp. 56, 58, 60, and 72. Thereafter, the scattered pianoforte trios : D minor, Op. 63, 1847; F major, Op. 80, 1847; and G minor, Op. 110, 1851 ; *Genoveva* Op. 81, 1847 and 1848 ; *Manfred* Op. 115, 1848 and 1849 ; further *Faust* music; further pianoforte and other instrumental and vocal works, ballads for chorus and orchestra, overtures, etc., etc.—the variety continuing until the end.

Schumann began composition as an amateur before he had studied his art professionally. Of course, a man of his distinguished talent divines more than he is taught. What he wrote of his first theory teacher, Heinrich Dorn, whose lessons he attended (or neglected) at Leipzig after his return from Heidelberg University, is therefore of the greatest significance (pp. 109, 110) and must be repeated here :

. . . All the same I feel that the theoretical studies have had a good influence on me. If formerly everything was inspiration of the moment, I now reflect more on the play of my enthusiasm, sometimes stop in the middle of it to take stock of where I am. . . . Dorn, my theory teacher, had advanced me inwardly a great deal. By dint of persevering study, I gained that beautiful clearness of which, indeed, I early had some idea, but which I often lacked. From now onwards my life becomes different, I am independent. I gave the manuscript out of my hands almost with hesitation : now it is printed. . . . So, firstly, I think of you [Dorn] almost every day, often sadly, because I studied so negligently; always gratefully, for I learned more than you believe. . . .

The most interesting thing about Schumann's Op. 1 is the dedication, which, let it be said at once, is a fraud and a mystification, though it gives itself out as *Thème sur le nom "Abegg" varié pour le Pianoforte. Dédié à Mademoiselle Pauline Comtesse d'Abegg.* Leipzig, Fr. Kistner. Composed 1830; appeared July, 1832. The name of Abegg was familiar enough in Mannheim, the neighbour town of

Heidelberg, where the composer then lived (1830). But Schumann could not boast an aristocratic acquaintance of that name, and there was, indeed, neither a Comtesse nor a Mademoiselle Pauline. In fact the son had a hearty laugh at his mother, who examined him with suspicion in a letter in which she asks for information about the dedication. Writing to her on November 25, 1831, Schumann says :

. . . the Countess is an old maid of twenty-six, very clever and musical, but sharp and ugly. But not to deprive your imagination of all hope of a future aristocratic connection, I must admit that the younger sister is really like an angel (Emily is her name), only too ethereal for your son. . . .

The theme, opening with the notes A, B, E, G, G (B flat in German is called B), which appear later in reversed order, is in form wholly sequential and, as Rellstab, editor of the Berlin music journal *Iris*, tells the composer, monotonously so. You have only to note the reversed form of the melody in the second part :

and you will agree with the critic and disagree with the composer, although he blindly refuses to admit the criticism. The worst that can be said of the variations is that structurally they leave something to be desired here and there. On the whole the talented amateur could not help writing pleasingly. But how Rellstab had the heart to compare them to those of Czerny and Henri Herz—Schumann's *bêtes noires*—it is difficult to understand. The last movement, the *Finale alla Fantasia*, is musically the most satisfactory. Let us note the first appearance here and there of chromaticism, especially harmonic, but not yet in Schumann's characteristic manner. The publication caused him a great deal of excitement. He wrote to his family speaking of the birth of a healthy, thriving child, saying that he was revelling in the first joys of the author which could fall short only of the state of courtship, and he reminds them of the Doge and the Marriage of the Adriatic. But the most touching thing was his illusion that all the world took a lively interest in him.

* Op. 2. *Papillons pour le Pianoforte seul. Dédiés à Therese, Rosalie et Emilie.* Leipzig, Fr. Kistner. Composed 1829 and 1831; appeared 1832.

This was, unlike Op. 1, a very real dedication, to his brothers' wives, for whom the composer had a sincere regard and kind liking. Let us not forget that at this time Schubert was his darling composer, and no doubt the waltzes of " my only Schubert " had some influence on the composition of the *Papillons.* Op. 2 consists of an Introduction of six bars and twelve more or less short pieces of dance-like character (waltzes, polonaises, etc.), in a variety of keys. The *Finale* is based on the old tune, the *Grossvatertanz* (grandfather's dance, the last dance of the evening), combined with the theme of No. 1 ; towards the end a superscription tells us " The noise of the carnival dies away. The tower clock strikes six," the melodies gradually breaking off, *diminuendo, ritardando, p., pp., ppp.,* and a slowly vanishing chord. Schumann had something in his mind, struggled hard to express it, but failed. Try to follow him in what he says about Jean Paul's romance, *Die Flegeljahre,* to his family, Clara, his friends, Rellstab, and others. The quest is not hopeful, the composer does not succeed in his self-revelation. In the course of a letter to Rellstab (April 19, 1832):

. . . Not so much for the Editor of the *Iris,* but rather for the poet spiritually akin to Jean Paul, I venture to add a few words about the origin of the *Papillons,* as the thread which should bind them together is hardly visible. You remember the last scene of the *Flegel-*

---

* The substance of some of the following passages on Schumann's works is incorporated in the chapter on Schumann, pp. 183 sqq., of the Author's *Programme Music* (London : Novello & Company, Ltd., 1907).

jahre—masked dance—Walt—Vult—masks—Wina—Vult's dancing—
the exchange of masks—confessions—anger—revelations—hurrying off
—concluding scene, and then the departing brother. I kept turning
over the last page, for the end seemed to me only a new beginning—
almost unconsciously I found myself at the pianoforte, and so one
Papillon after another came into being. . . .

Part of a letter to his mother, sisters-in-law, and brothers
brings us nearer to the title—*Butterflies* (April 17, 1832):

The air is so sweet and heavenly that I can wish for nothing but a
carriage made of roses for an army of butterflies to draw home with
gold and silver threads. Then I should say to them : " Carry off
the *Papillons* to Therese, Rosalie, and Emilie, rejoice and flutter
them as lightly and happily as you will, tell the good old mother something of my dreams and thoughts and of my silence . . . then beg
them to read the last scene of Jean Paul's *Flegeljahre* as soon as possible,
and tell them that the *Papillons* have tried to turn this masked ball
into music. Then ask them if they do not find faithfully reflected in
the *Papillons* something of Wina's angelic love, of Walt's poetic nature,
and of Vult's swift-flashing soul. . . ."

It must have been for their lightness and gracefulness that
Schumann chose the title *Butterflies, Papillons.* He was
also quite aware that his originality broke out more and
more distinctly in this composition. The charm of the
particular scenes from the *Flegeljahre*—dancing and masking
—has a wonderful attraction at that age. The *Papillons*
are a prognostication of the *Carnaval*, Op. 9, one of the
most characteristic of the early Schumann works.

Op. 3. *Studies for the Pianoforte after 6 Caprices by N.
Paganini (Op. 1), with fingering, preparatory exercises, and
preface on their aims.* First book. Leipzig, Friedrich
Hofmeister. Composed and published 1832.

Op. 10. *Six Concert Studies for the Pianoforte after 12
of the 24 Caprices (Op. 1) by Paganini.* Leipzig, Friedrich
Hofmeister. Composed 1833, published 1835.

When after these publications Schumann produced his
Opp. 4 and 5, the Intermezzi and the Impromptus, he had
become a new man, a " maker "—in truth an artist, a creator.
The Paganini task gave him just the needed stimulus and

support. And yet it was not quite enough. Schumann missed Dorn; the Paganini basses were so doubtful, that without Dorn's help safety could only be attained by simplicity. In his desperation he turned to Wieck : " Receive the Caprices favourably. That was a divine task, if somewhat Herculean. Please sit down by Clara with pencil in hand and mark what strikes you. . . ."

One wonders that Schumann did not do what seems to us the obvious thing. Would not Moscheles, the brilliant pianoforte virtuoso and admired composer, have been a more suitable interpreter of the unique Paganini than a beginner who, however talented he might be, was not yet sure of himself ?

There is this difference in the character of the two books : the first book contains ineffective passages left unchanged for the sake of faithfulness; the second avoids this exactness, and to the advantage of the original. There never was a composer who set himself a task with greater zest and achieved it with greater contentment than Schumann. And we can add that no composer could have done so with more justification. He was unremitting in diligence and spared no pains.

Although Schumann, owing to his non-professional upbringing and his obstinate ways as a spoilt child, began the first part of his musical career as an amateur, he must not be confounded with the unfortunate geniuses who learn their art with difficulty, finding everywhere obstacles, such as established rules, etc. On the contrary, although for a time he might go his own way and make his guides desperate, yet in the long run he saw the usefulness of theory and the reasonableness of the examples of the older masters. Thus we find him neglecting the teaching of Dorn, yet valuing it and following his advice. Then, again, take his early and lifelong admiration of J. S. Bach—we have already heard his confession to the music master of his childhood, Kuntzsch, as to his musical and moral indebtedness to Sebastian Bach in general and the " Forty-eight " in particular. Then he writes to his brother Julius that he cannot say how courageously he is steering towards his goal, and how diligently and contentedly he works in his life element, the world spreading out so joyously before him. The further course of his development Schumann describes thus : " . . . Composing goes on easily and quickly, but afterwards in the working out I get involved in all kinds of artifices which are enough to make me despair." In arranging the Paganini Caprices, Opp. 3 and 10, he again did what was most useful for the development of his technique as a composer. He is perfectly conscious of this, and what he says on this point is most interesting and valuable.

It is a pity that Schumann is more communicative about his stepchildren the Caprices Opp. 3 and 10 than about the Intermezzi Op. 4 and the Impromptus Op. 5. Of the Intermezzi he says only that they are " longer *Papillons*," which is not enlightening.

Op. 4. *Intermezzi per il Pianoforte. Dedicati al Signore Kalliwoda, Maestro di Capella, etc.* Two books. Leipzig, Friedrich Hofmeister. Composed 1832, published 1833.

Of the six Intermezzi the first, third, fifth, and sixth have an *alternativo* (a middle part) preceded and followed by a part divisible into *ab* or *aba*; the second has a middle part indicated by the words, " My peace is gone " (" Meine Ruh' ist hin," Gretchen's song in Goethe's *Faust*).

Op. 5. *Impromptus sur une Romance de Clara Wieck, dédiés à Mr. Frédéric Wieck.* Leipzig, chez Hofmeister, et Schneeberg, chez Ch. Schumann, publié 1833, août.

The story of the different places and publishers is told in a letter of Schumann's to Hofmeister, in which Schumann, writing on July 31, 1833, says that he is anxious to give Wieck, to whom he has so many obligations, a birthday surprise with " Impromptus on Clara's Romance." But as the birthday falls in the middle of August he feels he cannot ask Hofmeister to publish the composition at such short notice, and has therefore asked his brothers to do it ; he begs Hofmeister, however, to allow his name also to appear on the title-page for the sake of the prestige. Hofmeister himself republished the work a month later, September, 1833.

In these Impromptus (variations) Schumann uses most often as his theme the bass of the Romance, but now and then also the treble melody. The first edition, Hofmeister tells us, contains eleven variations; an edition that appeared in 1850 had only ten, the eleventh having been omitted. The reader who wishes to study the several readings of the different editions should consult Clara Schumann's edition of Schumann's Pianoforte Works (Breitkopf and Härtel), and Ernst Pauer's edition of Schumann's Pianoforte Works (Augener, London), which (i, p. 89) gives the preface of the publisher, Fr. Hofmeister, Leipzig, with additional information.

Schumann has advanced as a craftsman, but has not yet assimilated the ripe advice of his teachers. He feels that he does not know where to stop—and goes on against his better self. Hence the above remark about the artifices in working out that bring him to despair.

What reception did the musical papers give to Schumann's early publications? Neither very bad nor good. It cannot be said that they showed any inclination for a conspiracy of silence, the worst fate that can befall a beginner. His letters show that he was, on the whole, pleased with the critical utterances of the editors. Chopin fared much worse. The most cavalier treatment came from Gottfried Wilhelm Fink, the editor of the widely-read *Allgemeine Musikalische Zeitung* of Leipzig, who inserted only one of Schumann's articles (the famous criticism of Chopin's *Là ci darem la mano*, Op. 2, 1831), and for a long time paid no attention to the publication of his compositions. This—who could have believed it?—induced the proud Schumann to write the following letter to Fink (August, 1833):

Strange and mortifying to the undersigned as is your silence on various compositions sent to you in the past, especially as he knows of no reason for this slight, he makes a last attempt, in case the accompanying Impromptus should induce you to give a critical notice. I beg you not to count me among those who wish to make more difficult the difficult enough position of an editor, and to be assured that I should never have taken this, perhaps, bold step were it not that a despondent old mother asks anxiously in every letter, " But why is there nothing about you in the Leipzig paper ? " And every time I have to answer, " Mother, I don't know." For this reason I beg you to excuse my letter.

Schumann felt greatly flattered by the journals that took notice of his compositions, and they agreed on the whole in describing these as the work of a clever promising youth. For instance, the Vienna *Allgemeine Musikalische Anzeiger*, edited by I. F. Castelli, who chose Grillparzer as reviewer—both dramatists of wide musical experience ; the Berlin *Iris im Gebiete der Tonkunst*, edited by H. F. L. Rellstab, best known as a poet, story-teller, and conservative music critic, with an exaggerated admiration for his masters, Ludwig Berger and Bernhard Klein ; and in Mayence Gottfried Weber's *Cäcilie, eine Zeitschrift für die Musikalische Welt*. Weber's reputation was that of a theorist and general musical authority, and it was a great honour to have such an esteemed personality to treat the first five works seriously, and so benevolently and handsomely. But much more valuable than the critical voices of the press was that of a friendly correspondent of Schumann's—in fact, no less a musician than the virtuoso and composer Johann Nepomuk Hummel. This pupil of Mozart, friend of Beethoven, and master of Hiller, wrote Schumann an encouraging and characteristic letter—characteristic of his position in the art as a virtuoso and as a composer. Hummel, now, of course, near the end of his career, was not personally known to Schumann, which is no doubt to be regretted, for, if perhaps a narrow individuality, he was a simple honest soul, and had played an important part in the development of his art. One likes to read about him in the Goethe-Zelter correspondence. He writes to Schumann (May, 1832) :

I have looked through your last two works carefully, and have rejoiced in your lively talent ; the only thing I might remark on is an occasional quick succession of changing harmonies, etc. Also, you seem often to abandon yourself too much to the originality which is characteristic of you ; I should not like you to allow this to become habitual, for it would be disadvantageous to the beauty, freedom, and clearness of a well-ordered composition. Go on diligently and calmly, and I do not doubt that you will completely reach your object.

On November 18, 1833, Schumann lost through death his favourite brother Julius, and about the same time his beloved sister-in-law, Rosalie, wife of his brother Carl. We have already recorded the death, about a year later, of Ludwig Schunke. In every case Schumann's health is affected —in 1833 most alarmingly. It becomes more and more clear that his mental constitution will not stand the emotional wear and tear of life. We cannot read the following distressful correspondence without knowing that Schumann's doom is a foregone conclusion. The Düsseldorf tragedy can already be foreseen.

Writing in autumn, 1833, to his mother, who kept urging him to come on account of the illness of his brother Julius :

. . . But you seem not to have the least idea of my agonizing illness, otherwise you would not keep inviting me. I hardly need to assure you that only a word would have been necessary had I been well. But as I refused in the last letter, that should have convinced you that I was certainly not flourishing, for almost every current of air brings attacks with it (I have not been able to go out for a fortnight). I dare not even wash myself. It might easily happen that I should have to go straight from the post-chaise to bed, perhaps never to leave it again. . . .

Again, November 27, 1833 (Julius and Rosalie had died) :

Of the past weeks, nothing. I was little more than a statue, neither cold nor warm ; by dint of forced work life returned gradually. But I am still so timid and fearful that I cannot sleep alone and have with me a thoroughly good fellow whose education I can help a good deal, which stimulates and cheers me. Do you believe that I have not courage to travel alone to Zwickau for fear that something might befall me ? Violent rushes of blood, unspeakable fear, breathlessness, momentary unconsciousness, alternate quickly, although less now than in the last few days. You would certainly forgive my not having written if you had the least idea of the deep-seated sleep in which melancholy has sunk my soul. One thing more : do you know that a certain R. S. thinks hourly of you ?—do write to him very soon. Live happily ! Deep in my heart is something I would not be without at any price: the belief that there are still good people—and a God. Am I not happy?

On January 4, 1834:

My good Mother, I have only to-day read your letter. A week ago when I received it and at once guessed the dark colour of the whole, strength failed me to finish it. As now the mere thought of the sorrows of others so overwhelms me as to deprive me of all energy, be careful not to let me hear of anything that could in the least disturb me, otherwise I must renounce your letters altogether. Especially I beg you earnestly not to remind me in any way by word of mouth or in writing of Julius and Rosalie. I was without knowledge of pain; now it has come, but I have not been able to crush it and it has crushed me immeasurably. Yet for some days past I have felt better and fresher than for a long time; perhaps serene images will return gradually and then I will be good to my fellow-men who are so good to me now. You hardly believe me. If you think I am withdrawing more and more into myself you are mistaken: for every syllable spoken to me I should like to thank people. For the rest, I live very simply, have given up all alcoholic drinks, walk out every day. . . .

October 17, 1834:

. . . Shall you be glad when I arrive next week? I am only waiting for a good day, then you have me with my joys and sorrows. How much I have to tell you! The sad anniversary of Rosalie's death, which I still cannot forget, is drawing near—I foresee my fits of melancholy, made worse by Ernestine's absence. I thank heaven for giving me strength to tear myself away from here—I hope for recovery at home and you will certainly receive me kindly. . . .

Fifteen months later, on February 4, 1836, Schumann's mother died. He did not go home for her funeral; why, we do not learn. He may have felt it impossible to face it. Litzmann surmises that his journalistic duties may have detained him. But he writes to Clara some days after the event, on February 13, from Zwickau while waiting with other sleepy passengers for the mail coach, after 10 p.m., a snowstorm raging outside:

. . . This has been a day of many emotions; my mother's will; accounts of her death; but behind all the darkness is your glowing picture, and I bear everything more easily. . . .

The mention of Ernestine shows that a new character has come on the scene.   What we had previously heard of the intimate friendship between Clara and Robert seems to have taken a surprising turn.   And what specially aggravated the circumstances was the intimate friendship between Clara and Ernestine—in 1834 Ernestine had become the pupil of Friedrich Wieck and an inmate of the Wieck household.   Old Frau Wieck told me that Ernestine was just an ordinary fresh buxom girl without any mental distinction. Carl Banck, well acquainted with the Wiecks and Schumann, described her as physically luxuriant, emotionally strongly developed, and intellectually insignificant.   Of course Schumann would not have agreed with these views.   He talked of her Madonna head, believed her to be a brilliant jewel that could not be over-prized, and had no doubt that she had a splendidly pure childlike soul, tender and mild ; he talked of her attachment to him and everything artistic—to him she appeared extraordinarily musical ; to her was dedicated the *Allegro pour le pianoforte*, Op. 8 ;   in short he thought her all that he could wish for in his wife.   Well, those who have read Ernestine's letters know that the lover was wrong, that he idealized her " whom he loved above all."   Schumann could not have failed to have found out her intellectual inferiority very soon, and a lifelong disappointment must have followed.   Ernestine was the daughter of a rich Bohemian Baron von Fricken and Countess Zedtwitz.   Between him and Schumann there was the link of music—the Baron cultivated the flute, and on his C sharp minor theme Schumann wrote his *Études Symphoniques*.   The somewhat mysterious Clara-Ernestine-Schumann affair cannot be understood unless certain circumstances receive due weight—the connection of the love affair with the phases of Schumann's temporary mental unsoundness, and the absence of Clara in Dresden while studying composition under Reissiger and singing under Mieksch.

It is puzzling that while his love for Ernestine is going on, the country walks, the common friendship with Henriette Voigt, the affection and artistic admiration for Clara do not

in any way diminish. When father Wieck intended a visit
to his daughter in Dresden, Schumann proposed to accompany him. The entanglements do not stop even here. Carl
Banck was in love with Clara, whose step-mother suspected
her of a weakness for him; but the father did not favour
the intentions of the young man, and let him hear some of
his acid speeches. In the course of 1835, a letter of Schumann's to Ernestine brought the really impossible state of
affairs—impossible as far as suitability of temperament was
concerned—to an end. She married afterwards in her own
rank. The circumstances that led to the publication (after
Schumann's death) of Ernestine's letters are very regrettable,
and make this a veritable chapter of indiscretions in which
Schumann, his wife Clara, his sister-in-law Marie Wieck,
and old Frau Wieck are all more or less involved. Madame
Schumann had in her keeping the letters written by Ernestine
von Fricken to her and to some others. While on a visit to
Madame Schumann in Düsseldorf Marie Wieck got the
letters into her hands and, without her sister's consent,
published them with some other matter through the writer
Adolf Kohut. Madame Schumann threatened legal interference, which, however, came to nothing. And here we will
close what may be described as an episode of errors.

CHAPTER XII

Mendelssohn and Schumann : Their intercourse and influence on each other —Contemporary virtuosi and composers : Moscheles, David, Sterndale Bennett, etc.

FOR the musical life of the town in general, and for one of its most remarkable musicians, Robert Schumann, in particular, the coming of Mendelssohn to Leipzig in the autumn of 1835 as musical conductor was certainly an event the importance of which cannot be exaggerated, if we take into view his talents, upbringing, and parental, family, and social advantages. Felix Mendelssohn was born on February 3, 1809, at Hamburg, the son of the Jewish banker Abraham Mendelssohn and his wife Lea, a daughter of the banker Salomon. One of Abraham's first employments was that of clerk in the famous banking house of Fould in Paris. In 1811 the Mendelssohns went to Berlin, which henceforth became their dwelling-place and the place of education of their children. The grandfather of Felix was no less a man than Moses Mendelssohn (1729–86), the philosopher and friend of Lessing, whose best-known works are *Phaedo*, a dialogue on the immortality of the soul in the manner of Plato ; a *Defence of Judaism as a Religion ;* and *Morning Hours :* essays in refutation of Pantheism and Spinozism. The daughters of Moses, Dorothea and Henriette (" Aunt Jette," governess of the daughter of Count Sebastiani, one of Napoleon's generals and employed by the subsequent Governments), have likewise to be mentioned here. Both became Roman Catholics, Dorothea marrying as her second husband Friedrich Schlegel. Another noteworthy member of the family was the brother of Felix's mother, Salomon Bartholdy (Prussian Consul-General at Rome), proprietor of the Casa

146

Bartholdy (Casa Zuccari), where he had the famous frescoes picturing the story of Joseph painted by Overbeck, Cornelius, Schadow, and Philip Veit, of the Nazarene school. From him comes the name Bartholdy, which Abraham accepted for himself and his children when he decided to have them baptized, in which he followed the advice of his brother-in-law, who had done the same some years before against the wish of his parents. Felix had two surviving sisters and one brother : the elder sister, Fanny, after Felix the most musical of the children, who married William Hensel ; Rebecka, who distinguished herself in Greek, and became the wife of the mathematician P. G. L. Dirichlet ; and Paul, a banker, who was brought up in partnership with his father and his uncle Joseph. And the mention of Joseph reminds us that he was a friend of Alexander von Humboldt.

Felix was a musician born. The executive and creative parts came to him quite easily. Like Mozart, he had all the natural endowments and readiness, and his parents gave him all the teachers he could desire and require. His mother was his first instructress at the pianoforte ; the excellent teacher Madame Bigot continuing, during a visit in Paris, where the mother left off. Ludwig Berger, the famous pianist, and the authoritative Zelter, the composer, were chosen as his principal masters, and afterwards he had the benefit of some finishing lessons from the greatest virtuoso of his time, Moscheles. General education went hand in hand with musical education—the best masters, private as well as university, and those of special accomplishments, were requisitioned. As to music, the father did not approve of amateurishness. He did not object to his son's becoming a professional musician, but it must be the real thing. So he insisted that Felix should show that he could make a living by his art, and not look to his well-to-do parents to provide the funds for supporting him in his career. Apart from the masters that came to instruct the children there were other educational factors that furthered their education : the intellectually alive and morally superior parents, the delightful life of the whole family, the society of artists, musicians, poets, savants, and other men and women of distinction that gathered round them—here were more advantages than schools can give. Nor as they grew older did they lack the advantages of travel, that powerful means of culture, of which from an early age Felix had a good share : first in short tours in Germany, later on in Switzerland (1822), Paris (1816, 1825, 1831–32), Italy (1830–31), and England and Scotland (1829, 1832, 1833, etc.). And not the least of the many great privileges that had fallen to Felix's lot was that of being the nephew of his famous uncle, Bartholdy of Rome.

These excursions to foreign parts prepared the young man for his professional career. From Düsseldorf came the first acknowledgment of his maturity, an invitation to conduct the Lower Rhenish Music Festival of that year (1833, May 26–28). He was then twenty-four, and the authorities were so pleased with what they saw of him that they soon after offered him the musical directorship of the town. He accepted the offer, and held the Düsseldorf post for about two years, until 1835, when he was induced by Leipzig to exchange the charms of Düsseldorf for her superior musical attractions.

Mendelssohn was not altogether a stranger in Düsseldorf —artist friends from Berlin had preceded him there. In Berlin the Mendelssohn family had been on friendly terms with the Schadows, father and son, the sculptor and the painter, and this double friendship was continued in Düsseldorf after the younger Schadow, Wilhelm, was appointed Director of the Academy of Fine Arts. The master brought his brilliant pupils with him to Düsseldorf—Bendemann, Hübner, Köhler, Lessing (historical and landscape painter), Hildebrandt (historical and character), Karl Sohn (character and portrait), etc. Soon after settling down, Mendelssohn writes : " I am very much pleased with my position here." He looked forward to a quiet time for composition, and thought the concerts promised to be brilliant. But it was not music alone that occupied his mind. Having rooms in Schadow's house, he lived among artists, and discussed art with Schadow and his pupils ; took regular painting lessons from Schirmer, and was sociable and gay. His friend Klingemann recalls an occasion which must have been one of many: " . . . Do you not remember playing and singing it [*Die Walpurgisnacht*] to me and Hildebrandt and Schadow in your room at the Schadows'? . . ." He also kept a horse and rode it a good deal. At this time Immermann, the poet, was trying to improve the theatrical conditions of the town, and induced Mendelssohn to imitate his own enthusiasm by undertaking the improvement of the opera. But after giving a few master-performances (*see* p. 156) Mendelssohn withdrew, Immermann and he having failed to divide the management harmoniously between them. The various duties as Music Director—the concerts and the church functions—although not taking up too much of his time, were sufficient to keep his hand in practice. Happy, on the whole, as the Düsseldorf episode was, the life with the artists, for instance, which he enjoyed, and by which he profited, there came a time when the greater resources and opportunities of Leipzig afforded wider scope for his talents. I wish here only to point out what, I think, has never been pointed out before, the inspiration the musician received from the painters—from Wilhelm Schadow's criticisms of the works of art they saw together in the Italian galleries, and from chats with Lessing, Bendemann, Hildebrandt, and others, while he viewed their pictures, and they communicated to him their thoughts on pictorial form and expression.

These remarks on Mendelssohn I intend to serve as an introduction to a comparison of Mendelssohn and Schumann. What were their relative positions? How much is true of what is told and presumed of them? The problem—and it is one—is worth discussing. Unfortunately, it is not always treated impartially—indeed, far from it. In my inquiry I have made use of the most trustworthy information.

With Joachim, a long and intimate acquaintance of Schumann and Mendelssohn, I often had leisurely conversations about this curious subject, and I quite agreed with him in what he wished to impress upon me first of all and emphatically. " The relation between Mendelssohn and Schumann

is frequently misunderstood," he used to say. " There can
be no question of envy and jealousy." In fact Joachim thought
that Mendelssohn really loved Schumann personally. In his
account, however, there was a " but," for he went on : " But
in Schumann's music Mendelssohn often found faults. He
said, for instance, on one occasion : ' It is remarkable that a
man who has created such beautiful things can be so awkward.' " This awkwardness Mendelssohn found, for instance,
in the instrumentation and sometimes even in the notation,
of the B flat major Symphony. Joachim remarked that this
was no wonder, as Mendelssohn was already a perfect master
when Schumann was only making his way out of dilettantism.
Joachim mentioned as important what occurred one morning
when he presented himself for a lesson : " This time,"
Mendelssohn said, " we must miss the lesson, for to-day
there is a performance of a work you must hear." This
work was *Paradise and the Peri.*

Madame Schumann remarked, when I consulted her on
the question, that she knew that Mendelssohn did not care
for some of Schumann's compositions ; for instance, the
second Symphony and the Pianoforte Concerto. The editors
of the Mendelssohn letters, by the omission of all reference
to Schumann, were to blame, she said, for the misunderstanding that arose later concerning Mendelssohn and Schumann. Mendelssohn's son wrote to Madame Schumann
when a new edition was contemplated, and asked if she had
anything to contribute. She sent him some of Mendelssohn's
letters to herself—they were charming and Schumann was
kindly referred to. These were returned with the remark
that they were unsuitable. It is my impression that she was
suspicious of the answer ; at any rate, she distinctly remarked
that the entire absence of her husband's name from the
correspondence was strange, seeing that they had been so
much together, walking, talking, and playing billiards.

There can at no time be any doubt as to Schumann's
references to Mendelssohn in his private correspondence and
public criticism—warmth and admiration speak for themselves,
especially the private utterances.

To his sister-in-law, Therese Schumann, April, 1836:

I should like very much to go with Mendelssohn to the Düsseldorf music festival. . . . I look up to Mendelssohn as to a high mountain. He is a real god and you ought to know him. . . .

Again, November, 1836:

Mendelssohn has a *fiancée* and is quite full of this Only One . . . not a day passes without his producing at least a few thoughts that might straightway be engraved in gold. . . .

To A. W. v. Zuccalmaglio, January 31, 1837:

. . . Mendelssohn, with whom I take my midday meal every day . . . has a face (a splendid, eternal one) that reflects all that goes on within him. . . . Do you know his *St. Paul?* There one beauty succeeds another. And he is the first to assign a place in God's Temple to the Graces who should certainly be admitted, but whom incessant fugues have hitherto not allowed to be heard. . . .

To Simonin de Sire at Dinant (Belgium), March 15, 1839:

. . . I regard Mendelssohn as the foremost musician of the day, and take off my hat to him as to a master. He just *plays* with everything, especially with the orchestral masses, but how freely, how tenderly, how artistically, in what masterly manner throughout. . . .

To Dr. E. Krüger, May 15, 1840:

. . . I know no one among the musicians who could be compared with Mendelssohn. He knows too that this is my opinion, and for this reason he likes me, and some of my music as well. In Berlin we spent some hours together at the pianoforte, unforgettable for me. I have written a great deal for the voice lately. He sang all this accompanied on the pianoforte by my *fiancée* (who, as you may be aware, plays well), making me feel utterly blissful. And in other ways, too, I know a good deal of him. Before his marriage we saw each other almost every day. . . .

To C. Kossmaly, January 8, 1842:

. . . Mendelssohn, I believe for certain, returns to Leipzig next winter. Dear friend, he is after all the best musician in the world just now. Do you not think so? An extraordinary man—or, as Santini in Rome says of him, a *monstrum sine vitio.* . . .

To Clara, October 25, 1838:

. . . Vienna is richer in resources than perhaps any other town, but a chief is needed, such as Mendelssohn, to co-ordinate and command them. . . .

To Clara, April 22, 1839:

. . . The mere sight of Mendelssohn must make one rejoice; he is the worthiest artist imaginable; moreover, he likes me very much. . . .

To Mendelssohn, October 22, 1845:

. . . It is indeed true, dear Mendelssohn—nobody else writes such pure harmonies, ever purer and more transcendental [*verklärter*]. Have I praised you again? May I? Truly, what does the world (including many of its musicians) understand about pure harmony? . . .

To Verhulst, November 4, 1848:

. . . You will find everybody again—except the One who was the best of all [Mendelssohn had died]. It is exactly a year to-day since he departed from us. . . .

After a period of apparently serene friendship the time came when suspicion was sown, and on one side seemed to fall on receptive ground. In the case of Schumann, the above letter to Verhulst shows that the impression was not permanent.

To Clara, Leipzig, April 13, 1838:

. . . I have not gone often to Mendelssohn, he has come more often to me. After all, he is the most eminent man I have met so far. I am told that he is not sincere with regard to me. That would pain me, as I am consciously loyal to him, and have proved it. But tell me some time what you know. . . . I know exactly how I compare with him as a musician, and for years to come I could learn from him. But he could also learn something from me. If I had grown up in circumstances such as his, destined to music from childhood, I should outsoar you one and all—the energy of my ideas makes me feel it. Well, every life has its peculiarity, and I will not complain of my own. My father, a man whom you would have admired even if you had merely seen him, understood me at an early age and intended me for a musician, but my mother did not consent; afterwards, however, she often spoke very nicely, indeed approvingly, of my change of profession.

Schumann's comparison between himself and Mendelssohn is very interesting and very true. As to Mendelssohn's view of the story, it is short, abrupt, and without solution. It is contained in the course of a letter to Klingemann, of January 31, 1847, a harsh dissonance that remains unresolved:

> . . . I shall not be able to give you a letter of introduction to Frau Schumann; her husband has behaved very ambiguously (or more than ambiguously) to me, and has stirred up a very ugly story about me here [Leipzig], about which I shall not waste any words, but which has damnably cooled my former zeal to help him on and be obliging to him. More by word of mouth if you think it worth the trouble. . . .

Here Mendelssohn must have rashly lent his ear to idle scandal and have let his judgment be over-ruled by his hot-headedness. The condescending tone is offensive. He should have known Schumann's character better than to be ready to attribute any meanness to him. As a rule a most lovable and charming personality, Mendelssohn had the defects of his qualities. His friends, relatives, and he himself shall be allowed to speak for him.

Eduard Devrient, in his *Recollections of Mendelssohn*, gives us interesting intimate hints concerning his friend's character. (*Meine Erinnerungen an Felix Mendelssohn Bartholdy und seine Briefe an mich*. Leipzig, J. J. Weber. Second edition, 1872.) His nature was sensitive to an extraordinary degree—in fact, Devrient thought the atmosphere of love and admiration in which he grew up was to him a necessity of his existence. Anyone who was cold to him and his music he regarded as hostile, and the feeling concerning them went so far as to prevent his perceiving the real worth they actually possessed. Even the *mal à propos* behaviour of anyone, or a single utterance that rubbed him the wrong way, could quite alienate him and make him perverse and intolerable. The truth is that Mendelssohn loved only those who loved him in return. In his affection he was abnormally prejudiced—it was a matter of prejudice. Here lay the sole dark spot of his being, otherwise as clear as sunlight. He had been nurtured by the happy conditions amongst which he grew up. He was a pampered child—that was the truth of the matter. In the circumstances it is to be wondered at that his nobility of soul did not fall a victim to the egoism of exclusiveness. His mistrust even of his confidential friends was really incomprehensible : an unconsidered utterance, a silly joke, made him unexpectedly lower his eyelids, and drew from him the suspicious question : " What do you mean ? "

The foregoing peculiarities may be illustrated further by actual occurrences. Mendelssohn's intercourse with his excellent teacher Ludwig Berger must often have been noticed for its curious want of warmth and its reticence—nay, sometimes even antipathy. Rellstab surmises that the conscientious, truth-loving Berger now and then told Mendelssohn unpalatable truths regarding his composition, and made him peevishly break out to Klingemann (1832): " Berger is more distrustful and unbearable than ever ; there is no getting on with him. . . ." Here is another instance of Mendelssohn's sensitiveness to and treasuring up of a disagreeable impression. He told Eduard Devrient that he had never forgotten how once as a boy he was sitting beside Bernhard Klein in a theatre box, dangling his legs from the high chair, and his companion exclaimed half aloud : " Why can't that boy keep his feet still ? " His sister Rebecka thought him easily upset ; a word too much or too little spoken by his ailing mother in 1835 at Düsseldorf made him most anxious, in spite of the calmness of his father. And this led her to the reflection how fortunate it was that he was not married, for cares did not suit him ; that such a peaceful marriage as that of hers with Dirichlet was a rare exception. Mendelssohn's playfulness was at least as remarkable as his seriousness. He was witty, but more in a boyish way than intellectually, and he did not despise practical jokes. He had a real passion for insinuating sand and stones into his sisters' hair and pockets. His love of fun is also evidenced by his games with the Moscheles children, the many comical pictures he drew for them, and all the fun that can be read of in the intimate correspondence with this family.

Among Mendelssohn's idiosyncrasies is his inveterate dislike of writers on music. The scorn of creative for non-creative musicians can easily be understood, also the small respect of the non-literary musician for the mere talker on the art.   But Mendelssohn's contempt for the whole class of contributors to music journalism cannot be understood with equal ease.   Was he not aware of the valuable contributions of the creative musicians of his time—Weber, Schumann, Berlioz, Liszt, Wagner, etc. ?

Schumann approached Mendelssohn through Henriette Voigt to inquire whether he or the poet Immermann could be prevailed upon to write an article on the musical life of Düsseldorf for the *Neue Zeitschrift für Musik*, and received the following answer :

. . . . Immermann would be the last who could furnish one, for he hates all music, never hears or wishes to hear any.   I, however, am the last but one, for if I were to write anything coherent with the thought that it might be printed, I should sit over it a fortnight and strike out the beginning when I got to the end. . . .

Mendelssohn began Schumann's acquaintance with two prejudices which he never quite overcame : that against literary writers on music, and that against dilettantism, of which he suspected his brother artist, but which Schumann had in a lesser degree than Mendelssohn imagined.   Of Mendelssohn's own powers as a writer on music we get a fairer and more favourable opinion than his own from his letters to Ferdinand Hiller and other correspondents.

Nor must we overlook the characteristic inability of the well-to-do Mendelssohn to negotiate with his less fortunate fellow-musicians—choristers and orchestral players—which drew down upon him the blame of his severe father.

Throughout the early part of the year 1835 negotiations went on between Leipzig and Mendelssohn—between Heinrich Conrad von Schleinitz, advocate, the representative of the directors of the Gewandhaus concerts, and the fortunate young genius in a position to stipulate for conditions in a way that very few conductors could afford to do.   I mention only the questions of teaching and concert-giving to eke out the salary, and insistence on six months' leave of absence during spring and summer to give time for composition and travel. It was pleasant to me in after years to talk with the old friend Schleinitz about these opening days of their friendship. Düsseldorf was for Mendelssohn the time of preparation as *Capellmeister*, and in much else—in concert-conducting, orchestral and vocal, a small amount of church music, experience at festivals of conducting large forces (1833, Düsseldorf; 1835, Cologne); theatrical master-performances—*Don Giovanni*, *Egmont*, Calderon's *The Steadfast Prince* with music by Mendelssohn * (choruses and ghost effects, etc.), *Les deux Journées*—and composition of the overture † *To the Story of the Lovely Melusina*; *St. Paul* (the greater part); some *Lieder ohne Worte*; four-part vocal songs, etc. Of the classes of society he came in contact with, the painters never lost their charm for him, but his sympathy with the poets, especially with Immermann, turned into intense dislike. He found only one family, the Woringens, to whose house he could go to hear and make music. "I am as solitary here as in Noah's ark." "I lead a very quiet and lonely life; often for a whole day I speak less to any man than to my horse." No doubt Mendelssohn felt it was time for a change. In Leipzig he could be sure of a musical public, musical families, etc. On December 14, 1835, he writes from Leipzig to Klingemann:

. . . The new faces and new acquaintances do indeed alarm me doubly at present, all the same it is fortunate for me that I have made the change from Düsseldorf, where, except at the Woringens', I could hear no music at all, while here it is very plentiful and good. But it is strange how little satisfaction the thought of my art has given me in the past; for long it was hateful to me, and even now I only have moments in which I love it wholly again. . . .

(Felix Mendelssohn Bartholdys Briefwechsel mit Legationsrat Karl Klingemann. Essen, G. D. Baedeker, 1909.)

* This music, unpublished, is in the collection of Mendelssohn's autograph MSS. in the Royal Library, Berlin.

† The overture *Calm Sea and Prosperous Voyage*, composed in 1828, and performed both in private and in public, underwent thorough revision in Düsseldorf. Mendelssohn wrote to Schubring (August 6, 1834) that he thought it now " about 30 times better."

In September, 1835, some members of his family found Mendelssohn already in Leipzig, no doubt preparing for the commencement of the Gewandhaus concert season in October. At first, before new friends were made, the new-comer felt, as we have seen, a certain loneliness, almost emptiness, in the new *milieu*. But in the ordinary course, want of variety would be the last sensation to be experienced in busy Leipzig, that place of passage and meeting for all the world, even out of season when the places of amusement are closed. The coming of Chopin, on his way home after a visit to his parents at Carlsbad, caused a great sensation among the few connoisseurs. The busybody Friedrich Wieck announces the visit, bubbling over with excitement : Chopin will arrive in a day or two, will stay one day only, has no intention of giving a concert. What interests the proud father most is to disprove the declaration of some ill-disposed tongues that there is no one in Germany who can play Chopin's compositions. " We will see what Clara can do." There are several interesting reports of this visit of Chopin's, but perhaps their accuracy leaves something to be desired. I confine myself to Clara's diaries and a letter of Mendelssohn's. From the Diary we learn that as Chopin was staying only one day and found Clara not at home, he waited fully an hour for her return to greet her and hear her play. She played Schumann's F sharp minor Sonata, the last movement of his own Concerto, and two of his Études. He overwhelmed her with praise, and expressed his thanks by giving her one of his latest works. At Clara's request he played to her, one of his nocturnes, with the most delicate *pianissimo*, but, she thought, too arbitrarily, capriciously. He was already so ill and frail that he could produce a *forte* only with spasmodic movements of the whole body [Clara somewhat exaggerates, I think, his then state of health]. His character appeared to Clara that of a typical gallant Frenchman. On taking leave he expressed the hope and intention of returning next winter. It goes without saying that on this occasion Schumann and Chopin became personally acquainted.

Mendelssohn's meeting with and impression of Chopin is

much more interesting. His account is in a letter of October 6, 1835, addressed to his family—especially to Fanny and his father—in which he tries to correct their criticisms of Chopin (from Mendelssohn's *Briefe*, 1830–1847. Leipzig, Hermann Mendelssohn. Fifth Edition, 1882):

. . . I cannot deny, dear Fanny, that I have found lately that your criticisms do not do him [Chopin] justice; perhaps when you heard him he was not in the mood for playing, which may often happen with him; but his playing has charmed me afresh, and I am convinced that if you and father had heard some of his better things as I heard them you would say the same. There is something radically original, and at the same time so very masterly in his playing, that one can call him a truly perfect virtuoso; and as I love and rejoice in all kinds of perfection this has been a most agreeable day for me, although so different from the day before with you Hensels. It was a pleasure to me to be once more with a proper musician, not with these half-virtuosi and half-classics who would fain unite in music *les honneurs de la vertu et les plaisirs du vice*, but with one who has his perfectly defined style. And even if it is as far from my own as heaven from earth, I can get on with it splendidly—only not with these half-folk. Sunday evening brought a strange experience—I had to play him my oratorio while inquisitive Leipzigers pushed in on the sly in order to have seen Chopin; then between the first and second parts he dashed off his new Études and a new concerto to the astonished Leipzigers, then I went on with my *St. Paul*—as if an Iroquois and a Kaffir had met and were conversing. He has also a very pretty new nocturne, of which I have remembered a good deal by heart to play to Paul [Felix's brother] for his pleasure. So we were merry together, and he promised in all seriousness to come back in the course of the winter if I would compose a new symphony and perform it in his honour. We both took our oath upon it before three witnesses, and we shall see if we both keep our word. . . .

Clara's sixteenth birthday had been celebrated on September 13, with champagne, speeches, poetry, the gift of a gold watch from the " Davidsbündler," and music. She played with Mendelssohn his Capriccio for two pianofortes, Bach's C sharp major fugue, and, by Mendelssohn's special desire, the *Scherzo* of Schumann's F sharp minor Sonata. Mendelssohn emphatically refused to listen to Herz, but he played a Bach fugue and other things, in which he very cleverly imitated the style of playing of Liszt and Chopin.

About the 1st of October, 1835, Moscheles (1794–1870) came to Leipzig, perhaps in the hope of concert engagements. Of course Mendelssohn, his pupil, intimate friend, and delightful companion, being already on the spot, Moscheles soon betook himself to him, and was received " in the old childlike, friendly way "; and Moscheles is as " fresh and merry as ever." The two friends had consequently a good time together, enjoying each other's compositions and pianoforte playing. Moscheles " plays quite splendidly," was Mendelssohn's opinion. " Yet another kind of perfect virtuoso and master." Moscheles found Mendelssohn agreeably and suitably housed in Reichel's Garden, outside the town. He thought him " not improved in looks (half youth, half man) and not looking well, but merrier, wittier and cleverer than ever." He describes Mendelssohn's room—his Erard in the middle, in a bookcase a beautifully-bound Handel and his wealth of scores, on a table a silver inkstand, a gift from the Philharmonic Society ; on the wall two charming copperplates —Titian's daughter and a portrait of the singer Schätzel ; on the pianoforte a pretty disorder of scores and novelties, but otherwise everything neat and clean. " We drank tea and chatted, and I am invited to tea at his house every night." (*Aus Moscheles' Leben. Nach Briefen und Tagebüchern. Herausgegeben von seiner Frau.* Leipzig, Duncker *und* Humblot, 1872.) Felix played his three latest *Songs without Words* ; Moscheles played his Concerto *fantastique* and the *pathétique,* and the Rondo dedicated to him by Felix ; together they played Moscheles's overture, *The Maid of Orleans,* and Mendelssohn's Octet ; then the two tried together the newly written *Hommage à Hændel* for two pianofortes, which Moscheles intended to play with Mendelssohn at his concert. At the first evening tea with Mendelssohn, Schleinitz came in and sang some of his friend's newest songs. On another occasion the oratorio *St. Paul* was the subject of the music-making, and Felix also played two pianoforte Caprices and a fugue in F minor. Among those the friends visited together were Hauser, the singer and stage-manager at the Opera, collector of manuscripts, and to whom are addressed the

famous letters of Moritz Hauptmann ; and Friedrich Wieck
and his daughter Clara, who played them Schumann's
manuscript Sonata in F sharp minor, which Moscheles found
" very far-fetched, difficult, and somewhat confused, but
interesting " ; Clara's playing he found unaffected, excellent,
and solid. Moscheles and Mendelssohn repeatedly met
Schumann at Moscheles's hotel dinner-table.

The pleasant days of Moscheles's Leipzig stay soon came
to an end, but they comprised the first Gewandhaus concert,
Mendelssohn's ardently awaited début, October 5, 1835, and
Moscheles's own concert on October 9. Mendelssohn shall
give us his own report of the beginning of his world-famous
concert series (to his family, October 6, 1835) :

. . . It is not possible to tell you how satisfied I am with this beginning,
and with the whole outlook of my position here. It is a quiet, proper
business post ; one can see that the institution has existed for fifty-six
years ; moreover, the people seem friendly and fond of me and my
music. The orchestra is very good, thoroughly musical, and I think
it will be still better in six months, for the love and attention with which
these people received and immediately acted upon my remarks in the
two rehearsals we have had so far was really touching—there was always
an improvement, as if it were a different orchestra each time. Some
inefficient players there are, but they will be gradually replaced.

Between the functions of Mendelssohn's predecessors in
the direction of the Gewandhaus concerts and Mendelssohn's
functions there lay a whole age. The previous Music Director,
Christian August Pohlenz, had under him the rehearsing and
direction of the vocal forces ; and the *Concertmeister*, Heinrich
August Matthäi, had command of the whole of the instrumentalists, whom he led now with his bow, now with all the
vigour of his example. The new style of conducting gave
the supreme and sole power into the hands of Mendelssohn :
the direction was no longer in several hands, there was no
longer a vocal and instrumental division, the *Concertmeister* now
had functions strictly subordinate to the *Capellmeister*. Matthäi
(pupil of his predecessor, Campagnoli, Leipzig, and of
Rodolphe Kreutzer, Paris) fell ill in the summer of 1835, and
died on November 4 of that year ; his last solo performance—a

concertino of his own composition—took place at a Gewandhaus concert. He had the reputation of being an extremely neat and smooth player. The post of the Gewandhaus *Concertmeister* was thus thrown open and two old friends and most able and sympathetic colleagues—Mendelssohn and David— were brought together.

Ferdinand David, son of a Jewish merchant, was born at Hamburg in 1810, one year after Felix Mendelssohn. The Mendelssohn and David parents knew and esteemed each other, and in after years, when the Mendelssohns had settled in Berlin, Ferdinand became almost a child of the family, as may be seen from the letters of the mother, daughters, and Felix, which are appreciative, hearty, humorous, altogether charming. Old Abraham acted as guardian. After his early musical studies at Hamburg the young man showed himself talented and precocious, and eyes were turned on Louis Spohr, the most solid German violinist of the day, who at that time had become *Capellmeister* at Cassel. With Spohr David studied assiduously for two years (1823–25), during which time he had the clever, thoughtful Hauptmann for his teacher in theory. Next followed a concert tour with his sister the pianist, Louise (afterwards Madame Dulcken, of London fame, teacher of Queen Victoria), to Dresden, Leipzig, Berlin, and Copenhagen. At the Leipzig concert, December 28, 1825, Ferdinand David played Spohr's eighth Concerto (*in modo d'una scena cantante*) and a Potpourri on Irish songs, also by his master; his sister played the G minor Concerto and the variations on the Alexander March by Moscheles. In the middle of August, 1826, David consulted Mendelssohn about taking steps to get pupils and a place in an orchestra in Berlin, and he obtained a post in the orchestra of the Königstädter theatre. The year 1829 brought him a more promising situation, again with Mendelssohn's help. A rich Livonian landed proprietor and *Landrat* (administrative government official at the head of a district) was engaging a private string quartet, and was only too glad to take Mendelssohn's advice to choose David as first violin. The conditions were all that could be desired—an amiable family, plenty of

M

leisure time for his own musical and other studies, and the stimulus of a university. And thus David accepted the offer of von Liphardt to take up his abode in the university town of Dorpat, near to which was his patron's estate where the musical meetings took place. But all the advantages have not yet been mentioned, for among the daughters of von Liphardt David found a wife, an heiress who, as rumour went, had a fortune of 100,000 thalers. In this delightful situation he remained six years, from summer, 1829, till autumn, 1835. He then returned to Germany for the purpose of finding a better post than this out-of-the-way one in the Baltic provinces, and Mendelssohn advised him to show himself and what he could do to the Leipzigers. Just then Mendelssohn had experienced a great loss in the death of his idolized father, November 4, 1835, the event taking him for ten days to Berlin, where he met David and persuaded him to accompany him to Leipzig. With what result the history of the next months will show. On December 10, 1835, David played two compositions of his own, a violin concerto and a set of variations, and was heard with general applause ; on February 25, 1836, took place his début as *Concertmeister* of the Gewandhaus concerts ; and in January, 1836, he opened his Chamber Evenings with Ulrich, Queisser, and Grabau, followed by a second series of three on February 27, and March 12 and 19. The rest of his life was spent in the exercise of his various musical capacities—first, as a devoted friend and fellow-worker of Mendelssohn as long as the latter lived, and then of his successors, until his own death, July 19, 1873. A good deal of Mendelssohn's own success must be ascribed to David's model qualities as *Concertmeister*. But David was as good a solo player as an orchestral leader. And he made an excellent substitute for Mendelssohn himself when he was absent. This advantage had, of course, the drawback that it left the *Concertmeister's* place vacant. Also as leader of chamber music David occupied a distinguished position. As to his activity as a composer, he left five violin concertos, two symphonies, a sextet for strings, one string quartet, and concertos for other orchestral instruments—viola, violoncello,

clarinet, trombone, etc. Of virtuosic violin music he pro-
duced several sets of variations and shorter pieces, *Bunte
Blätter*, etc.; then a *Violin School*, and *Die hohe Schule des
Violinspiels*—that is, editions of the concertos of the olden time.
And to show the range of his productivity an opera, *Hans
Wacht*, has yet to be mentioned. In 1843, when Mendelssohn
founded the Leipzig conservatorium, David became, in
addition to his other activities, head of the violin department.
The two old friends lived a charming artist's life to the
benefit of both, in which Schumann gradually took a fuller
and fuller share.

One of the first great musicians to be attracted to Leipzig
by Mendelssohn's fame was the Englishman William Sterndale
Bennett; he went out to see one genius, and behold, he found
two—Schumann as well as Mendelssohn. They received
him with open arms—he won their hearts at once, both as an
artist and as a man. The whole story of the intercourse is
charming, and should be read in the delightful biography of
Sterndale Bennett, by his son. (Cambridge: at the University Press, 1907.) The biographer tells us how Mendelssohn
first saw Bennett during one of his visits to London on the
occasion of the Royal Academy of Music Midsummer Concert
in Hanover Square Rooms, on June 26, 1833, when the seven-
teen-year-old Bennett performed his D minor Concerto to the
great pleasure of the twenty-four-year-old Mendelssohn.
Mendelssohn sought the boy's acquaintance, and invited him
to come to Germany. "If I come," said Bennett, "may I
come to be your pupil?" "No, no," was the reply, "you
must come to be my friend."

When at Whitsuntide, 1836, Mendelssohn was to produce
his oratorio *St. Paul* and conduct the rest of the Lower Rhenish
Festival at Düsseldorf, a London party of three set out—
Bennett and his intimate young friend Davison under the guidance of Mendelssohn's diplomatic friend, Karl Klingemann.
The English travellers had a kind reception, and when the
Festival was over, Mendelssohn made music or played billiards
with them. When Mendelssohn examined the compositions
that Bennett had brought with him from England he told

Davison that he knew of no young composer in Germany, of Bennett's age, with equal gifts; and he wrote afterwards to England that—

> . . . . His Concerto [No. 3 in C minor] and Symphony [No. 5 in G minor] are so well written, the thoughts so well developed and so natural, that I was highly gratified when I looked over them yesterday, but when he played this morning his six studies [Op. 11, *Six Studies in form of Capriccios*] and the sketches [Op. 10, *Three Musical Sketches, The Lake, The Millstream, and The Fountain*], I was quite delighted. . . .

On Mendelssohn's advice the two young Englishmen made a tour up the Rhine before returning to England. When Mendelssohn and Bennett met again it was in Mendelssohn's favourite *milieu*. Bennett announced his coming to Leipzig at the beginning of October; Mendelssohn answers on October 10, 1836: " . . . Pray bring your Symphony and the Concertos, if possible with the instrumental parts, with you. . . ." Could a conductor write more agreeably to a composer?

On Saturday, October 29, 1836, Bennett arrived at Leipzig, Hôtel de Russie. A note dispatched to Mendelssohn brought this friend at once to his side, who took him to his own lodging and saw to the immediate wants of the new settler, even providing an interpreter, a Scotsman, one Monicke, a teacher of languages. In the next few days he became acquainted with David (the *Concertmeister*), Stamaty (Camille Marie, son of a Greek and naturalized Frenchman), the pianist and composer, Eduard Franck, of Breslau, pianist, etc. And then we read in a letter to Davison:

> I have found a new friend, a man who would be just after your own heart. How I wish you could know him. His name is Robert Schumann.

Finally Bennett took lodgings with Dr. Hasper, Katherinen Strasse, 364, dining at the Hôtel de Bavière, where Mendelssohn and Schumann dined regularly at this time. For the very next Gewandhaus concert Mendelssohn gave Bennett a ticket, and about this main event of the Leipzig musical season Bennett writes as follows in his diary:

. . . The Symphony [Mozart in E flat] was performed really well. The band is rather small, but quite perfect, and possesses great animation. Mendelssohn played Beethoven's Concerto [in G] very splendidly and his two cadences [*sic*] were magnificent. The people were enthusiastic. The overture to *Oberon* was not so well played as I have heard it in London. I mean as regards the style of playing it. I have this afternoon been to the rehearsal of *Israel in Egypt* in the church. Upon consideration, I do not think that they understand the manner of playing this Oratorio, but I will say nothing until I hear it performed. . . . I have been again to the church to hear *Israel in Egypt*, and still have the same opinion with regard to its performance. . . . The opera began at six. The price of admission to the boxes or the stalls is sixteen groschen (two shillings). The opera was one of Marschner's, entitled *Hans Heiling*. I cannot say that I think it was in any way well performed, but I like some of the music, and I admire also some points of the orchestra, which altogether is *rather* more musician-like than our orchestras in England, though it is far inferior in *force* and *spirit*.

Bennett also attended one of David's string quartet performances, which he thought capital except the 'cello. Concerning Beethoven's E minor quartet, Rasoumoffsky):

I should think that the Scherzo was one of the most beautiful things ever written. The Trio is certainly a *little too* much of a good thing. . . . After dining at the hotel, I went with David, Schumann, and Mendelssohn to play billiards at some gardens a little way out of town [Rosenthal]—where afterwards heard some waltzes played by Mr. Strauss's band. They tell me that the master of the gardens, Mr. Queisser, is the finest trombone player in Europe.

Bennett made his bow to Clara Wieck, who played him her Pianoforte Concerto, which he thought required " *weeding*." He thought her a capital player.

Schumann introduced Bennett to his friends Henriette and Carl Voigt, who adopted him at once as one of their family circle. He also introduced him to Walther von Goethe, grandson of the poet. An introduction of another kind was to Friedrich Kistner, the publisher, brother of Julius Kistner, landlord of the Hôtel de Bavière. Then the great princes of the publishing trade—Brockhaus, and Breitkopf and Härtel— honoured the young musician from Britain.

Sledge parties, Christmas festivities, and all kinds of joyous

social occasions we take for granted, and go straight to the
musical events of the season that concerned Bennett most.
He made his début on January 19, 1837, at the Gewandhaus
concert with his C minor Concerto. Mendelssohn, we are
told, described the performance as " masterly," and wrote
to his sister Fanny :

> Bennett played his C minor Concerto amidst the triumphant applause
> of the Leipzigers, whom he seems to have made his friends and admirers
> at one stroke ; indeed, he is the sole topic of conversation here now.

Bennett himself was not quite so pleased :

> . . . According to all accounts made a satisfactory début.   I did not
> play so well as I can when I am thoroughly comfortable.   I had a bad
> *clavier*, not *strong* enough.   However, I was perfectly satisfied with the
> whole affair. . . .

The second event was the performance of his overture
The Naiads, which was received with great applause (February
13, 1837).

> I directed it myself, and did not know what to do with my left hand.
> I rather liked it myself, but I do not think the people understood it,
> with all the compliments which were paid me. . . .

The Gewandhaus concerts closed on March 13, 1837,
and with this close began Mendelssohn's statutory spring and
summer holiday.   He was perhaps conscious of some neglect
of Bennett and, as soon as he became a free man, tried to make
up for it by breakfast invitations.   Bennett accused himself
of having kept out of the way of the busy Mendelssohn, who
on his part twitted Bennett with being always with Schumann.
But the two were at the same time on good terms, as was
shown by the farewell present which Mendelssohn gave
Bennett of the autograph score of his *Hebrides* overture, and
the gold pencil-case with inscription which Bennett sent him
afterwards from England.   Now, however, Mendelssohn's
departure was near, and the business which for the present
filled his heart and soul was his coming marriage with Cécile
Jeanrenaud, the second daughter of the widow of a Frankfurt

clergyman of the French Reformed Church, who became his wife on March 28, 1837.

Schumann seems to have outrun the enthusiasm of Mendelssohn in the province where Mendelssohn's own force seemed to lie, and where Schumann was, in the opinion of most people, deficient, namely, in structure and the formal *finesses*. His criticisms show this ; and he writes as enthusiastically to his friends about Bennett as he does in his critical pages. Beginning with a few of his letters we find him writing, for instance, to his sister-in-law, Therese, Eduard's wife, on November 15, 1836 :

. . . There is a young Englishman, William Bennett, in our daily circle, an out and out Englishman, a splendid artist, a poetic beautiful soul ; perhaps I may bring him with me too. . . .

To Simonin de Sire, March 15, 1839 :

. . . And *how* they both [Mendelssohn and Bennett] play the pianoforte, like angels, almost as unassuming as children. . . .

To Zuccalmaglio he calls Bennett " an angel of a tone-poet." To Henselt, August 31, 1837 : " . . . Have a look at Bennett's compositions, you will find much for yourself and your heart. . . ."

From Schumann's many appreciations of Bennett and his compositions in the *Neue Zeitschrift für Musik* we may glean the following, from the criticism of the C minor Concerto, Op. 9 :

. . . We cannot but marvel at this early-developed master-hand, at the calm ordering and cohesion of the whole, at the euphony of the language, the purity of the thought. . . . Throughout we find nothing unessential, nothing but what is inwardly related to the fundamental feeling. . . . What a treat for once to come across an organic living whole. . . . In the case of our artist we must understand the modesty which makes him reject everything striking. . . . After the first movement, a purely lyrical piece full of fine human feeling such as we find in the best examples only, we were of course quite clear as to the main point, that here we have to do with an artist of the higher orders. . . .

About the overture, *The Naiads*, he writes :

. . . What blossoming poetry in the work, how deeply lyrical and delicate in construction, what lovely soft instruments [*welch' schöne weiche Instrumente*]! . . .

From the criticism of the *Three Sketches*, Op. 10 :

. . . True, his personality is bewitching ; but it also seems to me that the merits and beauties of these pictures are striking. . . . We have never wished to hold Bennett up as a miracle, we wish only to make sure that he receives the honours due to such a combination of artistic virtues. . . . [The *Sketches*] seem to me to surpass in delicacy and naïveness of expression all I know of musical *genre* painting ; the composer, like a true poet, having indeed caught Nature in some of her most musical scenes. . . . *The Fountain* we preferred to hear played by him, he put his whole soul into it. . . .

About the *Three Diversions*, Op. 17 :

. . . These are also small forms, but what delicacy of detail and how artistic the whole! The great artist is distinguished from the mediocre one in that he treats his smallest works lovingly and carefully, while the other throws them off anyhow, thinking that the stuff deserves nothing better and may be treated in an offhand way. Indeed, among living composers I know of none but Mendelssohn who could say so much so unpretentiously, who could so plan and round off a piece, in a word, who could write such *Diversions*. Bolder and cleverer things there are ; more delicate and dainty, hardly. The pieces breathe an amiability which only the roughest hands could mar, a wealth of the choicest grace in the simplest movements, everywhere poetry and innocence. It would seem as if this rare foreign flower were just now at its sweetest blossoming ; let us hasten, then, to behold it. Foreign countries, moreover, are giving us so little. Italy sends only butterfly dust across to us, and the gnarled excrescences of the amazing Berlioz frighten us. But of all foreigners this Englishman is most akin to German sympathy ; a born artist, even Germany can show few of his like.

About Op. 24, *Suite de Pièces :*

. . . Here we have not the profound, the grand, to arouse thoughts and to impose ; rather the delicate, playful, often elfish, that leaves its small but deep traces in our heart. No one will call Bennett a great genius, but there is much of genius in him. In these days when so much unenjoyable music is prevalent, the external, the mechanical, being carried to a degree of excess and nonsense, let us rejoice doubly in the natural grace, the quiet inwardness of Bennett's compositions. . . . If only he wrote more ! But he himself seems to realize that he is moving within a small territory and should not always restrict himself to this; for, as has been said, we like fairy sportings, but manly deeds still more, and for the accomplishing of these the small domain of the pianoforte seems too limited. . . .

In comparing the friendship of Mendelssohn and Schumann for Bennett we may perhaps say that that of the former was more reticent, more distant, that of the latter more familiar, more romantic. When Mendelssohn entered a room (for instance, the dining-room at the Hôtel de Bavière) it seemed to Bennett that a silence fell on the company, the effect of the young master's authoritative and dignified bearing. Of no such impression of restraint was Bennett aware in the case of Schumann—as yet, of course, unknown to fame. The respective ways of address of the friends may also have some significance :—Mendelssohn writes : " Dear Bennett "; Bennett writes : " My dear Mr. Mendelssohn," and " Dear Schumann," or " Dear, good Schumann," etc. We are also glad to find in Bennett's letters something more than mere acquaintanceship : one feels through the words something of attachment, of loving-kindness, and above all one feels the sincerity of his praise. He had made himself acquainted with those of Schumann's compositions that were already in print, and greeted with pleasure the subsequent ones as they appeared. He writes, for instance, to Schumann from Cambridge, in August, 1837 :

My dear Friend, you really were most kind to send me such a charming letter. You show yourself, my dear fellow, in so happy a mood, and I trust that your joy springs from the heart. Yes! as you say, your style is no longer that of an *Editor*, but of a maiden of eighteen years. I have so often had you in my thoughts, wishing at the same time that you were with me here. . . . Do come and stop with me for six months. Say *yes*, and I will fetch you.

Coventry and Hollier [London publishers] will gladly print your *Études*. I have been playing them a great deal and with much enjoyment. . . . And now, dear Schumann, before you quit this world, do visit England. I very often think of Zwickau, of your brother and of his wife. I must soon come and see you all again, so when I *can* then I *will*. . . . I am hoping for a copy of your *Études* and for one of the *Carnival*. . . .

In a later letter, November 11, 1838, written from Leipzig to Schumann in Vienna, Bennett says :

. . . I have here seen for the first time your *Fantasiestücke*, and they greatly delight me. Madame Voigt plays your music very industriously, but to my mind with too great *hardness*. . . .

Bennett's first visit to Leipzig had lasted about eight months ; on June 10, 1837, he writes in his Journal : " Well, I'm off on Monday. . . . Schumann has been to spend an hour with me and drink a bottle of Porter. I am so sorry to part from him, for I think he is one of the finest-hearted fellows I ever knew. . . ." After some time spent at Frankfurt, where he saw Mendelssohn and his wife, and at Mayence, he reached London about the middle of July. In the autumn of the following year he again set out for Leipzig, arriving on October 15, 1838, and remaining this time rather more than four months. The conditions of Leipzig life were on the whole the same as in the preceding year, but there were changes among his friends. Schumann had left for Vienna, and they could only correspond ; Walther von Goethe had left the University and gone home to Weimar, and in this case too only epistolary intercourse was possible, Bennett not being able to accept a cordial invitation to spend Christmas at Weimar. But a friendship begun during his first Leipzig visit now developed into intimacy with Count Reuss, afterwards his Highness Henry II, Prince of Reuss-Koestritz, who had received part of his education in Yorkshire and seemed to Bennett quite English. Of the old friends there remained Mendelssohn, now a happy family man, the ever-faithful Voigts, husband and wife, and others. (Henriette Voigt died on October 15, 1839.) During the fifteen months' absence in England, correspondence had passed between Mendelssohn and Bennett, and Bennett had promised a new concerto and, if possible, an overture for the Gewandhaus concerts. Three days after his arrival at Leipzig, he and the two Englishmen who accompanied him dined with Mendelssohn, who invited Bennett to his weekly musical parties, and also to breakfast and music-making on Friday mornings, after the weekly

Thursday night Gewandhaus concert. Then Bennett played his F minor Concerto at a Gewandhaus concert on January 17, 1839, with, on Mendelssohn's advice, the Barcarolle as slow movement; and on January 23, his new overture, *The Wood-Nymphs*, Op. 20, was performed. In a letter to Schumann from Leipzig, January 23, 1839, he tells of his " contemplating a Symphony " for the London Philharmonic Society. Schumann must have requested a piece of music for the supplement of his paper, for in the same letter Bennett answers : " . . . Are you anxious about a composition for the Supplement ?—for a later number ? because at present I have too much on hand, and I should like to do it properly for you." And lastly :

The only thing I miss here, dear Schumann, is your presence. In about a month's time I shall set out, with David, for London. That makes it impossible for me to come to Vienna ; but how delightful it would have been for me to be always able to pass an hour with you, talking over music and musicians, and then sometimes about our every-day concerns. But you really must come to England. We would make you very welcome.

Of your newer compositions I always place the *Davidsbündler* first. They are certainly very charming. . . .

On Christmas Day a festive dinner *à l'anglaise* was given at the Hôtel de Bavière by the English circle, Bennett one of the foremost, and among the guests were Mendelssohn, David, Brockhaus, and others. On March 2, 1839, Bennett, accompanied by Ferdinand David, once more left Leipzig for home. In later years he visited Spohr at Cassel, and some of his Leipzig friends : his hope of seeing Schumann in England was not fulfilled.

CHAPTER XIII

Schumann's compositions, Op. 6 to Op. 17—Further contemporary composers and virtuosi: Hirschbach, Verhulst, Gade, Chopin, Henselt, Thalberg, Liszt, etc.

THE first of Schumann's published compositions, discussed in Chapter XI, consisted, we saw, of partly amateurish work and of early efforts of a more serious tendency. Now we shall have to do with weightier endeavours and the earliest revelations of the master's original genius: Op. 6, *Die Davidsbündler (Tänze)*; Op. 7, *Toccata pour le Pianoforte*; Op. 8, *Allegro pour le Pianoforte*; Op. 9, *Carnaval*; [Op. 10, *Six Études de Concert pour le Pianoforte composées d'après des Caprices de Paganini*—see Chapter XI]; Op. 11, *Grande Sonate pour le Pianoforte*; Op. 12, *Fantasiestücke für das Pianoforte*; Op. 13, *Études en forme de Variations*; Op. 14, *Troisième Grande Sonate pour le Pianoforte*; Op. 15, *Kinderscenen*; Op. 16, *Kreisleriana*; Op. 17, *Fantasie für das Pianoforte*.

Op. 6. *Die Davidsbündler-Tänze*, 18 *Charakterstücke für das Pianoforte*. Dedicated to Walther von Goethe. J. Schuberth and Co., Leipzig and New York. Composed 1837. Published February, 1838, in original edition by Robert Friese in Leipzig with the title: *Davidsbündlertänze für das Pianoforte, Walther von Goethe zugeeignet von Florestan und Eusebius*, in two books of nine numbers each. On the title-page was the old German saying:

> In all und jeder Zeit
> Verknüpft sich Lust und Leid.
> Bleibt fromm in Lust und seid
> Beim Leid mit Muth bereit.

> (Aye hand in hand go weal and woe,
> In weal be good, in woe thy courage show.)

Second edition, October, 1850, and January, 1851 (revised by the author); third edition, July, 1862, "containing the variants of the two earlier editions, revised and with a preface by 'Das.'" ("Das" was a name invented for himself by Wieck, the old schoolmaster, "Der Alte Schulmeister.")

The first piece opens with a two-bar musical motto by "C. W." (Clara Wieck), continued by Schumann in the next two bars. The eighteen dances have no titles, but indications of *tempo* or of general character, such as: lively; tender and singing; wild and merry; with extremely strong emotion; as if from a distance; in ballad style; impatiently; with humour—somewhat roughly, ponderously [*etwas hahnbüchen*]; etc. They were also signed "F," or "E," or "F and E" (Florestan and Eusebius, the chief of the "Davidsbündler," the fighters against the Philistines), except the last of each book, which bore the respective superscriptions: (No. 9) "Hereupon Florestan finished, and his lips quivered painfully"; (No. 18) "Quite superfluously Eusebius remarked as follows, but his eyes beamed blissfully the while." These and other romantic extravagances of the composer disappeared from later editions, with the exception of the Schuberth and Co. 1850–51 edition.

The reader remembers Bennett's favourable comment on the *Davidsbündler*; but now I have to record Schumann's remarks to Clara Wieck, written to her at Vienna from Leipzig, January 5, 1838:

. . . There are many marriage thoughts in the dances—they originated in the most joyful excitement I can ever remember—I will explain them to you some time. . . .

A month later:

. . . But my Clara will discover what is in the dances which are dedicated to her more than anything else of mine—the story is a whole *Polterabend* [festivity on the evening before marriage], and now you can picture to yourself the beginning and the end. If ever I was happy at the pianoforte it was when I was composing these. . . .

February 11:

. . . At the end of the *Davidstänze* it strikes twelve, as I have discovered (twelve repetitions of Great C crotchet near the end).

Again, March 17, 1838 :

You pass very hastily over the *Davidsbündler ;* I think they are *quite different* from the *Carnaval,* and are to it as faces are to masks. But I may be wrong, as I have not forgotten them yet. One thing I know, that they arose in happiness, the other often in toil and trouble. . . ."

That Schumann himself had no mean opinion of the *Davidsbündler* emotionally, intellectually, and musically, is clear from his remarks to Clara, but an opposite opinion had much support among his contemporaries. In answer to Bennett's question as to how he liked Schumann's *Davidsbündler,* Walther von Goethe said : " Some of these please me very much, but some—Oh no !!!! " It would be extremely interesting to learn what his objections were. Among those of our own time we should be surprised to find any who do not appreciate their charming piquancy and are not delighted with the variety of syncopations, auxiliary notes, surprising harmonies and modulations, and all the intellectual ingenuities and emotional subtleties and species of humour. There is only one word that adequately characterizes the infinite variety of the *Davidsbündler.* Whether the dances are boisterous or dreamy they are equally perfect and teach us the meaning of the term " romantic " of which the adepts make such a secret.

Op. 7. *Toccata pour le Pianoforte. Dédiée à son ami Louis Schunke.* Leipzig, Friedrich Hofmeister. Composed 1830, revised 1833, published May, 1834. When Schumann published his first compositions and wished to give some member of his family a share in the dedications, he said humorously of the Toccata : " a big study in double notes for the brothers to practise." But he had a great deal of difficulty in completing the composition to his satisfaction, in persuading the publisher to accept it, and in making up his mind finally about the dedication. He applied to Härtel of Leipzig and to Haslinger of Vienna before he was successful with Hofmeister. His first idea was to dedicate it to his old master Kuntzsch as a birthday offering ; and I think there must also have been an idea of dedicating it to Clara Wieck—an appropriate gift for the great virtuosa. He finally decided to dedicate it to his friend, the virtuoso, Ludwig Schunke. The Toccata is a genuine pianoforte piece—intended for virtuosic display. The composer himself said of it, "perhaps one of the most difficult of pianoforte pieces." In short, Schumann did not intend to furnish in the Toccata one of his poetic compositions, but a pianistic virtuoso-piece pure and simple. The Toccata seems to me to stand as a piece by itself. And the pianists seem to have approved of it so strongly that they have given it a place in their repertory.

Op. 8. *Allegro pour le Pianoforte. Dédié à Mademoiselle la Baronne Ernestine de Fricken.* Leipzig and New York: J. Schuberth and Co. Composed 1831. Published March, 1835, originally by Robert Friese, Leipzig. Schumann wrote from Leipzig on February 6, 1835, to Töpken: "Have you the *Allegro* ? There is not much to be found in it except good intentions—and it was composed four years ago immediately after my return from Heidelberg [to Leipzig]." We dare not contradict the composer's opinion, although he may have judged himself too severely. And, further, we may not neglect the report of a friend who examined a volume preserved in the master's family, and found there several versions of the *Allegro* which proved his carefulness and his dissatisfaction with the work. Writing to Clara on January 11, 1832, while working under Dorn, he mentions having ready a sonata in B minor and a book of *Papillons.* By sonata in B minor he doubtless means what he elsewhere calls *Allegro di Bravura.* But whatever the composer's corrections of his first ideas, I do not think that the somewhat unfavourable judgment of the public to-day will differ from the composer's own opinion expressed to Töpken.

Op. 9. *Carnaval. Scènes mignonnes composées pour le Pianoforte sur quatre notes. Dédiées à Monsieur Charles Lipinski.* Leipzig, Breitkopf and Härtel. Composed 1834 and '35. Published September, 1837. In sending the *Carnaval* to Moscheles on August 23, 1837, Schumann writes :

. . . To figure out the Masked Ball will be child's play to you ; and I need hardly assure you that the putting together of the pieces and the superscriptions came about *after* the composition. . . .

Again, a month later :

> . . . The *Carnaval* came into existence incidentally, and is built for the most part on the notes A, S, C, H [*H* is the German name for *B*], the name of a small Bohemian town where I had a lady friend [Ernestine von Fricken], but which, strange to say, are also the only musical letters in my name. The superscriptions I placed over them afterwards. For is not music itself always enough and sufficiently expressive? *Estrella* is a name such as is placed under portraits to fix the picture better in one's memory; *Reconnaissance*, a scene of recognition; *Aveu*, an avowal of love; *Promenade*, a walk such as one takes at a German ball with one's partner. The whole has no artistic value whatever; the manifold states of the soul alone seem to me of interest. . . .

Schumann, in saying that the whole has no artistic value, had, no doubt, in his mind the fragmentariness from the purely formal point of view. The *Carnaval* is a higher kind of *Papillons*. Somebody called it a glorification of the ballroom, of its noisy rejoicings, its motley masquerade, and its secret whisperings of love. Schumann himself referred to it as a *Maskentanz*, a masked ball, and before adopting the present title thought of *Burlesques* and of *Frolics* [*Schwänke*] *on Four Notes*. The *Carnaval* does not give one comprehensive view, but rather a series of glimpses. In comparing it with the *Papillons* we find that the young master's drawing shows greater firmness of line and more forcibleness of characterization. In short, both as a man and as an artist Schumann proves himself maturer. The reader will remember his own comparison between the *Davidsbündler* and the *Carnaval*: " I think they are *quite different* from the *Carnaval*, and are to it as faces are to masks." The *Carnaval* comprises twenty-one pieces, each having a superscription. Some of these have already been explained in Schumann's letter to Moscheles. Of the others the greater number do not stand in need of explanation—*Préambule, Valse Allemande, Valse Noble; Pierrot, Arlequin, Pantalon et Colombine; Coquette; Lettres Dansantes; Chopin, Paganini, Florestan* and *Eusebius*, whom we already know as the representatives of Schumann's dual nature. *Réplique* is no doubt a mocking reply to *Coquette. Papillons* may this time be real butterflies. *Chiarina* is Clara

(*Clärchen*), *Estrella*, Ernestine von Fricken. The *Sphinxes* (musical equivalents of the letters in the word A S C H on which the *Carnaval* is built) may be unriddled when the reader remembers that E flat is called *Es* (hence S) in German, A flat is *As*, and B is *H*. Thus:

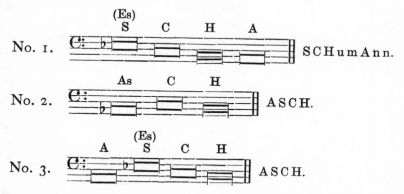

The last piece but one is entitled *Pause*, during which preparations for a great fight are going on—a hurrying to and fro, everyone hastening to join his standard for battle. And then begins the *Marche des Davidsbündler contre les Philistins*, the march of the champions of progress and idealism against the upholders of tradition and commonplace—the climax of the composition. Exuberance of youth and faith in their good cause animate the valiant band of the " Davidsbündler." The Philistines, represented by the old tune, the *Grandfather's Dance*, show pluck, but in the end are completely routed.

On March 30, 1840, Liszt gave at Leipzig, in addition to other concerts, one for the benefit of the pension fund for aged and infirm musicians, choosing compositions by three composers then in Leipzig—Mendelssohn, Hiller, and Schumann. Of Schumann he played several numbers of the *Carnaval*. Schumann had expressed a doubt as to whether a rhapsody of this kind on carnival life would make an impression upon an audience, to which Liszt replied that he confidently hoped so. Schumann, however, thought that Liszt was mistaken, that he had not considered the fact that

N

while much of the composition might charm some hearers, the musical moods changed too quickly for a whole public to follow. And sympathetically and inspiredly though Liszt played, individuals may have been impressed, but not the whole mass. Since then many virtuosi have made the experiment of performing the *Carnaval* or a selection from it without the result feared by Schumann. If the fragmentariness and manifoldness constitute a real drawback, we have to put against these qualities the great piquancies and indescribable beauties. And the first surprise of strangeness must soon give way to the delights of familiarity. The *Carnaval* with its kaleidoscopic moods is in its way one of Schumann's most marvellous compositions, each number a complete, condensed, and convincing psychological study of irresistible charm—his most unique and brilliant composition before the *Fantasiestücke*, Op. 12, *Kreisleriana*, Op. 16, *Fantasie*, Op. 17, and the *Novelletten*, Op. 21.

Op. 11. *Grande Sonate pour le Pianoforte*. *Dédiée a Mademoiselle Clara Wieck, Pianiste de S.M. L'Empereur d'Autriche*. Leipzig, Fr. Kistner. Composed 1835 (begun 1833). Appeared June, 1836, with the title " Pianoforte Sonata. Dedicated to Clara by Florestan and Eusebius." Appeared August, 1840, with the name of the composer himself.

I feel inclined to think that the following passage in a letter of Schumann's to his mother (December 31, 1831) may be connected with some of the earlier stages of the F sharp minor Sonata, Op. 11 :

. . . My holiday was so quiet that I really neither spoke nor heard a sound. I sank into a kind of lethargy which for some years past has been apt to seize me at times. Then I started on a gigantic work, which requires my whole strength, and at this moment I am more fresh and healthy and proud than I can tell you. God grant that the work may remain gigantic. I will dedicate it to Moscheles in London. . . .

As to Moscheles's opinion of the work we get a sincerer one in a letter to his wife (Leipzig, October 1, 1835) than

in his later criticism in the *Neue Zeitschrift :* " . . . I was
at Wieck's, too, and heard Clara play a great deal, among
other things a manuscript sonata by Schumann, which is
very laboured, difficult, and rather confused, interesting
nevertheless. . . ." Schumann asked Moscheles to review
for the *Neue Zeitschrift* his Sonata Op. 11, by " Florestan
and Eusebius," and the criticism (October 25, 1836), began
as follows : " This work is a genuine sign of the newly-
awakened and spreading Romanticism of our day. . . ."
The article, however, is really a make-believe. Moscheles
did not want to speak the truth and nothing but the truth,
but covered the truth with benevolent banalities. The greater
part treats not of the Sonata but of Romanticism and the
relation to it of Mendelssohn, Berlioz, Liszt, Hiller, Chopin.
Then, coming to Schumann's Sonata, Moscheles summarizes
the emotional contents, and lastly touches on a few technical
features with some remarks of an ambiguous nature. This
sentence, however, may be quoted : " Among the Romanticists Florestan is the one who least desires to create effects
at the expense of purity of style by means of dissonant
incivilities and musical imprecations." In sending the Sonata
to another friend, one of the contributors to the *Neue Zeitschrift*, Schumann writes : " . . . I send you herewith the
Sonata, several more are to follow later. If you regard it
lovingly it will respond to you. Much of my old heart's
blood has gone into it. . . ."

Another great European pianist, Franz Liszt, wrote in the
Gazette Musicale (November 12, 1837) a criticism on the
following works of Schumann : *Impromptus sur une Romance
de Clara Wieck*, Op. 5 ; *Sonate*, Op. 11 ; *Concert sans orchestre*,
Op. 14. Bearing in mind the different characters of the two
men, we can almost accuse Liszt of writing criticism similar
to that of Moscheles, for we have to call it a case of benevolent
criticism, of course on different grounds. Schlesinger asked
Liszt to contribute to his *Gazette Musicale* a eulogistic article
on some new phenomenon of the art world. After many
months' casting about, Liszt came across the above-mentioned
compositions of Schumann, whose name and work were

hitherto unknown to him.*   How he faced the problem the following sentence will show.

. . . We shall draw the attention of musicians to the works of the young pianist, which of all the recent compositions known to us—the music of Chopin excepted—are those in which we have noticed the greatest amount of individuality, novelty, and knowledge. . . .

Liszt characterizes the movements of the Sonata as follows (I abridge greatly) :

. . . The introduction is of a simple and sad solemnity. . . . The first *Allegro* which follows is written in a vigorous style ; the logic of the ideas is close, inflexible—qualities, moreover, which are the distinguishing mark of the works of M. Schumann. . . . The *Aria* is one of the most perfect things we know.   Although the composer has written *Senza passione*, its character is that of the most passionate abandon.   M. Schumann's music appeals more especially to meditative souls, to serious minds that do not stop on the surface but can dive to the depths of the waters to seek the hidden pearl. . . . The *Scherzo* is extremely remarkable in its rhythm and harmonic effects.   The melody in A [*legatissimo leggierissimo*] is ravishing.   The *Intermezzo* in D, *lento, alla burla*, followed by a recitative for the left hand, surprises and astonishes ; it is a *tour de force* to give by the disposition of the preceding parts a new meaning to a phrase in itself common and trivial. . . . The *Finale* is extremely original.   Nevertheless, however logical the course of the main ideas, and in spite of the rapture of the peroration, the general effect of this piece is often broken up, interrupted.   Perhaps the length of the developments contributes to the uncertainty of the whole.   Perhaps, too, there is need for an indication of the poetic import. . . .

A few weeks after the publication of this criticism, Schumann wrote to Clara (December 22, 1837) that Liszt had written " a long, very just article " on him in the French paper ; " it has greatly pleased and surprised me. . . ." Clara, to whom the Sonata was dedicated, lost no opportunity of playing it in private to people likely to listen to it sympathetically—Moscheles, Chopin, Mendelssohn, Täglichsbeck, Vieuxtemps, and others.   As a rule, of course, friends were

* Jansen points out that Liszt may have been mistaken, as he is said to have known the " Abegg " variations as early as 1834.   See Jansen's *Die Davidsbündler*, p. 224.

critical, and it was a long time before publisher and composer found a demand for it. The work is, indeed, something gigantic, but has the formal deficiencies which we have seen Moscheles and Liszt to have felt. The formally particular Mendelssohn seems to have had similar thoughts in his mind when, having heard Clara play the whole work on a previous occasion, he limited his request at her birthday festivities to the *Scherzo*. And Schumann himself in later years referred to his early work as " confused stuff " (Wasielewski's report).

Op. 12. *Fantasiestücke für das Pianoforte.* Dedicated to Miss Anna Robena Laidlaw. Leipzig, Breitkopf and Härtel. Composed 1837. Appeared March, 1838. Book I, 1–4; Book II, 5–8. [Miss Laidlaw was an Englishwoman and gifted pianist (pupil of Berger and Herz) whom Schumann heard with admiration in Leipzig.] No. 1. *Des Abends (In the Evening)*. Three-against-two rhythm—a piece woven of twilight. 2. *Aufschwung (Soaring)*. Impassioned and impatient. 3. *Warum ? (Why ?)* Tenderly longing and passionate. 4. *Grillen (Whims)*. Delightfully humorous. 5. *In der Nacht (At Night)*. A passionate piece—" Hero and Leander." 6. *Fabel (Fable)*. A chatty piece. 7. *Traumeswirren (Dream Visions)*. In the main a dizzily rushing piece. 8. *Ende vom Lied (End of the Song)*. A joyous conclusion. On January 5, 1838, Schumann informed Clara that in a week these compositions would be finished : *Die Davidsbündler* and *Die Fantasiestücke*. Of the latter work he always spoke with entire satisfaction ; he seems to have felt that it was a real success, that it had flowed from his pen with perfect ease, and was spontaneous and expressive. " I am often overflowing just now, do not know where to stop," he writes to a friend. Schumann frequently remarked about this time that none of his things were really suitable for public performance, but he excepted some of the *Fantasiestücke*, especially *Traumeswirren* and *Des Abends—In der Nacht* he thought too long. He suggests to Clara not to play the *Carnaval* to people who know nothing of his, but rather to choose the *Fantasiestücke*. " In the *Carnaval* each piece kills the other, while in the *Fantasiestücke* one can settle down comfortably."

A musician friend, Krägen, wrote expressing his enthusiasm for the *Fantasiestücke*, especially for *In der Nacht ;* and Schumann confesses to Clara that this is his favourite too. On the same occasion he gives the following interesting information about the piece (April 21, 1838):

> . . . After I had finished I found to my joy the story of Hero and Leander in it. When I play *Die Nacht* I cannot forget the picture—first, how he plunges into the sea—she calls—he answers—through the waves he safely reaches land—then the cantilena where they embrace—when he must away again, he cannot bring himself to part—then night once more shrouds everything in darkness. . . .

On the one and only occasion on which Henselt heard Schumann play, he played *Des Abends,* " which he certainly played very charmingly," says Henselt. Schumann thanked his friend Henriette Voigt for taking up the *Fantasiestücke* so warmly—" I need such Amazons. The music of many composers is like their handwriting—difficult to read, strange to look at, but once understood it is as if it could not be otherwise. . . ." Writing to his friend Kossmaly in 1843, he says that his best pianoforte compositions are the *Kreisleriana,* six *Fantasiestücke,* four books of *Novelletten,* and one book of *Romances.*

> But [he continues] the earlier ones too will give you a picture of my character, my endeavours ; the seeds of the future are often to be found in these very experiments. So accept them kindly with all their faults. . . . They are all still little known, for natural reasons. (1) On account of the intrinsic difficulty of form and content ; (2) because I am not a virtuoso who could perform them publicly ; (3) because, being editor of my paper, I could not mention them ; (4) because Fink, the editor of the others, would not. But many things have changed. . . .

And he adds that the public are beginning to take more interest in his music. On the showing of the publishers, Breitkopf and Härtel, four years earlier (1839), 250–300 copies of the *Carnaval* and *Fantasiestücke* had been sold ; and of the *Kinderscenen* 300–350 within half a year of publication. So that things could not be said to be so very bad. But Schumann's reputation was of slow growth—not one of his works produced a decisive effect on the public, still less a widespread general effect. Till much later times, times subsequent to his death, his adherents and admirers were only a minority, for a time only a clique. Outside Germany he was received with greater reluctance than within. Next to his native country, Holland received him most readily. Austria showed itself very reticent. England had to be educated to the cult of the composer. In France only a few individuals—notably Gounod—were charmed by his personality, which remained uncomprehended by the many. In the south, in Italy and Spain, Schumann's music found no echo in the hearts of the people.

Op. 13. *Études en forme de Variations (XII Études Symphoniques) pour le Pianoforte. Dédiées à son ami William Sterndale Bennett.* Composed 1834. Appeared August, 1837, original edition by Haslinger, Vienna, with the title: *XII Études Symphoniques.* Revised edition 1852. Leipzig and New York, J. Schuberth and Co. The variations are written on a theme composed by an amateur, Hauptmann von Fricken (the father of Ernestine), who sent a composition of his own, a theme with variations for flute, to Wieck and Schumann for criticism. Schumann was attracted by the theme, found in it " character and feeling," showed how it could be improved by omitting the introduction, which weakened the impression of the simple, serious theme, and by slight changes, inversions, repetitions, and simplifications in the theme ; and was himself inspired to write variations on it, which became the *Études Symphoniques*, Op. 13. " I may call them pathetic ; but I have to show in varied lights whatever there may be of the pathetic in them." In the last Étude, called *Finale*, the theme proper becomes of secondary importance. The rousing opening melody is based on an air used by Marschner in his *Der Templer und die Jüdin*, the Romance, with the words " Wer ist der Ritter hochgeehrt ? " ("Who is the highly-honoured knight ? " an allusion to Richard Cœur-de-Lion) and " Freue Dich, Du stolzes England " (" Rejoice, proud England ")—meant by Schumann as a tribute to Sterndale Bennett, to whom the work

was dedicated.   In March, 1838, Schumann wrote to Clara :
" . . . You have done well not to play my Études ; they are
not suitable for the public, and it would be foolish if I were
to complain of their not having understood what was not
intended for their approval but exists solely for its own
sake. . . ."   Indeed, the composition was not taken up for
good till long after, when Rubinstein's powerful rendering
revealed its full significance.   Rubinstein, whatever single
pieces he may have played at other concerts, gave in 1885–86
in the chief European capitals a series of seven historical
concerts, of which No. 4 was a Schumann programme :
Fantasie, C major, Op. 17 ; *Kreisleriana* (1–8) ; *Études Symphoniques* ; *Sonate* F sharp minor ; *Fantasiestücke* (*Abends,
Nachts, Traumeswirren, Warum ?*) ; *Vogel als Prophet* ; *Romanze*
D minor ; *Carnaval.*   It was a revelation to hear the unique,
original, forceful virtuoso interpret the immortal works of the
master of Romanticism—to hear his interpretation of the
Études Symphoniques, the essence of the *Kreisleriana*, the new-
born F sharp minor Sonata, *The Bird as Prophet*, the D
minor Romance, the humorous *Carnaval*, etc.

Op. 14.   *Troisième grande Sonate* (*Concert sans orchestre*)
pour le Pianoforte.   Dédiée à Monsieur Ignace Moscheles.
Leipzig and New York, Schuberth and Co.   Composed 1835
(1836) as a second Sonata in four movements.   Published
November, 1836, original edition by Haslinger, Vienna, with
the title " Concert sans orchestre " without the *Scherzo* ;
second (revised) edition September, 1853, as " Troisième
grande Sonate " ;   third edition (revised by " Das ") May,
1862.   It was at the desire of Haslinger that the work was
named " Concert sans orchestre," Schumann consenting, and
it was published without the *Scherzo* to keep it within the
usual number of movements.   As Op. 14 is of little practical
interest nowadays, I confine myself to some benevolent
criticism of Liszt and Moscheles.   Liszt says that this sonata
is unjustly called a " concerto," which, intended for a large
public, must be clear, brilliant, and on a large scale ; this
composition is of the class of intimate works, of a nature to
be appreciated by the few only.   Regarded as a sonata it is

a rich and powerful work. The introduction and the melody
of the first *Allegro* are magnificent; in the procedure are to
be found the same qualities admired elsewhere. The *Finale*
above all, a kind of toccata in 6/16/, is extremely interesting
in its harmonic combinations, the strangeness of which might,
however, shock the ear, but for the excessive speed of the
movement. Moscheles (to whom the work is dedicated)
wrote of it in a letter to Schumann who published part of the
letter in the *Neue Zeitschrift* (February 24, 1837). Moscheles,
like Liszt, points out the unsuitability of the title " concerto " ;
and dwells more explicitly on Schumann's use of dissonance,
which, he says, could be understood only by the ear of an
educated musician.

Op. 15. *Kinderscenen. Easy Pieces for the Pianoforte.*
Leipzig, Breitkopf and Härtel. Composed 1838. Published September, 1839. 1. *Of Foreign Parts and People.*
2. *Strange Story.* 3. *Catch me if you can.* 4. *Entreating
Child.* 5. *Happiness enough.* 6. *Great Event.* 7. *Dream-
ing.* 8. *At the Fireside.* 9. *The Knight of the Hobby Horse.*
10. *Almost too serious.* 11. *Frightening.* 12. *Child falling
asleep.* 13. *The Poet speaks.* In sending the *Kinderscenen*
to the publisher, Härtel, in March, 1838, Schumann says
that at first he intended them as a beginning to the *Novelletten*,
but thought afterwards that they would be best as a separate
volume, and that the nature of the contents and their easiness
make them suitable for gifts. For payment he asks " the
same as for the other things "—three louis d'or, with several
free copies to give away (a louis d'or was 15s.). Anxious
that the get-up of the volume should be in keeping with the
contents, he makes detailed requests about type, margin,
lines, " something pretty for the title," etc., which were duly
carried out. The *Kinderscenen* came into being, Schumann
tells Clara, as an echo of a remark of hers, that he sometimes
seemed to her like a child. March 17, 1838 :

. . . I felt as if I had wings, and wrote about thirty neat little things
from which I have chosen twelve [thirteen] and called them *Kinderscenen*. You will like them, but you must forget your virtuosic self.
. . . I am very proud of them, make a great impression—especially on

myself—when I perform them. . . . Romanticism is not a question of figures and forms, but of the composer's being a poet or not. At the pianoforte and with some *Kinderscenen* I would show you all this much better. . . .

The criticism of the work by the Berlin critic Rellstab, who wondered whether the composer was in earnest or joking, called forth the following from Schumann in a letter to Dorn, September 5, 1839:

Anything more inept and narrow-minded than Rellstab's remarks about the *Kinderscenen* I have never come across. He seems to think that I place a crying child before me and then seek for tones to imitate it. It is the other way round. However, I do not deny that while composing, some children's heads were hovering round me (for instance, Ottilie Voigt), but of course the superscriptions came into existence afterwards and are, indeed, nothing more than delicate directions for the rendering and understanding of the music.

In April, 1838, Schumann writes to a friend : ". . . Things have never flowed so freely from my heart as lately. . . . *Kinderscenen*, very easy, for children, by a grown-up." Elsewhere he compares them with the *Christmas Album (Album for the Young)* : " The *Kinderscenen* are reminiscences of an old person for old folk, whereas the others are rather foreshadowings, anticipations, for young folk." In a letter to Henriette Voigt, Schumann sends greeting to " Ottilie, whose big blue eyes go well with my *Kinderscenen*." To Zuccalmaglio Schumann wrote on August 8, 1838 : ". . . Gottschalk will find his name on the *Kinderscenen* about to appear with my name. He will enjoy some of them—they came from my heart." (" Gottschalk Wedel " was a pseudonym of Zuccalmaglio's in the *Neue Zeitschrift für Musik*. Strange to say, the dedication of the *Kinderscenen* was omitted.) Again, later, to the same : ". . . I wish you would look at the *Kinderscenen* and say some of your nice Wedelish things about them. . . ." In reading the composer's comments on the *Kinderscenen*, one of his favourite works, we realize that it is also one of his most characteristic masterpieces.

Op. 16. *Kreisleriana. Phantasies for the Pianoforte.* Dedicated to his friend F. Chopin. Leipzig, Gustav Heinze.

Composed 1838. First published by Haslinger, Vienna, October, 1838; new edition by F. Whistling, Leipzig, September, 1850; December, 1858, transferred to Gustav Heinze, Leipzig. 1–8, without superscriptions. Schumann was impatient to have the *Kreisleriana* published more quickly than could be done by Breitkopf and Härtel, who had already published four of his compositions in this year. Through Fischhof he applied to Haslinger of Vienna, who published the work within the stipulated time. A new edition was published in 1850, by Whistling of Leipzig, to whom Schumann writes: "The *Kreisleriana* are thoroughly revised. In earlier times I unfortunately often spoiled my things, and quite wantonly. That is all done away with now. . . ." About the origin and significance of the work we learn from various letters. Schumann tells Dorn that certainly much of his struggle for Clara is contained in his music, and that the "Concerto [Op. 14], the Sonata, the *Davidsbündler*, the *Kreisleriana*, and the *Novelletten* were inspired by her alone." To Clara he writes on April 13, 1838:

. . . This music in me now, and always such lovely melodies! Think, since my last letter I again have a whole book of new things ready. *Kreisleriana* I am going to call them, in which you and a thought of you play the chief part, and I will dedicate it to you—yes, to you and to no one else. You will smile so sweetly when you recognize yourself. My music now seems to me so wonderfully complex for all its simplicity, so eloquent from the heart, and it has the same effect on all to whom I play it, which I now do gladly and often. . . .

Again, to Clara, one of Schumann's interesting comparisons :

. . . Play my *Kreisleriana* sometimes. An out and out wild love is to be found in some places, and your life and mine and many of your looks. The *Kinderscenen* are the opposite—peaceful and tender and happy, like our future. . . .

The key to the title is given in a letter to Simonin de Sire, March 15, 1839 :

. . . The title is intelligible to Germans only. Kreisler is a creation of E. T. A. Hoffmann's, an eccentric, wild, clever *Capellmeister*. There is much about him that you will like. . . .

Writing to Moscheles about sending him the *Kreisleriana* shortly, Schumann says : " . . . If I am not quite mistaken they will please you more than anything else of mine you know. . . ."

Op. 17. *Fantasie for the Pianoforte.* Dedicated to Herr Franz Liszt. Leipzig. Breitkopf and Härtel. Composed 1836. Appeared April, 1839. Motto :

> Durch alle Töne tönet
> Im bunten Erdentraum
> Ein leiser Ton gezogen
> Für den, der heimlich lauschet.
> FR. SCHLEGEL.

" To be played fantastically and passionately throughout." Schumann at first intended this work—its pecuniary profits— as a contribution to the projected Beethoven monument for Bonn. In December, 1836, he writes to the publisher Kistner that Florestan and Eusebius would like to do something for the Beethoven monument and have written a composition for the purpose with the title : " Ruins. Trophies. Palms. Grand Sonata for the Pianoforte. For Beethoven's Monument. By " etc. The title underwent many transformations, but the idea was abandoned and the work was published two and a half years later as *Fantasie,* with the dedication to Liszt and the Schlegel motto, which may be literally rendered thus : " Through all the tones in Earth's many-coloured dream there sounds one soft long-drawn note for the secret listener." The rest of the inward history of Op. 17 is to be found in Schumann's letters to Clara. March 17, 1838 :

I have finished a *Fantasie* in three movements, which I sketched down to the details in June, 1836. I do not think I ever wrote anything more impassioned than the first movement ; it is a profound lament about you. The others are weaker, but need not be ashamed of themselves.

April 22, 1839 :

The *Fantasie* you can understand only if you transport yourself back to the unhappy summer of 1836 when I resigned you. Now I have no reason to compose in so miserable and melancholy a way.

June 9, 1839:

Tell me what you think in hearing the first piece of the *Fantasie*. Does it not call up pictures to you? . . . Don't you think the " note " in the motto is you? I almost believe it.

Lastly, Schumann writes to Hirschbach in 1839:

. . . Look at the first movement in which at the time (three years ago) I thought I had achieved the highest. Now I think differently. . . .

Turning to some of Schumann's contemporaries, we find among the greatest pianists of the first quarter of the century Hummel (1778–1837—7 concertos, septet, F sharp minor Sonata, concert pieces, etc.—Weimar), and John Field (1782–1837—7 concertos, 20 nocturnes, etc.—St. Petersburg, Moscow). Somewhat later came F. Kalkbrenner (1788–1849—the master of the " belle méthode " and of the *Grande méthode théorique et pratique à l'qide du guide-mains*) and Henri Herz (1803–1888—of " l'éternelle jeunesse "), whom the writers of the *Neue Zeitschrift* characterize with a newer vocabulary than we find in the critique of the banks of the Seine. These two Paris masters, although great in the estimation of those who place finger skill highest, had little value in the eyes of the romanticists that rose about this time, and of whom Chopin was one of the first. Chopin paid his first visit in the winter of 1835 to Leipzig, where were Mendelssohn and Schumann, and where he made Clara's acquaintance, as we have seen, returning for a second visit a year later. Let us recall the following passage which shows something of Schumann's feeling for Chopin and his music (to Dorn, September 14, 1836):

. . . Just as I had received . . . your letter the day before yesterday who should come in but Chopin! That was a great pleasure. We spent a delightful day, and yesterday I held an after-celebration. . . . I have a new ballade of Chopin's [G minor]. It seems to me his work of greatest *esprit* (not of greatest genius), and I said to him that it was my favourite of all. After long consideration he said with great emphasis, " I am glad, it is my favourite too." He played besides a number of new *études*, nocturnes, mazurkas, all incomparable. It is touching to see him at the pianoforte. You would love him very much. . . .

Ignaz Moscheles, one of the oldest pianists in years, still remains one of the youngest, as his *Concert pathétique* and his latest studies prove. And Thalberg, one of the most up-to-date virtuosi, can play the older masters as well as his own wonders. Henselt was the newest star that dazzled Schumann, until, of course, the coming of Liszt to Leipzig in 1840 and again in 1841 set up a new standard for the pianist virtuoso—the genius-virtuoso, the last word. A few words must be said of the violinists. In the earlier part of the century Schumann heard Paganini and was influenced by him. Then he became intimate with the young Vieuxtemps, and contracted a close friendship with the Dresden Polish violinist, Lipinski, and admired the Norwegian violinist, Ole Bull. Of course Spohr (1784–1859—symphonies, concertos, operas, etc.—Cassel) interested him more than Friedrich Schneider, the master of oratorio of a quarter of a century before (1786–1853—symphonies, *Weltgericht*, 1819, etc.). Johannes Wenceslaus Kalliwoda, Director of the Prague Music School, has to be mentioned, not as a genius of the first rank, but as a master of great talent (1800–66—symphonies, overtures, string quartets, etc.). The same holds good of J. F. Kittl and Franz Lachner, who likewise contributed very honourably to the Gewandhaus programmes.

Among the contemporary creative artists of Schumann's acquaintance we must mention one in particular who could at no time boast of great success for his work, but who, because of the great impression he made on Schumann by his example and his ideas, deserves a more special description of his personality—Hermann Hirschbach. Schumann thought that in the nature of the man he discovered something akin to his own nature—many qualities that were common to both of them. That he made a grandiose impression on Schumann

will be apparent from the first allusion to him in a letter to
Clara (July 13, 1838), although it is also apparent that
Schumann is unsuccessfully wrestling to express all he felt:

> . . . There is much of Faust, of the black art, about him. The
> day before yesterday we were doing quartets of his, deficient in style:
> in invention, endeavour, the most colossal to be met with to-day. In
> tendency, some resemblance to myself—states of the soul. But he is
> much more passionate, tragic, than I. The forms quite new, as also
> the treatment of the quartet. Some things moved me most deeply.
> Where there is such overwhelming imagination one does not notice
> small faults. Further, a *Hamlet* overture, ideas for a *Paradise Lost*
> oratorio. The quartets are scenes from *Faust*. There you have a
> picture. Everywhere the deepest romanticism joined to perfect sim-
> plicity and touching truthfulness. . . .

Schumann exhorts Hirschbach to compose more vocal
music, " or are you like myself?—all my life I have placed
vocal music on a lower level than instrumental, and have
never regarded it as a great art. . . ." Schumann also
availed himself of Hirschbach's contributions to the *Neue
Zeitschrift*, sometimes differing from his heterodox opinions—
for instance, with regard to Beethoven's Ninth Symphony and
the counterpoint of the latest string quartets—always treating
him most sympathetically in the practical matters of performances and publications. He regarded him, too, with
the greatest friendliness—" dear friend and fellow-fighter,"
" my precious friend," " best greeting and kiss," and other
affectionate expressions and suggestions abound in Schumann's
letters to him.

> . . . You must know me as a composer in order to realize how near
> we are to one another—you know nothing of my larger compositions
> . . . where, I believe, you will find many and new forms. . . . Your
> endeavour is the most colossal I have seen in new art tendencies, and
> has great force behind it. . . .

Camille Marie Stamaty was the first of the young Europeans
to be attracted to Leipzig by the star of Mendelssohn. The
Dutchman Jean J. H. Verhulst, and the Dane Niels W.
Gade, proved more talented and congenial. Music-lovers in
his own country enabled Verhulst to continue his studies

abroad, especially at Leipzig under Mendelssohn, through whose patronage he was appointed director of the second Musical Society. He became extremely intimate with Schumann, who esteemed him highly as a man and a composer (symphonies, overtures, short orchestral pieces, requiem, etc.). Niels Gade became famous at one stroke when, in 1841, his overture *Echoes of Ossian* gained him the prize of a Copenhagen Society on the decision of Spohr and Schneider. In 1842 he completed his first symphony, in C minor, and ventured with much diffidence to send it to Mendelssohn, who received it with enthusiastic appreciation and produced it at a Gewandhaus concert on March 1, 1843, writing to Gade to tell him of its immense success. In the same year Gade came to Leipzig, and became the idol of the Leipzigers—Mendelssohn at their head. Mendelssohn appointed him his substitute during his own absences, and on Mendelssohn's death Gade succeeded him for a short time (1847–48), returning afterwards to Copenhagen. From the mass of his varied compositions may be singled out, in addition to the above-mentioned overture, symphonies in C major, E major, A minor, and B flat major ; the cantata *Comala*, produced by Mendelssohn, and a great favourite of Schumann's ; a sonata for violin and pianoforte, Op. 6 ; and the overture *Im Hochland*. Ferdinand Hiller, the intimate friend of Mendelssohn and Schumann, cannot be omitted, although his creative endeavours are not always successful (the programmes of the Gewandhaus concerts show him as an instrumental and oratorio composer). Then we have to speak of a master of one of the most important departments of music successfully cultivated at the time, H. A. Marschner, of whom I mention only the operas *The Vampire* (1828), *The Templar and the Jewess* (1829), and *Hans Heiling* (1833). And, lastly, the unfortunate Albert Lortzing (1801–51), the composer of comic operas—*Die beiden Schützen, Zar und Zimmermann, Wildschütz*, and *Waffenschmidt*, and a grand opera, *Undine* (1845).

CHAPTER XIV

Robert's struggle for Clara Wieck (1836 to 1840): Wieck's opposition—Carl Banck—Clara's Vienna, etc., concert tour (October 1837 to May 1838)—Robert's Vienna visit (September 1838 to March 1839)—Clara an exile in Paris (February to August 1839)—Robert and Clara decide to appeal to law (June 1839)—Obstacles at last overcome—Marriage, September 12, 1840—Schumann's compositions, Opp. 18–23, Op. 26, Op. 28, and Op. 32.

THE story is now well known, especially since the publication of the English version of Litzmann's *Clara Schumann*, of the severe trials that Schumann and Clara had to endure from Father Wieck's hostility to the union for more than four years before they were happily married in the autumn of 1840.

The friendship of Schumann and Clara Wieck, begun in her childhood when he came to Leipzig in 1828, and always more or less close, need not be followed in detail through its various phases. This could, however, be done, bearing in mind the nine-years' difference in age between the two, and, in Clara's case, the difficult combination of immature child psychology and the *Wunderkind* phenomenon; and the love episode, curious but not psychologically inexplicable, between Schumann and Ernestine von Fricken (1834–36). Leaving the early girlhood friendship, we start with the troublous time of Schumann's courting, when Clara was barely seventeen years old, and when Wieck quickly decided (January, 1836) that it would be wise to send his daughter to Dresden for a time so as to separate the lovers; at the same time dropping a hint that he considered the match unsuitable and wished to keep them apart. The centre of Wieck's grievance was his pride in his daughter-pupil, who might indeed be called his handiwork. He was ambitious for her to pursue undisturbed the virtuosic career for which he had destined her, looking forward to brilliant years of glory for her and for himself, and was exasperated at the thought of any interference with his plans —and scouted the thought of " Clara with the perambulator."

In his objections to Schumann Wieck ignored the most important one—his tendency to mental instability; laying chief stress on Schumann's early indulgence in beer and his insufficient income. Old Frau Wieck, in my interview with her in 1890, referred to the fact that Schumann's mental weakness was there from the first, and said that she knew also that his drinking indulgences repeatedly led his friends to watch him lest he should throw himself out of the window. But Wieck and his family seemed to be anxious only about the drinking habits and the inadequate income. Schumann's confessions to his mother, relatives, and friends and his determined amendment show his own opinion. Marie Wieck stated with regard to the drinking habits that " he gave them up after marriage." As to the question of income, it is not hazardous to say that Wieck had no correct notion, had indeed extravagant notions, of the needs and desires of artists, at one time maintaining that Clara would be unhappy unless she could give large parties. Old Frau Wieck represented Schumann's circumstances to me thus : from his father six thousand thalers, from his mother the same, and a legacy from his brother. From Schumann himself we know that in his student days he spent money freely, and that in later days his literary and musical work brought him in extremely little.

Wieck's objections were undoubtedly, in themselves and for the time being, reasonable. But as time went on and conditions improved, the objections at last becoming invalid, he did not withdraw his opposition, but grew more and more unreasoningly hostile, amply justifying Schumann's name for him—*Rappelkopf* (crack-brained, hot-headed, madcap, *fou enragé*) ; and we have already learnt of his notoriously volcanic and domineering disposition. Clara, now transported to Dresden, found means of communicating with Schumann, who seized the opportunity of a short absence of Wieck's to go to Dresden, where Clara's friends facilitated the meetings of the pair. The fact was made known on his return to Wieck, who broke out in violent anger against Clara, her friends, and Schumann, intimidating Clara by threatening to shoot Schumann if he ventured to approach her again, and demanding from her Schumann's letters and her promise to break completely with him.   Schumann was informed of all this in the harshest and most offensive way, and forbidden henceforth all intercourse with the Wieck household.   On February 23, 1836, Wieck left Dresden with Clara, and for eighteen months from that time Robert and she, both living for the most part in Leipzig, were completely cut off from each other.   Clara's troubles were now upon her in real earnest—determined to be faithful to Robert, she was not only without means of seeing or hearing of him, but at home had daily to hear him spoken of in the most injurious way by her father, step-mother, and their friends.   Wieck's case against Schumann and Clara consisted in the main of a network of gossip, slander, misrepresentations, intrigues, obstinacy, and eventually sheer malice, and he used every possible means to discredit Schumann in her eyes.   There was at this time the unpleasant Banck episode (1836–7).   Carl Banck often came to the Wiecks', favoured by the parents as a friend of the house, and, so to speak, as assistant singing master ; and Clara played him the classical repertory she had recently been studying and her own compositions for his criticism.   Such at least was his explanation to me of his function.   They seem to have been very intimate, and she wrote to him during her absences on concert tours. Old Frau Wieck said that Banck was constantly about Clara and that she (Clara) liked him.   Banck said that Clara had complete confidence in him, and told me that at first Wieck may have favourably regarded her liking for him as a counterpoise to Schumann.   Later, however, the variable Wieck changed his mind, and one evening returning from a restaurant he broke out, saying, " This must come to an end," the upshot being that Banck left Leipzig suddenly.   In any case, he was dependent on his parents, and not in a position to marry, nor had he any serious wish for marriage.   On the other hand, Schumann held Banck responsible for trying to make him believe that Clara had forgotten him.   Banck talked to him

of his " surprise at Clara's frivolity in thinking nothing more
about it." And later, on hearing of this from Schumann,
Clara indignantly declared that Banck had taken advantage of
her friendly attitude towards him to try to prejudice her
against Schumann : " So he abused my friendship. Was
that the thanks for my genuinely friendly letters from
Berlin ? I am amazed at this bad heart ! He wished to
deceive you [Schumann] and slandered me. . . ." Later
Schumann wrote : " It is certainly Banck's fault that we
were separated for so long."

In May, 1836, Schumann had sent Clara his F sharp minor
Sonata, dedicated to her, and which he later described as his
heart's cry for her ; but we hear of no acknowledgment, and
it was just after this that the return of their respective letters
was insisted on by Wieck. After an interval of two years
Clara appeared again before the Leipzig public, giving a
recital on August 13, 1837, and Schumann was present.
On the programme was his F sharp minor Sonata, of which
Clara afterwards wrote : " . . . Did you not think that I
played it because I knew no other way of showing you something of my inmost heart ? I could not do it in secret, so I did
it in public." Their friend, E. A. Becker, had come from
Freiberg for the concert, and Clara begged him to get from
Schumann his letters to her, which Wieck had obliged her to
send back to him ; to which Schumann's answer was that the
old letters could not now be had, but that she could have new
ones. And thus they came into touch again, this time for
good, although their intercourse had to be carried on secretly
and mostly by letter. On August 14 they became formally
pledged to one another, and it was settled that on Clara's
birthday, September 13, Schumann should venture on a letter
to Wieck again asking for his consent. In this letter Schumann points out that he has been on trial for eighteen months,
and is willing to undergo a further probation of the same
length without seeing Clara, but only writing to her, and that
his character, talent, and position entitle him to a considerate
and full answer. The answer was so confused and indefinite
that nothing could be made of it, and an interview a few days

later was terrible. Robert and Clara were utterly cast down ; he adjures her to be faithful and strong, and resolves that if Wieck carries things to extremity and still withholds his consent after about two years, they must then let the law settle matters.

On October 30, 1837, Wieck started with Clara on a concert tour *via* Prague to Vienna, one of the great cities where she had to make her reputation and be tried against her compeers, and where she triumphantly held her own. She met Thalberg first and Liszt later. Liszt did what the exquisitely aristocratic Thalberg would never have done—to show his anxiety to meet his young colleague, choosing the quickest channel, he threw his visiting card in at her window ! Robert and Clara managed to exchange letters secretly—his specially rich in revelations about his compositions, hers about the Vienna experiences, apart from their own love affair with its ups and downs, misunderstandings and reconciliations. Then there were the moods which her biographer, Litzmann, speaks of when he alludes to her echoings of some of her father's critical remarks on Robert and fears of possible domestic deprivations—moods of which she repented later ; also, of course, Robert's passing moods of dissatisfaction with her for one reason or another. May, 1838, saw the Wiecks back in Leipzig after a highly successful tour, and for a few months Robert and Clara had plenty of opportunities to meet and discuss plans, and in spite of Wieck's increasing opposition they decided, come what might, to marry in 1840.

Schumann's long-standing intention of visiting Vienna was now carried out—on September 27 he started on the journey. He liked Vienna as most people do—he was attracted by the town itself, its people, its surrounding country, and its historic musical past. Then there was the Grand Opera, the Popular Opera, the spoken drama, and the concerts. He made the acquaintance of Schubert's brother, Ferdinand, and was the first to discover Schubert's grand C major Symphony, which Mendelssohn produced at Leipzig in 1839. But very soon Schumann came to realize that Vienna was not as favourable a place as he had hoped for his literary and musical work—the censorship and political illiberality, and the cliques and want of a musical authority, such as Mendelssohn at Leipzig, were too formidable obstacles. And at the end of March, 1839, on hearing of his brother Eduard's serious illness, he hurriedly left Vienna. If he had failed to find a new home for the *Neue Zeitschrift für Musik*, he had at least made pleasant musical friendships—for instance, publishers, virtuosi new and old, professional and amateur, such as Thalberg, Liszt, Vesque von Püttlingen, Baron Pasqualati, Seyfried, J. Fischhof, and Ferdinand Schubert.

Meanwhile (February, 1839) Wieck had sent Clara to Paris, this time accompanied by a French lady, wishing her to feel the unpleasantness of being without his help and protection in the troublesome business of concert and other arrangements. On this occasion she played at one of Schlesinger's famous *Gazette* concerts, also at one of Professor Zimmermann's private concerts, and elsewhere, besides giving a concert of her own. She met many of the distinguished musicians and literary men ; dining at Meyerbeer's, she met Heine and the journalist Jules Janin. But the six months were not happy ones, with frequent persecution on Wieck's part and anxious correspondence with Robert. One more appeal was made for Wieck's consent ; this being refused, Robert and Clara decided to force his consent by law, their lawyer friend Einert assuring them of success in time. Although, in accordance with Saxon law, the main business of the legal question was done in writing, the progress of the case required Clara's presence in Leipzig at times ; and her father's door being now closed to her, she had found a temporary home in Berlin with her own mother, Frau Bargiel, whose sister, Frau Carl, living in Leipzig, sheltered Clara when she had to be there. Litzmann relates that on one occasion when leaving Leipzig Clara sent to ask her father for her winter cloak. The maid brought back his answer : "Who, then, is Mamsell Wieck ? I know only two Fräulein Wieck, my little daughters here. I know no other." During Clara's concert tours in Berlin, Hamburg, and Bremen, Wieck behaved so as to cause doubt of his sanity, writing letters attacking even the moral character of both Robert and Clara, slandering them to their friends and supporters. For instance, to Herr Behrens, in whose house in Berlin Clara stayed for a time and who lent her his Wieck pianoforte for two concerts, notwithstanding a spiteful message from Wieck warning him not to let her play on his instrument, as she was now used to the hard English mechanism and spoiled all others, the passionate parent wrote : " Out of consideration for me and my business you should not again have exposed my instrument to the Rellstab criticism for which a girl demoralized by a miserable fellow shamelessly gives you the opportunity. (She *had* broken a string, of which the critic, Rellstab, wrote : ". . . but only at the end, and like a cry of victory.") (Litzmann, i, p. 375, etc.) When the end of the case was thought to be near, news of a painful set-back reached Clara from Robert—Wieck's objections were all disposed of but one, for which he had to furnish proof within six weeks and three days —a considerable delay ; and this objection was that Schumann was a drunkard. While much comfort came from the staunchness of Schumann's friends—Count Reuss, Mendelssohn, and David volunteered to testify in court against the charge, and Friese, Verhulst, and all the others were equally to be depended on—this was one of the most painful stages for the sensitive Schumann, telling on his mental condition, and so increasing the anxiety of Clara, who was already miserable enough. Another source of satisfaction and counterblast to Wieck's public machinations was the news of the honorary doctorate conferred on Schumann by the University of Jena. In the end Wieck withdrew his objection, and at last, as late as August 12, the way was clear. The banns were published for the first time on August 16, and the wedding took place quietly at Schönefeld, near Leipzig, on September 12, the day before Clara's twenty-first birthday. The long harrowing history with its supremely happy ending is told in detail in Litzmann's biography.

We must now resume the review of Schumann's pianoforte works composed before 1840.
Op. 18. *Arabeske for Pianoforte.* Dedicated to Frau

Majorin F. Serre of Maxen. Vienna, C. A. Spina. Composed 1839. Published 1839, by Mechetti.*

Op. 19. *Blumenstück (Flower Piece) for Pianoforte.* Dedicated to Frau Majorin F. Serre of Maxen. Vienna, C. A. Spina. Composed 1839. Published 1839, by Mechetti.

Op. 20. *Humoreske for Pianoforte.* Dedicated to Frau Julie von Webenau, *née* Baroni-Cavalcabò. Vienna, C. A. Spina. Composed 1839. Published 1839, by Mechetti.

Writing from Vienna to de Sire on March 15, 1839, Schumann says : " Within four or five weeks Op. 18, *Arabeske,* Op. 19, *Blumenstück,* and Op. 20, *Humoreske,* will be published by Mechetti." In August of the same year to Henriette Voigt :

. . . Three new compositions have arrived from Vienna and are awaiting you—a *Humoreske,* which certainly is rather melancholy, and a *Blumenstück* and *Arabeske,* which, however, are less important ; the titles describe them, and it is not my fault that the stems and lines are so fragile and weakly. [Perhaps Schumann is glancing at the titles of the pieces as well as the printing of the notes.]

In the *Arabeske* there is to be noted especially the syncopated " in conclusion," and the somewhat similar passage a few pages back, so characteristic of Schumann's romanticism. On March 11, 1839, he writes to Clara from Vienna :

I have been sitting the whole week at the pianoforte, composing and writing and laughing and crying all at once ; you will find all this beautifully depicted in my Op. 20, the " great Humoreske," already being engraved. See how quickly things go with me—invented, written down, printed, and that's what I like. Twelve sheets completely written in a week—you forgive me, don't you, for having kept you waiting a little ?

In connection with the word " Humoreske " Schumann laments that the French do not understand it, that they have no ·adequate word for " humour," the quality most deeply rooted in German nationality. " . . . Do you not know Jean Paul, our great writer ? I have learnt more counterpoint from him than from my music master. . . ." In this passage

* Pietro Mechetti's widow was succeeded by C. A. Spina.

Schumann describes humour as a combination of " *das Witzige und das Gemütliche (Schwärmerische)* " (approximately, wit and sensibility). At any rate, the English have not the same disadvantage as the French. In brief, a *Humoreske* may be said broadly to contain various capricious ideas of a humorous nature.

Op. 21. *Novelletten for Pianoforte*. Dedicated to Adolph Henselt. Four books. Leipzig, Breitkopf and Härtel. Composed 1838. Published July, 1839. The Intermezzo of No. 3 had already appeared in May, 1838, in the musical supplement to the *Neue Zeitschrift* with the motto from *Macbeth :*

> When shall we three meet again,
> In thunder, lightning, or in rain?

The *Novelletten* are among those works of Schumann's of which we have already heard so often that they were inspired by Clara, and that he considered them his best ; he describes these in particular as " longish connected romantic stories." To Hirschbach he writes of them as being " intimately connected and written with great zest, for the most part cheerful and on the surface, except now and then where I sound the depths." The following to Clara on February 6, 1838, is of interest :

. . . I have composed a frightful amount for you during the last few weeks—jests, Egmont stories, family scenes with fathers, a wedding ; in short, charming things. And I have called the whole *"Novelletten,"* because your name is Clara, and *"Wiecketten"* would not sound well [a playful allusion to Clara Novello, who, engaged by Mendelssohn, sang at two Gewandhaus concerts in 1838, taking Leipzig by storm] . . . [June 30, 1839] . . . In the *Novelletten* you appear in every possible attitude and situation and all else that is irresistible in you. . . . I assert that *Novelletten* could only be written by one who knows such eyes as yours and has touched such lips as yours. In short, better things might be made ; similar ones, hardly. . . .

In 1840 we hear of Schumann being much affected by Liszt's interpretation of the *Novelletten*, etc. The four books comprise eight *Novelletten*, without superscriptions, of which seven are in three sections, Nos. 2 and 3 having each a more independent middle section—" Intermezzo "; No. 8 is longer, containing more divisions.

Op. 22. *Sonate No. II for Pianoforte.* Dedicated to Madame Henriette Voigt *née* Kunze. Leipzig, Breitkopf and Härtel. Composed 1835 (begun 1833), the last movement 1838. Appeared October, 1839.

In March, 1838, Robert writes to Clara :

> . . . As to the last movement of the Sonata you are about right. It displeases me so extremely that (except for some passionate moments) I have rejected it altogether. And I have left the first movement as I originally conceived it, so not as you know it. But you will like it. . .

On August 29, 1839, Schumann writes begging Härtel to let him have a good copy of his G minor Sonata if possible by September 13, that he may give it to Clara Wieck on her birthday, as she is specially fond of it ; and this was accomplished. Early in 1840 Clara played the Sonata at a Berlin concert of which she writes to Robert :

> . . . Marx visited me to-day ; he spoke delightedly of your Sonata and I have already heard from several—connoisseurs, of course—that the Sonata was the finest thing of the whole evening. . . .

As with all his previous works in sonata form, Schumann spent much time and care over this work—no less than five years—with the result that the formal construction is admitted to be superior. The first movement begins " as fast as possible," becoming " faster," and finally " faster still." It will be found interesting to study the structure of this movement.

Op. 23. *Nachtstücke for Pianoforte.* Dedicated to E. A. Becker of Freiberg. Vienna, C. A. Spina. Composed 1839. Published June, 1840, by Mechetti. Schumann gives us definite information as to the prevailing mood of the *Nachtstücke* in a letter to Clara from Prague on April 7, 1839 :

> . . . I wrote to you about a presentiment I had from March 24–27 in the course of my new composition ; there is a passage I always returned to, as if someone were sighing deeply from a heavy heart :

" O God ! " During this composition I kept seeing funerals, coffins, unhappy, desperate people, and when I had finished and was casting about for a title I always came upon *Funeral Fantasy*—is it not strange ? While composing I was often so affected that tears came, and for no reason that I knew of. Then came Therese's letter and the matter became clear to me. [His brother Eduard was dying.] . . . Mechetti has been extraordinarily nice and decent to me and wished to have all my future compositions, to which, however, I have not agreed. But he is to have the *Funeral Fantasy*, which I am going to call *Night Pieces* [the title is taken from E. T. A. Hoffmann] . . .

In January, 1840, he writes :

. . . I have now made the *Night Pieces* quite right. What should you think if I were to call them as follows : 1. *Funeral Procession.* 2 *Strange Company.* 3. *Nocturnal Carousal.* 4. *Round with Solo Voices ?* Write me your opinion.

Op. 26. *Faschingsschwank aus Wien (Carnival Jest from Vienna).* *Fantastic Pictures for the Pianoforte.* Dedicated to Simonin de Sire of Dinant. Vienna, C. A. Spina. Composed 1839. Published September, 1841, by Mechetti. No. 1 *Allegro.* 2. *Romanze.* 3. *Scherzino.* 4. *Intermezzo.* 5 *Finale.* No. 4 had already appeared in December, 1839, in No. VIII of the musical supplement to the *Neue Zeitschrift für Musik.* Of the five movements the first alone contains the chief point of the jest—the smuggling in of the *Marseillaise,* at that time forbidden in Vienna. Schumann describes this composition as " a romantic show piece." To de Sire he writes : " That I have not forgotten you, you will see from a composition about to appear in Vienna, *Faschingsschwank aus Wien,* on which I have put your name. I hope you will look at it kindly and that it will please you." While engaged on the composition of the *Faschingsschwank* Schumann referred to it at first (to de Sire) as " a great romantic sonata," a few weeks later calling it " a romantic show piece."

Op. 28. *Three Romances for the Pianoforte.* Dedicated to Count Heinrich II Reuss-Köstritz. Leipzig, Breitkopf and Härtel. Composed 1839. Appeared October, 1840. The Romances Schumann reckoned among his best pianoforte works, but beyond this fact we hear little of them in his letters.

Clara admired them particularly and begged to have them
dedicated to her; to which Robert wrote: " . . . The
Romances are really not good enough for a girl like you,
all the same it pleases me genuinely that you would like to
have them dedicated to you. What shall the title be? Wait,
I know already." But no more is heard of it.

Op. 32.   *Four Pianoforte Pieces.   Scherzo, Gigue, Romanze
and Fughette.*   Dedicated to Fräulein Amalie Rieffel.   Leipzig
and New York, Schuberth and Co.   Composed 1838 (Nos. 1,
2, 3) and 1839 (No. 4).   Appeared April, 1841.   The Gigue
had already appeared in February, 1839, in No. V of the
musical supplement to the *Neue Zeitschrift*; the Fughette,
in June, 1840, in No. X of the same.   Of this *opus* Schumann
tells us next to nothing—writing to Fischhof on September 5,
1839, he says: " . . . In the Mozart album which *Capellmeister* Pott is bringing out you will find a little Fughette which
has given me much pleasure."

CHAPTER XV

OPUS 32 takes us to the end of the great group of pianoforte
works. And now we come to the second group—songs.
It is an important and rich group, great in quantity, originality, and beauty. Its main bulk belongs to the year 1840,
called by Schumann his " song year "—the year in which his
battle for Clara was won and their happiness launched, and in
which he composed nothing but songs. It has to be noted
that in each case where Schumann takes up a new department he unfolds new strength and inventions and becomes
almost a new man. After the songs there come orchestral
and chamber works, and each of these is a veritable revelation.
Unlike composers generally, Schumann had at first no particular leaning towards song composition—we have already
learnt his views from a letter to his friend Hirschbach :
" . . . All my life [before 1840] I have put vocal music on a
lower level than instrumental, and have never regarded it as a
great art. . . ." And we find him expressing the same views
elsewhere. Hence the first period of pianoforte creations.
But when the wells of his inner nature opened, songs gushed
forth in extraordinary abundance, and it was his love for Clara
that opened the floodgates, and made him produce in quick
succession the wonderful lyrics of 1840.

On February 22, 1840, Schumann wrote to Clara :

. . . Since yesterday morning I have written nearly twenty-seven
pages of music (something new) [it was his *Myrthen*] of which I can
tell you no more than that I laughed and cried for joy over it . . . all

this music nearly kills me now, it could drown me completely. Oh, Clara, what bliss to write songs! Too long have I been a stranger to it.

Again, a few weeks later :

Herewith something as a modest reward for your last two letters. The songs are my first printed ones, so pray do not criticize them too severely. I was quite wrapt up in you when I wrote them. Without such a sweetheart one cannot compose such music—in saying which I wish to praise you particularly.

Once more, on May 15, 1840 :

. . . I have again composed so much that it sometimes seems quite uncanny. Oh, I can't help it, I should like to sing myself to death like a nightingale. Twelve Eichendorff songs. But I have already forgotten them and begun something new.

Thus we have triumphant expressions about the songs as we had previously about the pianoforte works.

The essential quality of Schumann's songs is their spontaneity. With the pianoforte compositions we constantly found this quality, and noted how again and again he wrote of being overwhelmed with music, but this is even more the case with the songs. What strikes one especially with Schumann is the strength of mind with which he upholds his own estimate of his work. He ignores the opinion of others if they assure him that he is mistaken and tells them outright that they are wrong. So, for instance, his friend Wenzel after airing his views on the B flat symphony has to hear the master's own opinion :

. . . Was that your essay ? . . . How you have hurt me ! I was so happy. After a work written with so much love you talk of my *future* —in such cool words ! Yet it *surprised* you ? Words for which I have a deadly hatred. And I have been diligent and conscientious enough all my life to appear and to surprise *now*, without waiting for the future. That I know ! Be that as it may—at first I meant to keep these secret thoughts from you, but by you of all people I should like to be spoken of with the respect to which I am entitled. Now no more, and without resentment, Your Schumann.

Also to Kossmaly he writes, on May 9, 1841 :

. . . In your essay on *The Song* it vexed me a little that you put me in the second class. I did not ask for the first; but I believe I can claim a place of my *own*, and least of all am I pleased to be ranked with Reissiger, Curschmann, etc. I know that my endeavours, my means, far exceed those of the aforementioned, and I hope you will say that to yourself and not call me vain, which I am far from being.

Schumann went on developing his songs in all respects, first of all giving greatest attention to declamation and poetic interpretation. The pianoforte accompaniments are at first simple, consisting of rhythmically repeated chords and variously combined arpeggios. Then the instrumental melody becomes independent, now descriptive of the physical, the outward, now imitative of the psychical, the inward. Then we find alternation and mixture of the vocal and instrumental parts. For example, in *Der Nussbaum* (*Myrthen*, No. 3) the melody is divided, in alternating strains, between the voice and upper pianoforte part, supported by broken chord harmonies. In *Und wüssten's die Blumen* (*Dichterliebe*, No. 8) the extremely simple voice melody has a rapid constant demisemiquaver accompaniment suggestive of the humming of bees, birds, etc., among the flowers; the 6-bar concluding symphony bringing a new semiquaver triplet figure over a reminiscence in the bass of the voice melody. *Widmung* (*Myrthen*, No. 1), a fine example of psychic imitation, with—to indicate the main features only—its rapturous melody with arpeggio accompaniment breaking into emphasizing unison with the voice; the contrasting middle part where the character of the melody changes to one of supreme satisfaction, the triplet chord accompaniment producing the effect of suppressed palpitating excitement; and at the end of the song the characteristically romantic postlude with its thematic reminiscence. To take one more example—*Das ist ein Flöten und Geigen* (*Dichterliebe*, No. 9). Here the instrumental accompaniment is entirely independent and complete in itself, running along now with the voice, now without it—the melody illustrative, no doubt, of the *Flöten und Geigen* (fluting and fiddling), while the trumpets of the poem are perhaps to be heard in the rhythm of the bass chords. When the voice ends the accompaniment develops into a 20-bar concluding symphony with various modulations closing in the tonic major.

Among the first *Lied* compositions which Schumann wrote in 1840, the year of songs, there were these two: Op. 24, *Liederkreis* (Heine), nine songs; and Op. 25, *Myrthen*, "*seiner geliebten Braut*," a special bridal gift to his wife-to-be, twenty-six songs (four books) by Goethe, Rückert, Byron, Th. Moore, Heine, Burns, and J. Mosen. In the course of the same year there followed a multitude of characteristic significant songs, which may be said to have been intended for the same recipient, even if otherwise dedicated, the following of which may be mentioned: Op. 27, *Lieder und Gesänge* (Hebbel, Burns, Chamisso, Rückert, Zimmermann), Book I, five songs; Op. 31, Three Songs (Chamisso); Op. 35, *Liederreihe*, twelve poems (Kerner); Op. 36, Six Poems (Reinick); Op. 37, twelve poems from Rückert's *Liebesfrühling* (Nos. 2, 4, and 11 by Clara Schumann); Op. 39, *Liederkreis*, twelve songs, Eichendorff; Op. 40, Five Songs; Op. 42, *Frauenliebe und Leben*, eight songs (Chamisso); *Romanzen und Balladen* (Eichendorff, Heine, etc.), Book I, Op. 45; Book II, Op. 49; Book III, Op. 53; and Op. 48, *Dichterliebe*, sixteen songs from Heine's *Buch der Lieder*.

We are helped to a realization of the state of Schumann's bliss after his marriage by a letter to his brothers Eduard and Carl, written some two years earlier, March 19, 1838, about the grounds of his happiness. It reveals the whole inwardness of the affair, as well as his confidence in the harmoniousness to be:

. . . Of my good fortune in possessing such a girl to whom I am completely bound by art, mental affinity, habit of many years' friendship, and deepest, really holy love, I will say no more. My whole life is joy and activity. . . .

What their common interests and sympathies were we know. Does the reader understand what this means in the case of an artistically gifted pair, gifted, as here, in different ways, one being mainly creative, the other almost solely executive?

In the most favourable circumstances their art required that one, the executant, should be prepared to exercise renunciation, humility. Clara Schumann had this noble reverence— she saw the inequality of the creative and executive gifts, felt it overwhelmingly when her own slender creativeness was brought into comparison with her husband's superabundance; and she admired in him the greater musician and the superior intelligence, the eminently gifted pianist and prolific composer. When stimulated by Robert to compose some songs for a joint volume with him, she sighs: " . . . I have no talent at all for composition." (But the songs turned out charming —her Op. 12, and Nos. 2, 4, and 11 of Schumann's Op. 37, twelve songs from Rückert's *Liebesfrühling*.) Another time she remarks that " women as composers always betray themselves, which holds good of myself as well as of others." While her general education had been inferior, her musical education—studies in composition under Weinlig, Dorn, and Reissiger, in addition to her pianistic training—helped her, of course, to appreciate her husband's skill, breadth, fulness, imagination, and intelligence; although even in her musical education we find surprising limitations. Soon after marriage they took up together a systematic study of Bach's *Wohltemperirtes Klavier*, and Clara writes: " Robert points out the places where the subject reappears. . . ." And two years later, when Robert was occupied with string quartets, she confesses that she is only now beginning to enjoy quartet music, which hitherto had bored her as she had never been able to appreciate its beauties. In other studies as well Schumann guided and encouraged her, and we hear of her making acquaintance for the first time with Goethe, Shakespeare, etc. On the other hand, Clara's art had often to suffer from subordination to Robert's—a subject of tribulation to both of them. When Robert was composing, Clara's pianoforte had to be silent. Robert expresses his regret that he often hinders Clara in her studies, for she wishes to avoid disturbing him, and he realizes that every artist appearing in public must keep up technical practice. As far as deeper musical culture is concerned, she has made progress—

P

for she lives in nothing but good music, and so her playing is now certainly all the wholesomer and also more intelligent and delicate than before. But sometimes she has not the necessary time to bring mechanical sureness to the point of infallibility, and that is my fault and cannot be helped. Clara understands that I must cultivate my talent, that my powers are at their best, and that I must make the most of my youth. Well, that is the way in artist marriages—one cannot have everything at once; the chief thing is the happiness that remains, and right happy we certainly are that we possess and understand each other—understand so perfectly and love so whole-heartedly.

The Schumanns were, of course, anxious that Robert should have some regular work outside his journal and his composition. The following years seemed to give them some hope of this. Conducting they of course thought of first, but, alas! without realizing his unsuitability for it. A few months before the marriage, on May 31, 1840, Schumann wrote to Clara:

> . . . You speak in your last letter of a " right place " [Gewandhaus conductorship] where you would like to see me—don't be too ambitious for me—I wish no better place for myself than a pianoforte and you near me. You will never, in all your life, be a *Capellmeister's* wife, but inwardly we can compete with any *Capellmeister* couple, can we not? You understand me. . . .

Schumann seems to have understood his own defect better than did Clara and some other admiring friends. For she had no such reasonable ideas about her husband's fitness for a post of the kind, and consequently many disappointments were in store for her. No doubt she had in her mind the various substitutes for Mendelssohn during his Berlin absences— David, Gade, Hiller; but she forgot that it was Mendelssohn himself who determined the directors in their choice. In the course of my life I have come across only one musician who maintained that at first Schumann conducted quite well, but mark what he added: " that is to say, beat time distinctly." Well, that may be so, but beating time distinctly does not constitute good conducting. My informant was Woldemar Bargiel, Clara's stepbrother, the eminent composer, eventually director of the Berlin *Meisterschule* for composition.

The offer of a post, however, came and was accepted when the Leipzig conservatorium was founded. Whether the post was suitable for the uncommunicative Schumann, whom we know as the silent teacher, may well be doubted. After several years of negotiations Mendelssohn had at last succeeded in proposing plans for the foundation of a school of music at Leipzig. The King of Saxony took an interest in and furthered the scheme in every way, and various benefactors—Blümner and others—made gifts in money and in kind to the institution. A preliminary programme of January 16, 1843, announces a teaching staff of six; a later one gives the plan of study. We find Mendelssohn as teacher of solo singing, playing of instruments, and composition; Schumann for pianoforte and private composition; M. Hauptmann for harmony and counterpoint; C. F. Becker for organ playing and lectures on music; Ferdinand David for violin; Frau Grabau-Bünau and Böhme for singing (instead of C. A. Pohlenz, who had died before the opening). And E. F. Richter, the theorist, M. Klengel, the violinist, E. F. Wenzel, the pianist, and L. Plaidy, the pianistic technician, are added to the above. Moscheles settled in Leipzig and joined the music school in 1846. The conservatorium was opened in April, 1843, with some forty students, by the Minister v. Falkenstein in the name of the King of Saxony. Schumann's connection with the school was short, interrupted by the Russian concert tour with Clara (end of January to end of May, 1844), and severed by his breakdown in health in the autumn of 1844, and subsequent departure to Dresden. His actual teaching can have amounted to very little. Wasielewski, who was at the time a pupil at the conservatorium, relates that once he was called in to take part in a trio at one of Schumann's lessons, and that during the whole lesson the master hardly spoke a word, although there was ample occasion for criticism. The accounts we get of Schumann and his lessons always amount to the same thing— oblivion of the duties of a teacher.

Something further has to be said about Liszt and his remarkable doings, especially in connection with Mendelssohn and Schumann; and also of Thalberg, taking us back a few years. After a stay in Italy, a visit to Vienna, and a triumphal progress through Hungary, Liszt at last came to Dresden and Leipzig. Of the great musicians of Leipzig, Mendelssohn was already known to Liszt, who had met him in Paris, especially in company with Chopin and Hiller, as early as 1831–32. Liszt and Schumann knew each other through their compositions—we have already heard of Liszt's criticisms of Schumann's compositions in the *Gazette Musicale*; and Schumann in his paper had expressed urgent requests that Liszt would pay a visit long overdue in the north of Germany. At last the virtuoso appeared in Dresden on March 15, 1840, and two days later in Leipzig, alternating between the two towns. Schumann met him in Dresden, where the artist with the " Jupiter profile " had an overwhelming success. Schumann wrote of him in the *Neue Zeitschrift* (March 27, 1840):

. . . This power of dominating an audience, of uplifting, carrying along, and letting it go again, is probably not to be met with in any other artist—Paganini excepted. In the same second, delicacy, boldness, sweetness, madness, alternate, the instrument glows and glitters under its master. We have no longer pianoforte playing of this or that kind, but the expression of a daring personality to which Fate has for once allotted the peaceful ways of art instead of dangerous weapons as its means of dominating, conquering.

On March 17 Liszt gave his first Leipzig concert, which was not a complete success, chiefly because the Leipzig public had been prejudiced against him by newspaper and other intrigues. To counteract this, Mendelssohn resolved to give a musical soirée in the Gewandhaus with orchestra and chorus in Liszt's honour. The programme included Schubert's C major Symphony; Mendelssohn's 42nd Psalm and parts of *St. Paul*; and Bach's D minor Triple Concerto (with Liszt, Hiller, and Mendelssohn); Liszt playing as well his Fantasia on *Lucia di Lammermoor* and his transcription of the *Erlkönig* —and there was, too, a feast of punch, wine, and all imaginable delicacies. At other Leipzig concerts on this occasion Liszt played Mendelssohn's D minor Concerto, Weber's *Concertstück*, his own Fantasia on the *Huguenots*, Schubert's *Ave Maria*, *Ständchen*, and again the *Erlkönig*, carrying his audience off their feet. Schumann's letters to Clara in Berlin are full of Liszt, and as some of these are given more fully in Litzmann's *Clara Schumann* than in the *Jugendbriefe*, we draw from the former. On March 18, 1840, Schumann writes of being the whole day with Liszt:

. . . He said to me yesterday, " I feel as if I had known you for twenty years," and I feel the same. We are already quite rude to one another, and I often have reason to be so, for he is much too moody and spoilt by Vienna. But I cannot say in this letter all I have to tell you about Dresden, our meeting, the concert there, the railway journey here yesterday, and yesterday evening's concert, and this morning's rehearsal for the second concert. And how extraordinarily he plays, daringly and madly, and again tenderly and sweetly—I have heard it all. But this world, I mean his, is not mine. Art as you practise it, and as I often do at the pianoforte when composing, this fine inwardness (*Gemütlichkeit*), I would not give up for all his magnificence—and there is some, too much, tinsel with it all. No more to-day, you know what I mean.

Two days later, March 20, Schumann writes of being much affected by Liszt's playing of some of the *Novelletten*, *Fantasie*, and Sonata—

much of it differently from my own way of thinking, but always like a genius, and with a delicacy and boldness of feeling that one does not get every day even from him. Only Becker was there, and I am sure there were tears in his eyes.

The second concert was postponed—Liszt went instead to bed and sent word two hours before the concert that he was ill. " . . . I was glad, because I have him the whole day in bed, and besides myself only Mendelssohn, Hiller, and Reuss see him." To this letter to Clara Liszt added a postscript in characteristic fashion : " Permettez-moi aussi, mon grand artiste, de me rappeler affectueusement à votre gracieux souvenir . . ." and so on. One more view of the intimacy between Liszt and Schumann, dated March 22, 1840 :

. . . Life here is mad just now. . . . Liszt came here much spoilt by the aristocracy, and kept complaining so of the want of countesses and princesses and fine *toilettes* that I became annoyed and said to him that we here had our aristocracy too—a hundred and fifty bookshops, fifty printing houses, and thirty journals, and he had better be careful. But he only laughed; he does not trouble enough about the local customs, etc., and so he fares badly in all the papers. . . . But I tell you that Liszt seems to me more powerful every day. To-day at R. Härtel's he played Chopin studies and a piece from Rossini's *Soirées* and other things, making us all thrill and rejoice.

It is interesting to compare Mendelssohn on Thalberg with Schumann on Liszt. Writing to his sister Fanny, on December 29, 1838, Mendelssohn says:

. . . Thalberg gave a concert yesterday evening and pleased me extraordinarily. He restores one's desire for playing and studying as everything really perfect does. A Fantasia by him (such as, in particular, the *Donna del Lago*) is a piling up of the choicest, finest effects, and an astounding climax of difficulties and elegances. Everything is so thought-out, refined, with such sureness and knowledge, and full of the finest taste. Moreover, the man has incredible strength of hand, and yet such practised light fingers. . . . He wishes to be nothing more than what he is—a really *éclatant* virtuoso; and when a man does perfectly what he does one cannot wish him to be but what he is. (S. Hensel's *Familie Mendelssohn*. Berlin, B. Behr. [E. Bock], 1879.)

A few words have to be said, too, about the singers during the period of Mendelssohn's conductorship of the Gewandhaus concerts, on account of the influence they undoubtedly had on him and Schumann. There were the permanent local favourites, Frau Grabau-Bünau and Frau Livia Frege, the latter originally a professional musician, afterwards a rich amateur, and friend of Mendelssohn, Schumann, and others. Mendelssohn's intercourse with England led him to the recommendation, in the first years of his conductorship, of Clara Novello (1837) and Mrs. Alfred Shaw (1838), who became great favourites, as did also Elise Meerti of Antwerp. And Pauline Garcia and Madame Schroeder-Devrient must be mentioned as two wonderful vocal artists who astonished the world by their art and temperament. Remarkable in her more solid way was Sophie Schloss (1839, etc.). And to name only two more, there were Carl Löwe, the famous ballad composer and singer, and the interesting Franz Hauser, singer, *régisseur*, collector of Bach, etc., and friend of Mendelssohn and Hauptmann.

CHAPTER XVI

The symphony year, 1841—The chamber music year, 1842—Op. 46 and Op. 50, 1843—The Russian tour—Schumann gives up the editorship of the *Neue Zeitschrift für Musik*—His health breaks down—Removal from Leipzig to Dresden, December 1844.

THE Schumanns had taken up their abode at No. 5, Inselstrasse, and were living quietly for their artistic work. Here, after the songs of 1840, were created, first and foremost the B flat major Symphony and the D minor Symphony; then, among other works, the three string quartets, Op. 41, the Quintet for pianoforte and string instruments, Op. 44, and the Quartet for pianoforte and strings, Op. 47, received at once with the applause of the musicians—not merely the chatterers but real connoisseurs, such as Mendelssohn, Hauptmann, and others. Further, there were *Paradise and the Peri*, the Andante and Variations for two pianofortes, Op. 46, etc. Here, too, were born the Schumanns' first two children, Marie, on September 1, 1841, and Elise, on April 25, 1843. The godparents of Marie were Schumann's brother, Carl; Clara's mother, Frau Bargiel; Mendelssohn; and Frau Devrient (a lady in whose house Schumann once lodged, and from whom he received much kindness).

After the song year of 1840 an entirely new phase appears suddenly, and the first inkling of the new wonder we get, not from Schumann but from Clara, who notes in their joint Diary, January 17–23, 1841 (Litzmann's *Clara Schumann*, ii, p. 26) :

It is not my turn to keep the Diary this week; but when a husband is composing a symphony, he must be excused from other things. . . . The symphony is nearly finished, and though I have not yet heard any of it, I am infinitely delighted that Robert has at last found the sphere

for which his great imagination fits him.   [January 25] To-day, Monday,
Robert has about finished his symphony ; it has been composed mostly
at night—my poor Robert has spent some sleepless nights over it.   He
calls it " Spring Symphony." . . . A spring poem by [blank] gave the
first impulse to this creation.

Originally, Litzmann notes, the following superscriptions
were thought of for the four movements : *Frühlingsbeginn*
(Spring's Coming) ; *Abend* (Evening) ; *Frohe Gespielen*
(*Merry Playmates*) ; and *Voller Frühling* (*Full Spring*).   The
poet was, according to Jansen (*Die Davidsbündler*, p. 245),
Böttger, to whom Schumann sent, with his photograph, the
following dedication in his own hand-writing beneath the
two opening bars of the symphony (as in the printed version) :
" Beginning of a symphony inspired by a poem of Adolph
Böttger.   To the poet as a remembrance from Robert Schumann.   Leipzig, October, 1842."   And Böttger stated that
the poem in question was the following :

> Du Geist der Wolke, trüb und schwer,
> Fliegst drohend über Land und Meer,
> Dein grauer Schleier deckt im Nu
> Des Himmels klares Auge zu.
> Dein Nebel wallt herauf von fern
> Und Nacht verhüllt der Liebe Stern :
> Du Geist der Wolke, trüb und feucht,
> Was hast Du all' mein Glück verscheucht,
> Was rufst Du Thränen in's Gesicht
> Und Schatten in der Seele Licht !
> O wende, wende Deinen Lauf—
> Im Thale blüht der Frühling auf !

To return to the Diary : " . . . On Tuesday Robert
finished his symphony ; so, begun and ended in four days."
Schumann himself noted : " Sketched January 23 to 26,
1841."   The scoring was begun the next day, January 27.
Schumann had written to Wenzel :

A few days ago I finished (at least in outline) a work over which I
have been quite blissful, but which has also quite exhausted me.
Imagine, a whole symphony—moreover, a spring symphony. I myself
can hardly believe it is finished.   But the scoring has still to be done. . . .

On February 14, a Sunday, Clara's patience was rewarded when after dinner, in company with their friends Wenzel and Pfundt, they heard the Symphony for the first time. On February 30 the scoring was finished. Next, we find Schumann writing to the violinist Hilf:

> . . . I should like to play over with an expert violinist a symphony I have composed, especially as it will probably be performed next week, and it is always good if some of the chief supports of the orchestra know something of the work. . . .

Erler relates that Hilf received this (undated) letter on March 17, that Schumann consulted him about fingering, etc., and that Hilf, at Schumann's request, added various markings. The first rehearsal took place on March 28,

> and went off splendidly to the delight of all present. . . . Mendelssohn was greatly pleased, and conducted with the greatest love and care.

The performance took place three days later, March 31, at a concert given by Clara Schumann in the Gewandhaus for the benefit of the orchestra pension fund—Mendelssohn conducting. Schumann writes:

> Concert of the Schumann couple. Happy, unforgettable evening. My Clara played everything in such masterly manner and in such elevated mood that everyone was charmed. And in my artistic life, too, the day is one of the most important. My wife recognized this, too, and rejoiced almost more in the success of the Symphony than in her own success. Forward, then, with God's guidance, on this path. . . .

Clara wrote to her friend Emilie List: " . . . . My husband's Symphony was a victory over all cabals and intrigues. I never heard a symphony received with such applause. Mendelssohn conducted it, and throughout the concert was most charming, his eyes beamed with the greatest happiness. . . ."

Brilliant as was the performance of the B flat major Symphony under Mendelssohn, the reception was not all that it seemed to Clara. Dörffel relates that while the audience was extraordinarily stirred, many features of the Symphony had at first an effect of strangeness, and the players, too, were by no means at home in the spirit of the work. There was something risky for nearly every instrument, difficult of execution at that period ; only the redoubtable Pfundt was completely happy in that the composer had " written " for three drums instead of the usual two. But the general result was that the Symphony was much talked of, and Schumann, hitherto virtually unknown to the musical public in general, from now onwards began to be known and highly regarded.

Of the origin of the Symphony Schumann himself remarked that " it was born in a fiery hour." At the end of 1842, writing to Spohr, he says :

. . . I wrote the Symphony in that flush of spring which carries a man away even in his old age, and comes over him anew every year. Description and painting were not part of my intention, but I believe that the time at which it came into existence may have influenced its shape and made it what it is.

To Taubert, the composer and conductor, Schumann writes on January 10, 1843 (Erler, vol. i, p. 293) :

Try to inspire the orchestra with some of the spring longing which chiefly possessed me when I wrote the Symphony in February, 1841. At the very beginning I should like the trumpets to sound as if from on high, like a call to awaken. In what follows of the Introduction there might be a suggestion of the growing green of everything, even of a butterfly flying up ; and in the *Allegro*, of the gradual assembling of all that belongs to spring. But these are fancies which came to me after the completion of the work. Only of the last movement I will tell you that I like to think of it as Spring's Farewell, and that therefore I should not like it to be rendered frivolously.

What is it that suggests a kinship between Schubert's C major Symphony discovered by Schumann in Vienna, and produced by Mendelssohn at Leipzig in 1839,* and Schu-

* Different dates have been given for Mendelssohn's production at Leipzig in 1839 of Schubert's great C major Symphony. Dörffel in his *History of the Gewandhaus Concerts* gives March 21. The Symphony was repeated on December 12 of the same year, and Wasielewski remarks that this was " probably the first public performance of this important work." In 1840 the Symphony appears three times on the Gewandhaus programmes—on March 12

mann's B flat major Symphony composed in 1841 after an interval during which no such symphony was written ? Is it not the extraordinary freshness that characterizes both these symphonies ? After hearing the Schubert Symphony rehearsed, Schumann wrote to Clara on December 11, 1839— mark well the personal note in the words, the sympathetic touch :

. . . To-day I was blissful. A symphony of Schubert's was rehearsed. If only you had been there! It is indescribable ; all the instruments are human voices, and immeasurably *geistreich*—and this instrumentation, *pace* Beethoven—these heavenly lengths, like a novel in four volumes. . . .

And to his friend Becker of Freiberg :

To-day I heard parts of Schubert's Symphony rehearsed : all my life's ideals are realized in it ; it is the greatest that has been written since Beethoven—Spohr and Mendelssohn not excepted.

Almost immediately on the B flat major Symphony there followed another orchestral work, finally called *Overture, Scherzo and Finale*, Op. 52, sketched and scored in April and May ; then the Phantasie in A minor, which afterwards became the first movement of the A minor Concerto, Op. 54. In May and June a second symphony was under way. On May 31 Clara writes in the Diary :

. . . . He has again begun a new symphony. . . . As yet I have heard nothing about it, but from Robert's way of going on and D minor sounding wildly in the distance, I know already that another work is being created in the depths of his soul. . . .

On Clara's birthday, September 13, Robert surprised her with, among other things, the finished D minor Symphony (revised ten years later), and he writes in the Diary : " . . . . One thing makes me happy—the consciousness of being still far from my goal and obliged to keep doing better, and then the

---

and 26, and October 29. On March 12, Dörffel notes, the performance was interrupted at the second theme of the first movement by an alarm of fire near-by causing the audience to leave the hall ; and as the Symphony had been included in the programme " by request," it reappeared on the programme of the next concert, March 26.

feeling that I have strength to reach it. . . ." In August, 1841, Schumann writes: "Th. Moore's *Paradise and the Peri* has made me completely happy; perhaps something fine can be made out of it for music." But this came about nearly two years later. By November 10, 1841, " a little symphony in C minor " was sketched, but went no further.

As 1841 may be called the symphonic year—two symphonies composed and produced as well as other symphonic works— so 1842 may be called the chamber music year. In the spring of 1842 we find Schumann occupied with the study of Mozart and Haydn quartets, sharing this with Clara; then we find him writing: " . . . I have been busy in a new department and have ready and written down two string quartets, in A minor and F major." In June a third, A major, was finished, the three forming Op. 41. On August 4 he writes to Dr. Krüger: " To-morrow we start on a trip to the Bohemian watering-places. I have been working very strenuously of late (three string quartets) and need distraction." On Op. 41 there followed fast Op. 44—the Pianoforte Quintet in E flat, composed in September and October, and played by Mendelssohn at the Voigts' on December 6. Theodor Kirchner, who was present, told me that as Frau Schumann was unwell and unable to be there, Mendelssohn played famously at sight instead of her. He criticized the second trio as wanting in liveliness, and Schumann accepted the advice and composed another second trio. From *Die Davidsbündler* (p. 247) we see that Kirchner gave Jansen a somewhat similar account of the event. Schumann's composer friend, Hirschbach, remembered the first hearings of the string quartets, Op. 41, the pianoforte Quintet, and other works, at Schumann's own house. In November and December, 1842, were composed Op. 47, the Quartet in E flat for pianoforte and strings, and Op. 88, the pianoforte trio, known later as *Phantasiestücke*, for pianoforte, violin, and 'cello. A very interesting contemporary judgment of Schumann's new work is that of Hauptmann, the greatest critical authority of his time, who, writing of the A minor Quartet and the pianoforte Quintet, said :

These compositions are without reservation among the finest that recent times can show in this department. R. Schumann has already proved pleasingly in his first symphony that he knows very well how to combine artistic moderation with fresh, exuberant fancy; in these compositions it is confirmed afresh, but here we have to admire anew the freedom and security with which he moves in a branch of composition new to him, as if he had been long accustomed to it. It is a quality of genuine talent that it does not need long study and many experiments in each branch of its art in order to produce something good and sterling; it grasps the particular style, the essence and peculiarity of the means, and in this sense the idea shapes itself naturally and healthily just as the plant develops from its seed.

Hauptmann adds that the compositions are clear, spontaneous, easy to grasp and to follow in their technical form and development, euphonious throughout, and in conception and execution in the best style of the species; and with all these conditions, which concern rather the understanding and the outward aspect of the works, there is at the same time a beautiful and deeply-felt inwardness, free from all that is far-fetched and artificial in feeling, which attracts and interests us the more since there is so little obvious striving after effect. To Spohr Hauptmann wrote:

At David's I heard three quartets of Schumann's: his first, which pleased me greatly indeed, made me marvel at his talent, which I had thought by no means so remarkable, judging from his previous pianoforte pieces, which were so aphoristic and fragmentary, sheer revellings in strangeness. Here, too, there is no lack of the unusual in content and form, but it is cleverly conceived and held together and a great deal of it very lovely.

Schumann himself was much satisfied with the quartets. On October 15, 1842, he wrote to Raimund Härtel:

During the summer months I worked with great zeal at three quartets for violin, etc. We played them several times at David's, and they seemed to please players and listeners alike, in particular Mendelssohn. I do not care to say more about them. But you may be sure that I have spared no pains to produce something really good; indeed, I sometimes think, my best. . . .

The quartets were dedicated " to his friend Felix Mendelssohn Bartholdy with warm respect." Writing to Dr. Härtel a few years later (December 3, 1847), Schumann says :

. . . . My quartets which you published have gained fresh significance for me by the death of Mendelssohn, to whom they are dedicated. I still regard them as my best work of that time [1842], and Mendelssohn often spoke to me of them in the same way.

In a letter, also to Härtel, three years earlier, 1844, Schumann mentions a report (the truth of which, however, he disbelieves) that his quartets had been returned as "poor stuff" by the celebrated Müller Quartet of Brunswick to a Leipzig publisher ; and he suggests that, as the quartets have not yet been reviewed, it might be in his (Härtel's) interest to give them to a competent musician to review, for instance, Musik-Director Richter. There appeared, accordingly, a notice, signed "R.," in the *Allgemeine Musik Zeitung* of 1845, by the excellent Richter. Although Schumann's habit—strangely contrary to his advice to others—of composing at the pianoforte may have affected his style in writing for other instruments, we must not too readily follow Wasielewski in all he says as to Schumann's insufficient regard for the nature of the string instruments, and his particular complaint of the inconvenient characteristic use of syncopation in the accompanying parts in ensemble playing. Now remember Hauptmann's criticism of Schumann's quartets, remembering also that he was an excellent violinist, for whom the instrument held no secrets as to intonation, acoustics, etc. Did Wasielewski, who also was a violinist, overlook the important consideration that, in the development of technique, what may be a stumbling-block at one stage becomes a commonplace later on ?

It is not surprising that the spell of excessive creative activity should have resulted in an attack of "nerve exhaustion" (as Schumann called it) which obliged him to desist for a time from composition ; and the appointment early in 1843 to the newly started music school was welcomed as bringing in a much-needed supplement to the means of the increasing household. In the middle of 1843 Schumann writes : "The *Peri* and the music school took up my whole time during the past quarter."

After some eighteen months' preoccupation with the text of *Paradise and the Peri*, the musical composition was begun on February 23, 1843, on the completion of Op. 46, the Andante with Variations for two pianofortes, two 'cellos, and horn (afterwards rearranged for two pianofortes to facilitate performance) In the middle of March Robert played Clara the sketch of the first part; it seemed to her to be the finest thing he had ever written, but " he is working at it with body and soul, with a fervour that makes me sometimes fear it may harm him. . . ." By the end of March the first part was finished; by the end of April, the second. On May 25 Robert played her the newly finished sketch of part three; and on June 16 the *Peri* was completed " after several days of strenuous work. That was a great joy for the Schumann pair," he notes. How full of the new work Schumann's thoughts were we see from his letters written about this time. To Dr. Krüger, June 3, 1843 :

. . . . And so let me tell you that I have written many hundred thousands of notes lately and that on Ascension Day I completed a large *opus*, the largest I have as yet undertaken. The subject is *Paradise and the Peri* by Thomas Moore, an oratorio, but for cheerful people, not for the place of prayer; and while I wrote, a voice sometimes whispered to me, " What thou dost is not all in vain."

Again, to Verhulst, on June 19, 1843 :

. . . I finished my *Paradise and the Peri* last Friday, my largest work and, I hope, my best. With a thankful heart to heaven for preserving my strength while I worked, I wrote *Fine* at the end of the score. . . . I think I have already told you the story of the *Peri*; if not, try to get it, it is in Thomas Moore's *Lalla Rookh* and seems as if expressly written for music. The idea of the whole is so poetical, so pure, that it quite inspired me. . . .

The first performance took place on December 4, 1843, Schumann conducting. After a critical orchestral rehearsal he wrote to Clara who, to the distress of both, had to be in Dresden on that day :

It went excellently and I think your old man will do you credit. They were all very warm and I was really inspired in conducting.

Others were less satisfied, among them Livia Frege, who sang the part of the Peri, and wrote Clara a full report of the rehearsal :

. . . If your dear husband could only make up his mind to scold a little and to insist on greater attention it would undoubtedly go at once.

But the performance seems to have passed off well. Clara wrote in the Diary :

It is impossible to say how happy I was that evening (December 4). The applause was great, but at the second performance, on the 11th, it was enthusiastic. Robert was applauded as soon as he appeared, and found a beautiful laurel wreath on the conducting desk, which somewhat disconcerted him but must have pleased him. He was recalled after each part. . . .

Schumann takes the text of his first large vocal work from the second of the four parts of Thomas Moore's " Oriental romance " *Lalla Rookh*, his friend Flechsig doing the translating and adapting. In *Paradise and the Peri* the central idea is that of salvation through striving. The repentant Peri, the spirit of the air ejected from Paradise, learns from the angel at the gate of Eden that

> The Peri yet may be forgiven
> Who brings to this eternal gate
> The gift that is most dear to Heaven.

The first gift offered by the Peri, but rejected, is a drop of blood from a hero who died for freedom ; the second, also rejected, the last sigh of a maiden who in pure love shared death with her lover ; the third, the tear of a repentant sinner, is accepted and the Peri is readmitted to Paradise. There never was a composer more pleased with his text than Schumann was with *Paradise and the Peri*. He was not aware of the shortcomings of the poet—shortcomings in respect of genius and craftsmanship. The special charms of the poem which are seen at a glance, and were at this early time particu-

Q

larly notable—less familiar then than now—are the orientalisms of colour, form, symbolism, and picturesqueness. The striking feature of Schumann's composition is the entirely lyrical treatment, which eschews secco-recitative, and almost eliminates accompanied recitative ; and the developments of song that are employed do not exceed the simpler limitations of the aria. As specially charming and striking may be instanced the martial choruses of the first part and the Peri's first aria ; the Peri's slumber-song and chorus at the end of part two ; No. 13, tenor solo and quartet where the instruments play an important descriptive part ; No. 14, the wonderful characteristic harmonies, such as the combination of augmented fifth and major seventh (G, D sharp, F sharp, B, unprepared minims, G, E, G, crotchets *) ; the charming chorus of Houris introducing the third part and containing the climax and essence of orientalism—a *pianissimo* clash and clang of drums, triangle, cymbals, brasses, etc., accompanying the tuneful voices.

Op. 46. *Andante and Variations for two Pianofortes.* Dedicated to Miss Harriet Parish at Hamburg. Leipzig : Breitkopf and Härtel. Composed 1843. Appeared 1844. Schumann in the earlier times was often awkward until the natural ease of his genius asserted itself. It is really wonderful how frequently he hits on successes. His habit of seeking out the strange no longer strikes us in this *opus*. Yet, think of the instrumentation—two pianofortes, two 'cellos, and a horn. The difficulties of execution, however, decided him to re-instrumentate the work for two pianofortes. In its original form it was tried in March at the Härtels'. The first public performance of the altered form took place later in the same year, at a concert of Pauline Garcia's, by the hands of Clara Schumann and Mendelssohn, August 19, 1843. In later years, November 28, 1868, the work was played by Brahms and Clara Schumann in Vienna at one of her concerts. The

curious will be glad to hear that the original version can be had in the supplementary volume of Clara Schumann's edition (Breitkopf and Härtel). The composer wrote to Verhulst on June 19, 1843: "I have heard the Variations for two pianofortes, etc., only once: it did not go particularly well. A work of the kind requires study. It is very elegiac in tone; I believe I was rather melancholy when I composed it." The piece became one of Schumann's popular compositions. The impression made upon me by the pianists who first took it up is unforgettable.

In the course of the year 1843, finding that their income was not enough for their needs, Schumann resolved to take Clara on an often-planned Russian concert tour; and on January 25, 1844, having left the two babies at brother Carl's house at Schneeberg, the Schumann pair set out, by Berlin, Königsberg, and other towns, for St. Petersburg and Moscow, Clara giving many concerts on the way. At Dorpat they made the acquaintance of the Liphardt family, one of whom, as we learned, was the wife of Ferdinand David. In St. Petersburg Clara played at Court: and at a soirée specially arranged by the Wielhorskys Schumann conducted his B flat major Symphony. Then we hear of kindness shown by the Prince and Princess of Oldenburg, and of intimate and congenial intercourse with the Henselts. After an absence lasting four months the Schumann family were reunited on May 30. The tour was an interesting experience; it was also financially successful; but for the greater part of the time Robert was unwell and, as usual, suffered much chagrin from having to figure as the husband of his as yet more famous wife. Other expeditions, professional and recreative, were made during the four years' Leipzig residence—the concert tour to the northern towns Bremen, Hamburg, etc., in 1842; a short pleasure trip to Bohemia, in the course of which the Schumanns visited Prince Metternich; and frequent short excursions in the neighbourhood of Leipzig—the favourite walks of the Rosenthal and the more distant Connewitz.

Schumann's editorial work, interrupted by the Russian tour, was now abandoned altogether. On June 5 he wrote to

Verhulst : ". . . . I have entirely given up the *Neue Zeit-schrift* for this year to Lorenz, and hardly think I shall ever resume it.   I should like to live entirely for composition. . . ." In the following year the *Neue Zeitschrift* passed over to Brendel.

At the beginning of August, 1844, Schumann again took up work at the Conservatorium, but in the middle of the month he became seriously ill.   A visit to the Harz in September brought no benefit, and a visit to Dresden was decided on and carried out on October 3—Robert so ill that he feared he could not survive the journey.   Some terrible days followed : " Robert did not sleep a single night, his imagination painted the most terrible pictures, in the early morning I generally found him bathed in tears, he gave himself up completely," wrote Clara.   But the improvement hoped for from change of scene and society set in, and it was decided to remain in Dresden, a suitable house having been found (No. 35, Waisenhausstrasse).   After some weeks of comings and goings the Schumanns gave a farewell matinée for their friends on December 8, and on the 13th they left Leipzig for good to settle in Dresden.

CHAPTER XVII

Dresden (1844–1850)—Wagner and Schumann—Ferdinand Hiller and other artists—Op. 54—*Faust—Manfred.*

THE characteristic of Dresden was the Court, with its taste for art and literature, which led to the engagement of a variety of artists—painters, sculptors, architects, authors, and musicians. And there was also a personality with the ability to gather these men round him—I mean, of course, Ferdinand Hiller, who had sympathies in all these directions.

First of all let us see about the musicians brought together by the opera house and theatre. The most important musician of all, whether the public of the time knew it or not, was of course Wagner, who began his musical career nearly at the same time that Schumann began his; but what a different career! Born at Leipzig in 1813, he passed his early years in Dresden, where he attended the Kreuzschule from 1822–27; in the following year he was back at Leipzig, attending the secondary schools, then the University, having also a six-months course of harmony, counterpoint, and form with Cantor Weinlig. A symphony in C major, composed in 1832, was performed at a Gewandhaus concert in 1833. In 1833 Wagner was at Würzburg serving as chorus-master under his brother Albert, who was stage manager there, and there he composed *Die Feen.* In 1834 he became *Musik-Director* at Magdeburg, afterwards at Königsberg and at Riga; thereafter going to Paris, where he did hack work for publishers, studying and composing diligently as well (September, 1839, to April, 1842). He also wrote for Schumann's *Neue Zeitschrift,* appearing among the contributors as early as 1836—from Paris he sent a long article on Rossini's *Stabat Mater* ; 1842 found him back at Dresden, where on October 20 *Rienzi* was produced under Reissiger;

on January 2 of next year Wagner himself produced his *Flying Dutchman*. On January 10, 1843, he conducted his trial performance (Weber's *Euryanthe*), and by the end of the month his appointment as *Capellmeister* of the Court theatre was confirmed, in succession to Rastrelli and Morlacchi. In July of the same year he was appointed conductor of the *Männergesangfest*, for which he wrote his *Liebesmahl der Apostel*, for three separate choirs of male voices. A more important musical event entrusted to him was the direction of the music for the reinterment of Weber, on December 14, 1844, for which he composed a funeral march on motives from *Euryanthe*, the vocal and instrumental forces of the theatre performing other music as well. In 1845 (October 19) he produced *Tannhäuser*. Lastly must be mentioned his sensational performances of Gluck's *Iphigenia in Aulis*, revised by himself; and his very noteworthy performances with the Court theatre orchestra of certain of Beethoven's symphonies, including the *Eroica*, C minor, A major, F major, and the Ninth. In May, 1849, Wagner's Dresden period came to an end, for on the outbreak of the revolution he had to flee to Weimar, and, after a few days there with Liszt, he reached Paris in safety by Bavaria and Switzerland. Although there was, especially at first, a good deal of intercourse between Wagner and Schumann, the two were incompatible both as men and as artists, except in so far as they could jog along avoiding uncongenial topics. Schumann mentioned Wagner's presence at regular weekly gatherings, where Hiller, Bendemann, Hübner, Rietschel, and Reinick were present, and where Wagner surprised them with his *Lohengrin* text. The most obvious difference between their natures was, of course, the unwillingness of the one to unburden himself and the overwhelming need of the other to do so—Schumann complains that it is impossible to endure for long a man who talks incessantly, while Wagner complains that it is impossible to discuss with a man who will hardly open his mouth. Their minor peculiarities and tastes made real sympathy out of the question, although each was, to begin with, by way of appreciating the other. Theodor

Kirchner told me that at Zürich Liszt once came to him and said : " Can we not get something of Schumann's for four hands (*Manfred*, D minor Symphony, etc.) and try to convert Wagner ? " No sooner said than done. But Wagner was not appreciative of Schumann's music, had not the slightest understanding for it ; he called the D minor Symphony " *banal.*" As is well known, Schumann's opinion of Wagner's work became less and less favourable as time went on. Then there was the malignant article published in the *Bayreuther Blätter* in August, 1879, and written by Joseph Rubinstein, but known to be inspired by Wagner, in which it was sought to show that Schumann's writings were not coherent creations but complexes of rosalias, patch-work, and padding.

In 1845 Wagner had presented Schumann with the score of his *Tannhäuser* inscribed in his own handwriting : " To Robert Schumann as a souvenir from Richard Wagner," which occasioned the following remarks in a letter to Mendelssohn, October 22, 1845 :

. . . Wagner has another opera ready. Certainly a clever fellow full of mad ideas and infinitely audacious—the aristocracy are still raving about *Rienzi*—but he is really incapable of conceiving and writing four beautiful bars, indeed *hardly good* ones, in succession. That is where they are all wanting, in pure harmony, skill in four-part chorale writing. What lasting good can come of it ? And the score lies before us beautifully printed, with all the fifths and octaves, and he would like to alter and erase—too late ! [The score, Jansen tells us, is a transfer copy from Wagner's handwriting ; he was very skilful in the use of chemical ink.] Now enough ! The music is not a whit better than *Rienzi*, is indeed more feeble, more forced. But if one says so, " Oh, jealousy," they say ; so I say it to you alone, for I know that you knew it long ago. . . .

But writing again to Mendelssohn a few days later :

. . . About *Tannhäuser* perhaps by word of mouth soon. I must withdraw much that I wrote to you after reading the score ; on the stage everything works out quite differently. I was greatly affected by much of it. . . .

And in the same key Schumann tells Dorn that he wishes that he could see Wagner's *Tannhäuser.*

It contains things deep, original, a hundred times better than his earlier operas—certainly much that is musically trivial as well. In short, he can be of great importance for the stage, and as far as I know him he has courage for it. The technique, the instrumentation, I find excellent, incomparably more masterly than before. He has a new libretto ready, *Lohengrin*. . . .

After Robert and Clara had heard *Tannhäuser* together, Clara writes in the Diary : " . . . Robert was extremely interested in this opera, he finds it a great advance on *Rienzi* in regard to instrumentation as well as musically. I cannot agree with Robert, for me this music is no music—although I do not deny Wagner great dramatic vitality. . . ." Clara seems to have felt as did the majority of those who heard *Tannhäuser* for the first time, the verdict of whose unaccustomed ear was, " There is no melody in it." One of Schumann's last known utterances concerning Wagner occurs in a letter to C. van Bruyck, May 8, 1853 :

. . . He is, to express myself briefly, not a good musician ; he has no understanding for form and euphony. But you must not judge him from pianoforte scores. If you heard his operas on the stage, many parts could not but move you deeply. And if it is not clear sunlight that the genius radiates, it is often, nevertheless, a mysterious magic that overpowers our senses. But, as I said, the music apart from the representation is poor, often quite amateurish, empty, and repellent ; and it is a proof of the deterioration of taste that these should be put above the many dramatic masterpieces which the Germans possess. . . .

Had Schumann lived long enough to follow Wagner along his new revolutionary paths, watching the development and climax, one can hardly doubt that he would have followed appreciatively, even while still upholding the classical ideals of form and euphony. As it was, we must bear in mind that Schumann followed no farther than *Tannhäuser*—he did not hear *Lohengrin* ; and one cannot but feel that if he had known *Die Meistersinger* he would have withdrawn at least the statement that Wagner was " not a good musician."

Wagner's colleague was Karl Gottlieb Reissiger, whom neither Schumann nor Wagner seems to have considered a genius, but who wrote a large mass of easy-going music. Of his teachers we hear of Schicht at Leipzig and Winter at Munich. Among his operas are: *Yelva* (melodrama); *Libella*; *Die Felsenmühle von Etalières*; *Turandot*; *Adèle de Foix*; *Der Schiffbruch der Medusa*; etc.; and besides some church music a great deal of favourite chamber music, especially pianoforte trios. A late friend of mine, a London musician and pupil of Reissiger, characterized him to me as "an able and amiable master," and I am disinclined to accept the estimate of his mediocrity by such forceful geniuses as Schumann and Wagner. Reissiger's was an easy and popular style, which fact explains his successes in opera and chamber music.

Ferdinand Hiller was born in 1811, had Hummel as his master, and in 1831 was the friend of the romanticists Berlioz, Liszt, Mendelssohn, and the rest of the Parisian artists of that time. He then went to Italy to learn the art of opera-making, and later pursued it without much success at Dresden. His successes were mostly in the composition and performance of chamber music. His principal work was an oratorio, *The Destruction of Jerusalem*, performed at Leipzig in 1840. The operas had only a transitory success. He succeeded pretty well with his subscription concerts, given with an unofficial orchestra (1845–47). But the social qualities of well-to-do Hiller and his Polish wife (a singer) brought together the artistic elements of Dresden—at first they had gatherings at their own house, later at a restaurant of the capital. I knew Hiller in all his after stages from the time he came from Dresden to Düsseldorf, where he succeeded Julius Rietz as conductor, and in 1850 when he went for the rest of his days to Cologne, and I learned to know him as conductor, composer, director of the conservatorium, and teacher of Max Bruch and Humperdinck. He was one of the old school of conductors; not relying on the gesticulations customary nowadays. At the rehearsals he sat; gave his instructions with calmness and clearness. I soon had an example of other ways when on one occasion Berlioz conducted a concert in Hiller's stead, and at the end of the

concert testified to his satisfaction by embracing every one
of us players. To hear Hiller play a pianoforte concerto of,
say, Mozart, was a treat never to be forgotten. What
exquisite tone, what purity of style ! Hiller's writings and
conversations should also be mentioned, for they gave universal
satisfaction. His book *Briefe an eine Ungenannte* contains a
charming characterisation of Schumann's personality (Letter
xxii, pp. 85–89). Cologne, 1877. Dumont Schauberg.

The painters Eduard Bendemann (1811–89) and his
brother-in-law Julius Hübner (1806–82), who became faithful
friends of the Schumanns, were pupils of Wilhelm von Schadow
(son of the great sculptor, Johann Gottfried Schadow),
following their master from Berlin to Düsseldorf when he
founded the Düsseldorf school, and there making the acquaintance of Mendelssohn. From Düsseldorf they went to
Dresden as Professors and painters of historical and other
pictures, Bendemann afterwards returning to Düsseldorf as
Director of the Academy, Hübner remaining as Director of
the Dresden Gallery. Bendemann's " Lament of the Jews "
and " Jeremiah on the Ruins of Jerusalem " and Hübner's
" Disputation of Luther with Eck " may be known to the
reader. At Düsseldorf I became acquainted with Bendemann, appreciating to the full his scholarliness and refine-
ment and becoming the depository of many of his intimate
memories of Schumann's home-life. A student from another
art centre (Vienna and) Munich, was Schnorr von Carolsfeld
(1794–1872), the famous draughtsman and painter, whose
son and daughter-in-law became unequalled as interpreters
of Wagner's characters. The sculptors Rietschel and Hähnel
are too well known to need further remark here. Gottfried
Semper, famous both in the theory and practice of architecture, who served his apprenticeship in a great many schools,
has left traces of his glorious work wherever he lived. At
Dresden, for instance, he designed the present opera house
(carried out by his son), his first one having been burnt down
in 1869 ; museums, the Villa Rosa and the Palais Oppen-
heim (private buildings), etc., and in Switzerland and in
Vienna he conducted great building operations.

Among authors may be named Karl Gutzkow (1811–78), the novelist, dramatist, etc. (*Uriel, Acosta, Zopf und Schwert, Das Urbild des Tartuffe, Königsleutnant*—the most popular among his many plays); Eduard Devrient, author of a history of the play, and stage manager at Dresden, whom we already know as the friend of Mendelssohn ; Berthold Auerbach, the delightful teller of.stories ; and the poet and painter, Robert Reinick.

The most important of Schumann's works completed during the Dresden period are the *Pianoforte Concerto*, Op. 54 ; the *Scenes from Goethe's "Faust"* (without *opus* number) ; *Manfred*, Op. 115 ; and the *C major Symphony*, Op. 61.

Op. 54. *Concerto for Pianoforte with Orchestral Accompaniment*. Dedicated to Ferdinand Hiller in friendship. Leipzig : Breitkopf and Härtel.   1. *Allegro affettuoso*.   2. *Intermezzo*.   3. *Allegro vivace*.   Litzmann notes that the hand-written copy was inscribed : " First movement, which was a self-contained movement, composed at Leipzig in 1841 with the title ' Phantasie,' the other movements at Dresden, May and July, 1845." Clara writes on June 27, 1845 : " Robert has composed a beautiful last movement for his Phantasie in A minor for pianoforte and orchestra, so that it is now a concerto, and I shall play it next winter.   I am very glad about it, for I always wanted a large bravura piece by him."   And on July 31 : " Robert has finished his concerto and handed it over to the copyist.   I am as happy as a king to think of playing it with orchestra."   Schumann's concerto is a masterpiece of its kind, one of the greatest successes of Romanticism.   It is one of the happiest specimens of the solo-orchestral combination, and at the same time contains the most fascinatingly original, glorious material. Of the three contrasting movements, in the bold *Allegro affettuoso* the composer gives expression to all the heroic moods in him, loftiness, dignity, and pride, with intervening patches of darker colour and intenser pathos ; in the simple Intermezzo he is satisfied with more reticent qualities ; and in the dashing *Allegro vivace* all is impetuous, joyous—note the whirligig of quavers with breathless syncopations in the accompaniment. The Concerto, of course, found great favour at once, at first in the neighbourhood, then further afield. The first performance took place at a Leipzig Gewandhaus concert, played by Clara Schumann, on January 1, 1846; Dresden followed; and in time its adoption by virtuosi became general.

Faust and *Manfred* are not only larger in extent, but have also a greater qualitative range—a higher height, a deeper depth, and broader breadth than anything Schumann achieved before or after. In short, Schumann had grown to his full height as a composer, and the growth of the composer had become the growth of the man. But the question of advance is not a single one applicable to all musical categories and combinations. At a certain stage the changes in Schumann's development may be said to have become consolidated, so as to require a change in his musical language, and this stage is represented by *Faust*, in which the new language evidently reaches maturity.

The composition of *Faust* was spread over many years. From the Diary we learn that when Schumann was lying ill at Dorpat in the course of the Russian concert tour in the spring of 1844, he occupied himself closely with the reading of Goethe's *Faust*, and some musical drafting may have been done then; but the next we hear is that during a transitory improvement in his serious illness in August he was working at *Faust*, finishing the final chorus, but " with sacrifice of his last strength," and then came the complete nervous collapse which led to the removal to Dresden. In 1844, then, Schumann had composed the larger part of what became the great Part III of his *Scenes from Faust*—namely, the end of the second part of Goethe's *Faust*, *Fausts Verklärung* (Faust's Transfiguration). Of the seven numbers that make up this division, complete in itself, Nos. 1, 2, 3, and 7, the final *Chorus Mysticus*, were composed in 1844; Nos. 4, 5, and 6 not till 1848—the revised version of No. 7, the final chorus, belonging to 1847. In 1849 and 1850 Schumann added six more numbers as Part I and Part II, of which Part I (numbers 1, 2, and 3) and the first number of Part II (number 4) were composed in 1849, and the remainder of Part II (numbers 5 and 6) in 1850. The overture came last of all, not until 1853. Writing to Mendelssohn in 1845 Schumann says:

> . . . The scene from *Faust* reposes in my desk. I am thoroughly afraid to look at it again. The sublime poetry of the conclusion in particular moved me so that I ventured on the work; I do not know whether I shall ever publish it. . . .

But the revelation came in a very welcome and unexpected way. There had been a private performance in June, 1848, of which Schumann wrote to Nottebohm:

> A week ago we gave the scenes from *Faust*, which was a pleasure to me. The whole impression seemed to me stronger than that made by the *Peri*—no doubt because of the grander poem. . . .

On the same day he wrote the same to Brendel, adding:

> . . . What pleased me most was to hear from many that the music made the poem intelligible to them for the first time. For I often feared the reproach: " Why music to such perfect poetry ? " On the other hand I felt since I came to know this scene that here of all places music could enhance the effect. . . .

The first public performance took place most appropriately at the celebration of the Goethe centenary, August 29, 1849. In Schumann's own words to Dr. Härtel, July 28, 1849:

> . . . I was asked for my *Faust* music for performance at the coming Goethe celebration . . . the concert will be in the Palace of the large garden, and the *Walpurgisnacht* will also be given. . . . How strange, the piece has lain five years in my desk, known to nobody, almost forgotten by myself, and now comes to light at this very rare celebration.

The satisfaction was a threefold one, for Liszt at Weimar and Rietz at Leipzig also gave *Fausts Verklärung* on the same day. The Dresden and Weimar performances produced a profound effect; the Leipzig one less so, which Schumann, writing about it to Brendel, attributed partly to the placing of the work at the beginning of the programme. " . . . The whole formation (*Gestaltung*) of the scene has the character of finality. The separate parts are not self-contained—each must run straight and smooth into the next to form the climax, which seems to me to be at the first appearance of the words ' Das Ewig-Weibliche zieht uns hinan ' (shortly before the beginning of the lively final chorus)." Another drawback, thought Schumann, may have been the use of the original version of the final chorus (sent by him as the orchestral parts of the other were not written out) instead of the second version, " certainly far preferable." The first performance of the complete *Scenes from Faust* took place on January 14, 1862, at a Gürzenich concert at Cologne under Hiller.

We pass from *Faust* to *Manfred*, from the mainly idealistic in form to the realistic ; and without dwelling on the question of supposed psychological affinities between the two poems on the one hand, or between Schumann and Manfred on the other. We get very little enlightenment about the inwardness of the composing of *Manfred*. The Diary tells us that immediately after the completion of *Genoveva*, August 4, 1848, Robert began " a new work, a kind of melodrama, *Manfred* by Byron, that inspired him extraordinarily. . . . Robert has arranged the poem according to his own ideas to make it effective for the stage. . . ." By the second week of November the overture was finished ; on the 14th " Robert brought home a bottle of champagne for the birthday celebration of his first part of *Manfred* finished to-day." But Byron's determination to make his poem impossible for the stage proved more successful than Schumann's endeavour to adapt it for musico-dramatic treatment ; for although it has been staged, Schumann's *Manfred* lends itself better, if still imperfectly, to concert performance. The first staged performance was carried out by Liszt at Weimar on June 13 and June 17, 1852. The next one hears of was at Leipzig in 1863, which Dörffel, curiously, states to have been the first staged performance. The overture was first performed at a Leipzig Gewandhaus concert on March 14, 1852 ; the first complete concert performance took place there also, on March 24, 1859.

Richard Pohl (who collaborated with Schumann in some of his texts, and whose version of *Manfred* was published in 1858 by Breitkopf and Härtel, and is the one in general use), visiting Schumann on September 4, 1851, found him at work on *Manfred* for Liszt's prospective production of it at Weimar. Schumann told Pohl that he had used the translation of Posgaru in preference to that of Böttger; and he admitted that there were many difficulties in the way of scenic representation. Pohl was present at the Gewandhaus concert at Leipzig on March 14, 1852, when the *Manfred* overture was first performed, Schumann conducting. Pohl sat so that he faced Schumann, and he writes of it as follows :

His [Schumann's] mood was deeply serious; completely absorbed in the score, forgetting the audience altogether, taking little notice even of the orchestral musicians, he lived in his tones, identified himself as it were with his task, became himself Manfred. I felt that this work, more perhaps than any other, had been written with his heart's blood, that here he has spoken from his inmost soul. . . *

Of the several constituents of *Manfred* the overture is the greatest, is perhaps the greatest of Schumann's works—one of the grandest and most original compositions ever conceived, one of the most powerful but also one of the most unrelievedly sombre soul-portraits ever painted. Of the rest, the melodramatic parts (spoken words with instrumental accompaniment) are the finest.

* See R. Pohl's interesting *Erinnerungen an Robert Schumann*, in the *Deutsche Revue*, vol. ii, August and September, 1878. Berlin, Otto Janke.

CHAPTER XVIII

The C major Symphony—Opp. 56, 58, 60, 72, and further Dresden compositions—Schumann's health—Dresden reminiscences.

THE *C major Symphony*, Op. 61 (dedicated to King Oscar I of Norway and Sweden), known as the second symphony although actually the third in order of composition, the D minor Symphony in its first state having preceded it, was sketched in 1845 and finished in 1846. It was produced at Leipzig by Mendelssohn at a Gewandhaus concert on November 5, 1846; the first English performance was probably that at the Crystal Palace on December 9, 1865. Writing on April 2, 1849, to Otten, Music Director at Hamburg, about his performance of the Symphony there, Schumann says :

. . . I wrote the Symphony in December, 1845, when I was still ailing; it seems to me as if one could not but hear it in the music. It was only in the last movement that I began to feel myself again ; after completing the whole work I did actually feel better. But otherwise, as I said, it reminds me of a dark time. . . .

Further on he writes of " my melancholy bassoon in the *Adagio*," and of having written the passage for it with special fondness. In another letter he writes more specifically :

. . . I sketched it when I was still in a state of physical suffering ; nay, I may say it was, so to speak, the resistance of the spirit which exercised a visible influence here, and through which I sought to contend with my bodily state. The first movement is full of this struggle and is very capricious and refractory. . . .

In the four movements of the Symphony we recognize, as it were, four stages of a struggle ending in victory. In the first movement the composer seems to be wrestling actively

240

with evil powers ; the feverish *Scherzo* reveals indecision, more passivity ; the sweet *Adagio* is an outpouring of prayer, resignation, hope, and thankfulness ; and in the last move-ment he gathers up his whole strength and triumphantly begins the battle of life again. The youthful bloom and sprightliness of the earlier symphonies must not be sought in this work ; but in place of these qualities we find a noble independence and greater depth of thought—in short, while there is a loss in sensuous beauty, there is a gain in intellectual intensity.

Of the other compositions belonging to the Dresden period must be specially mentioned the contrapuntal works of 1845, the outcome of Schumann's indefatigable study of Bach about this time.

Op. 56. *Studies for Pedal-pianoforte.** *First Book : Six Pieces in canon form.* " *Also for pianoforte for three or four hands.*" These were dedicated to his old master Kuntzsch of Zwickau.

Op. 58. *Sketches for Pedal-pianoforte.* " These sketches may also be performed on the pianoforte by two players."

Op. 60. *Six Fugues on the name* " BACH." For organ or for Pedal-pianoforte.

Op. 72. *Four Fugues for pianoforte.* Dedicated to Carl Reinecke.

Of the *Six Fugues*, Op. 60, Schumann wrote to his pub-lisher Whistling in March, 1846 : " . . . This is a com-position at which I was working all last year, trying to make it in some measure worthy of the great name it bears—a work which, I believe, will perhaps longest outlive my others. . . ." Well, this masterpiece is much less in evidence to-day than it ought to be. To C. F. Becker he wrote on February 8, 1847 : " . . . Diligence and pains on my part

---

* A pianoforte provided with a pedalier or set of organ pedals, used by organists for home-practice. Clara Schumann notes (Litzmann, ii, 131) : " On April 24 [1845] we got on hire a pedal [pedalier] to attach below the pianoforte, and we had great pleasure from it. Our chief object was to practise organ playing. But Robert soon found a higher interest in this instrument and composed some sketches and studies for it which are sure to find high favour as something quite new."

R

have not been wanting; I have not worked and filed so at any of my other compositions. . . ." It was not till 1849 that Schumann heard this work on the organ—played to him for the first time at Leipzig by Radecke. Reimann justly says that this work is—

the best proof of how deeply Schumann had penetrated, in thought and feeling, into the spirit of the Old Master. Everywhere the fundamental contrapuntal principles of Sebastian Bach are recognizable. They rise up like mighty pillars; but the luxuriant tendrils, leaves, and blossoms of a romantic spirit twine about them, partly concealing the mighty edifice, partly enlivening it by splendour of colour and varied contrast and bringing it nearer to modern taste. The most obvious proofs of this are :—The second fugue with the characteristic Schumann rhythmic displacement (2/4 time in triple rhythm); the fifth, with its subject on quite modern lines; and the last, with its romantically treated counter-subject. (*Robert Schumanns Leben und Werke* by Heinrich Reimann. Leipzig, C. F. Peters, 1887.)

In 1847 fall the pianoforte trios Op. 63 in D minor and Op. 80 in F major; and the beginnings of *Genoveva*, Op. 81, opera in four acts after Tieck and Hebbel, completed in 1848. Also in 1848, the charming Op. 66, *Bilder aus Osten*, for pianoforte duet, dedicated to Frau Bendemann; some of the *Waldscenen*, Op. 82; Op. 68, the *Album für die Jugend*, forty (later forty-three) pianoforte pieces, with a title-page by Ludwig Richter—first part (" for young folk "), 1–18; second part (" for grown-up folk "), 19–43; the second edition (1851) containing the appendix: *Musical Rules for Home and Life*; and Rückert's *Adventlied*, Op. 71, for solo, chorus, and orchestra; etc. Op. 68, the *Christmas Album*, was a special favourite of Schumann's; the composing of it gave him " unspeakable joy." In sending it to Reinecke, he writes on October 6, 1848:

. . . The first pieces in the Album were written for the birthday of our eldest child, and the others were added gradually. I felt as if I were beginning composition all over again. And you will find traces, too, of the old humour. They are quite different from the *Kinder-scenen*, which are reminiscences of an old person for old folk, whereas the *Christmas Album* contains rather foreshadowings, anticipations, for young folk. . . .

To 1849 belong the rest of the *Waldscenen*, and a quantity
of works, vocal and instrumental, of great variety, including
the *Spanisches Liederspiel*, Op. 74; *Spanische Liebes-Lieder*,
Op. 138; *Neujahrslied* (Rückert) for chorus and orchestra,
Op. 144, 1849 and 1850; Introduction and Allegro for
pianoforte and orchestra, Op. 92, etc.

Let us see how far was fulfilled the Schumanns' hope of
benefit to Robert's health from the change from Leipzig to
Dresden. If we compare his health at the beginning and at
the end of the six-years' Dresden period, a great improvement
seems to have taken place. But in the long run this proved
illusory, although they themselves—Clara at all events—
thought otherwise. It was a time of ups and downs, of
freedom from, and recurrences and developments of, the
various symptoms of the disease, which was never really
arrested, but in the course of which there were longer or
shorter periods when Schumann was actively creative to an
amazing extent, as in the years 1848 and 1849. From
other than musical activity he had almost entirely withdrawn,
becoming more and more silently absorbed in himself and
inaccessible. Robert, as we saw, came to Dresden towards
the end of 1844 in a state of nervous collapse. The report
of the homœopathic physician, Dr. Helbig, who attended
him, is quoted at length by Wasielewski, and shows us
Schumann trembling and collapsing at the slightest mental
effort, possessed by terrors of various kinds, sleepless, suffering
from auricular delusions—unwilling to use what remedies were
ordered by the physician, and unable to carry out the advice
to abstain from the hearing of and working at music and to
occupy himself with some distracting interest. (Wasielewski
does not mention the date of Dr. Helbig's report; and
Litzmann thinks that some of the symptoms stated there as
having been contemporary were probably successive—fresh
symptoms arising in course of time while others disappeared.)
A very quiet life, walking exercise, and occasional sea and
mineral baths, seemed to conduce to his general well-being,
but the real evil could not in those days be ameliorated.
Schumann was not averse from describing his condition, and

we hear a good deal about it in his letters. Just before leaving Leipzig, near the end of 1844, he wrote to Dr. Krüger :

. . . Perhaps you do not know how very ill I was with a general nervous affection that came upon me as far back as a quarter of a year ago, so that the doctor forbade me all exertion, even mental. Now I am rather better; life has once more a gleam of light—hope and confidence are gradually returning. I believe I had had too much music, latterly much occupied with my music to Goethe's *Faust ;* at last mind and body refused to work. . . . I have not been able to bear the hearing of music for some time past; it cut into my nerves like knives. . . .

Five weeks later from Dresden :

I still suffer a great deal, and my courage often fails me entirely. I am not allowed to work, only to rest and take walks, and often I have not strength enough for it. Sweet spring, perhaps thou wilt restore me ! . . .

A few months later he tells Verhulst (May 28, 1845) :

The time during which you heard nothing from me was a bad one for me. I was often very ill. Dark demons dominated me. Now I am rather better and getting to work again, which for months I have been unable to do.

On July 17, 1845, to Mendelssohn :

. . . I have a great deal to tell you—what a bad winter I have had; how a complete nervous collapse, with an onslaught of terrifying thoughts in its train brought me to the verge of despair, but that the prospect is pleasanter now, and that music, too, is beginning again to sound within me, and I hope soon to be quite restored. . . .

In September of the same year :

. . . I am already rather better; Hofrath Carus has advised me to take early morning walks, which suit me very well but do not help everywhere—a hundred places itch and twitch every day. A mysterious trouble—when the doctor tries to lay hold of it it seems to fly away. But better times will come again, and to look at wife and children is joy enough. . . .

A month later, after bewailing his lack of enterprise :

. . . Every disturbance of my simple routine still upsets me, and brings on a morbid, irritable state. . . .

Again, still to Mendelssohn, on November 12, 1845 :

. . . Lately I tried to conduct, but had to desist; it was too great
an exertion.   But on the whole I am much better than when you
were here, and I feel more strength for work. . . .

In September, 1846, we find him complaining of being
often so tired that he can hardly even write a whole letter at
a time.   About the middle of 1847 he writes of often feeling
very exhausted.   Coming to 1848 we meet with more favourable reports.   In November, to Verhulst:

. . . We are all pretty well; sometimes melancholy bats flutter
round me, but music drives them away again. . . . I have been very
industrious this year—indeed, it is perhaps the most fruitful of my
whole life. . . .

The same expression—" my most fruitful year "—is used
in a letter to Hiller some months later (April, 1849): "as if
outside storms drove one more in upon oneself, I found that
work alone enabled me to resist all that was breaking in so
terribly from without [*i.e.* the general revolutionary atmo-
sphere]."   The Dresden rising occurred a few weeks later,
the Schumanns sheltering at Kreischa, a little village within
earshot of the tumult, where Robert worked away quietly at
composition—without a pianoforte, for there was not one in
the village.   Op. 79, *Lieder für die Jugend,* was completed
there, and other works finished and sketched.   In June, 1849,
he writes to Brendel of having worked a very great deal.
" . . . Never before have I felt so impelled to it, felt it so
easy."   He writes, too, of satisfaction with the recognition
his music has had from appreciative critics, also from publishers, from whom there is a pretty good demand for his
music, and who pay very highly.   " . . . Certain it is that
I have spared no pains, and for twenty years, regardless of
praise and blame, have striven for one object—to be called
a true servant of art."   Schumann summarizes his point of
view at this period in a letter to Dr. Krüger, written on
November 29, 1849:

. . . It has been the most stimulating possible time for me.   Never
have I been artistically more active, or happier.   I have completed a
great deal; still more remains for future plans.   And sympathy from

far and near assures me that I am not working in vain.   So we spin and
spin away, and at last spin ourselves in.   The house is very lively.
Five children jumping about, beginning already to listen to Mozart
and Beethoven.   The wife, as of old, always striving onwards. . . .

No word of health anxieties here, yet four days later he
complains to Hiller of headaches that hinder him from all
thinking and working.

For the six years in Dresden there was much to show—
the temporary improvement in Robert's health ; domestic
joys and sorrows in plenty ; great artistic accomplishment, if
also trials and disappointments.   In Dresden four children
were born ; but one, a boy, Emil, lived only some fourteen
months ; the death of Mendelssohn, November 4, 1847, was
a grievous blow ; and Schumann suffered another blow in the
death of his brother Carl (April 9, 1849).   The home-life—
in the autumn of 1846 the Schumanns had removed to
another house, 20, Reitbahnstrasse—was of the simplest, and
very quiet, Robert more and more withdrawing into himself,
Clara shielding and cherishing him with might and main.
Frau Bendemann related how, meeting Clara one day on her
marketing rounds, she inquired what was in her basket.
" Something tempting for my husband—mixed pickles," said
Clara.   Friends who visited the Schumanns all told the same
story of Robert's rarely-broken silence, Clara always bearing
the burden of conversation.

A faithful friend of the Schumanns, who visited them in
Dresden, has to be further spoken of—Gade, for whom they
had all along a great liking ; and when I came to make his
acquaintance I was impressed by his inexhaustible good-
nature.   When Schumann wrote or spoke of him it was
always something pleasant : " Gade is a splendid fellow and
musician.   He is above all a practical musician."   Schumann
found a " surprising likeness " between the heads of Mozart
and Gade—a surprising comparison truly !   Yet Gade's
portrait, prefixed to the forty-seventh volume (1845) of the
Allgemeine Musikalische Zeitung, drawn by G. Weinhold of
Dresden and printed by Braunsdorf of the same town,
confirms Schumann's statement inasmuch as the abundant

hair, high forehead, well-formed nose, bright eyes, full lips, smiling mouth, the general expression of serenity, frankness, and benevolence suffused over the whole countenance, remind one in many respects of Mozart. In August, 1846, Gade visited the Schumanns at Dresden, and Schumann writes: " . . . a fine, strong nature. I have rarely found anyone who harmonized so well with my views as Gade . . . whom one must love, quite apart from his talent."

A passing visitor to Dresden should also be mentioned— Félicien David (1810–76), whose " Ode-symphonie," *Le Désert*, had such remarkable success in France. But when the famous man came to Dresden to conduct his work the Schumanns were not favourably impressed by it, nor by the composer himself, who, with the Hillers, went after the concert to the Schumanns' to spend the evening. The rather amusing and characteristic *contretemps* that followed is related by Litzmann (vol. ii, p. 137). He tells that Clara asked David for his autograph for her album. David, however, had evidently no idea what she meant, nor what her artistic standing was, for soon after he wrote her a letter which was a testimonial pure and simple; expressed, moreover, in moderate, if elegant terms. Clara, unable to see the humorous side of it, was indignant, and in her best French answered as follows: " Madame Schumann n'ayant pas demandée une attestation pour son album remercie Monsieur David pour sa bonne volonté et prie du reste d'accepter l'assurance de sa parfaite estime."

The quiet home-life was varied by occasional absences— journeys for health and holiday purposes, and for the giving of concerts, especially in Vienna, Prague, and Berlin, during the winter of 1846 and spring of 1847, and in Zwickau, July, 1847, where a festival had been arranged at which Schumann conducted his C major Symphony and Clara played the Pianoforte Concerto, and great enthusiasm prevailed. These episodes were beneficial to Schumann as distractions; and the same holds good of two later activities in Dresden— the conductorship of the male choir, the *Liedertafel*, and that of the choral union founded by Schumann himself. In the conductorship of the *Liedertafel*—an inheritance from Hiller when he left Dresden for Düsseldorf in 1847—Schumann found a certain interest and stimulus, but after a year gave it up, for want of time, as he wrote when intimating his resignation (I possess a copy of the courteous letter); also, as he wrote to Hiller, because he found " too little musical endeavour, and found myself out of place there, nice people though they were." On the other hand, his own choral union, " . . . (sixty to seventy members) where I can have whatever music I like, gives me a great deal of pleasure. . . ."

Among Schumann's trials was the annoyance from the frequent postponement of the promised production at Leipzig of his *Genoveva*—the opera, finished in 1848, on which he had spent so many years of thought and work, and in which he confidently hoped to make a great contribution to the musico-dramatic repertory of his country. The production at last took place on June 25, 1850, a constellation of friendly artists having come to Leipzig for the occasion—Liszt, Hiller, Gade, Joachim, Spohr, etc. The opera, however, had no more than a *succès d'estime*, although both the Schumanns carried away an impression of great artistic success. But Spohr's opinion, expressed to Clara, that the opera contained " splendid dramatic life," is probably a solitary one; Schumann's genius lay in fields other than the dramatic. There were other trials—for instance, the discreditable ignoring of Schumann by official musical Dresden. Then the hope of a post at Leipzig, raised by the rumour of Rietz's transference to Berlin, came to nothing, as Rietz remained where he was. And a hope among Schumann's friends of an appointment for him in Dresden also fell through. Schumann had often felt and expressed a desire for some regular work apart from his own composing, and when the opportunity offered to leave Dresden for a good post elsewhere, he was glad to consider it.

At Dresden I was fortunate in making the acquaintance of two ladies, pupils of Frau Schumann—Fräulein Emilie Steffen (afterwards Frau Heydenreich) and Fräulein Marie von Lindeman, both trusty friends of the Schumanns (Frl. Steffen, for instance, took charge of the children and household when Robert and Clara went on a long-planned concert trip to Hamburg and elsewhere in March, 1850), who furnished me with many of their recollections. Of these, however, space permits of a few pictures only, some of which give us charming private views of the Schumanns' home-life.

The daily routine, said Frl. Steffen, was regular. If Schumann had been working hard in the morning and felt in need of a rest, a walk with his wife was his favourite recreation. In the afternoon he again worked hard till six o'clock, when he repaired to Dauch's restaurant to read the newspapers over a glass of beer. Punctually at eight he was home for supper. From six to eight Frau Schumann practised, Frl. Steffen often sitting by her listening and learning, and she was frequently invited to stay for supper. " When Schumann came in I saw at once whether my presence was welcome or not. If he looked at me kindly out of his deep soulful eyes and smiled, I knew that I need not go away; but if he was quiet, serious, absorbed, then I knew as surely that he was preoccupied with some work, and would rather be alone and undisturbed, so, making a pretext, I slipped quietly away." One year, when the 13th of September was approaching, Schumann requisitioned Frl. Steffen's help in preparing surprises for his wife's birthday. He begged her to teach his *Geburtstagsmarsch*, composed for the occasion, to the two elder children, Marie and Lieschen, aged eight and six (but on the day it was played by the father and the elder child); and a few days later Schumann again called her. " When I entered his room a messenger was laying hat boxes on the pianoforte, and Schumann beckoned to me. The hats were inspected and admired one after the other, and finally the loveliest and costliest one was chosen—nothing was too fine or too dear for his Clara." Frl. Steffen saw much of Schumann's innate kindness of heart, and relates, for instance, with regard to herself, how he, having heard from Clara of her coming birthday, wished to give her a treat, and she was invited to a select little party of friends, including the special friend, Becker of Freiberg—Schumann in so cheerful a mood that he actually made a speech proposing her health. When next year's birthday came round she was taken for a drive, and at table out of doors Schumann was again so cheerful that her own merriment, hitherto always suppressed by her great reverence, at last bubbled over, which pleased him heartily.   To illustrate another trait Frl. Steffen relates that one day Schumann asked her if she were studying Shakespeare and Jean Paul diligently, and whether she knew *Coriolanus* and *Siebenkäs*.   On receiving a negative answer, he looked at her with such surprise and at the same time so kindly that she at once began to read, and was grateful to him ever after. At the large parties often given in honour of the Schumanns, Schumann was mostly very silent, but his eyes lit up and he looked pleased if there was good music.   He assembled at his own house, chiefly in 1849, a small circle of distinguished artists, generally on Thursdays—*Concertmeister* Schubert, an excellent violinist, and his brother, an equally good 'cellist ; Madame Schröder-Devrient ; the opera singers Frl. Schwarz- bach and Frl. Jacobi (later Frau Dawison) ; and the opera singers Weixelsdorfer and Anton Mitterwurzer.   These de- lightful meetings were private, but Frl. Steffen was privileged to be present.   Anything new of importance was brought to a hearing, and while sometimes mediocre and insignificant music had to be tried over, yet never a word of condemnation came from Schumann.   His joy over every young outstanding talent was genuine and deep ; and far removed from any artistic jealousy, he tried to be helpful to talented musicians. Madame Schröder-Devrient was always eager when there was a prospect of something for her by Schumann, and when he brought his *Spanisches Liederspiel* shortly before publica- tion, she sang the songs with immense enthusiasm, making an overwhelming impression.   When Schumann had com- pleted a work, Frau Schumann would sometimes come with the kind words : " My husband has finished a composition, and is bringing home a bottle of wine and I will have the appropriate pancakes—come this evening and spend a cosy hour with us, and drink a glass to the new *opus* and my goodman ; he would like to see you cheerful again, and thinks a glass of wine the right prescription."

The story of the choral union Frl. Steffen leaves to her friend Frl. von Lindeman, whose recollections refer chiefly to the choral society founded by Schumann towards the end of his Dresden time. In response to a written invitation from Schumann, a number of musical ladies and gentlemen met on January 6 [should be January 5], 1848, in the Garden Hall of the Harmony Society, to form a new singing society. They were received by Robert and Clara Schumann, the personal impression produced by the great artist pair giving this first meeting a certain consecration. After a short speech, in which Schumann expressed his view that the foundation of choral singing must be the cultivation of a good tone, a solfeggio specially written by himself was sung ; he then intimated that the choir would make a special study of new music without neglecting the older classics. The name of the choir was then discussed, the simple one " Choral Union " being adopted : years after the master's death it became " The Robert Schumann Singing Academy." The choir met every Wednesday evening, and gave a first concert on April 30, 1848, when Gade's *Comala* and some part-songs of Schumann's were sung, Clara playing solos. Frl. von Lindeman, who attended the choir practices most regularly, said that her own feeling and that of the choir in general was that Schumann's influence as conductor was highly inspiring. True, he had neither the commanding voice nor the commanding eye that enforces immediate obedience. His voice was soft, a pleasant tenor ; his movements were quiet ; but his whole being showed the nobility of a great artist and bore the stamp of genius, and unconsciously he thereby raised the whole company to a high level of intelligence. Everybody felt that this was a question of serious artistic endeavour, and that each must do his best for the good of the whole. And technical drilling was not neglected —Schumann often had passages repeated five or six times for the sake of an exact entry, a dynamic effect, or a rhythmic precision. Frau Schumann accompanied at the pianoforte, and her example and influence contributed in a large measure to the choir's efficiency. The society had also social meetings, often excursions ; one, for instance, to Meissen, by steamboat, on a beautiful summer morning, when Schumann was in the happiest humorous mood. The choir sang in the open air; also, by permission, in the cathedral; a hearty midday meal was consumed in the park to the singing of quartets, and even a thunder shower did not damp the spirits of the party. Again, the ladies of the choir celebrated a birthday of Frau Schumann's by the presentation of a carpet sewn by one of them, while one of the gentlemen composed a cantata, the words by his wife, a well-known poetess, and a prologue was spoken by an actress, the festive evening ending with a dance, in which the Schumann pair took part. Among other works the choir studied under Schumann works of Bach, Handel, Palestrina; Mendelssohn's *Athalie* and *Lobgesang*; Hiller's *Geist über dem Wasser*; part-songs of Schumann's; his *Faust, Requiem for Mignon, Paradise and the Peri*. Christmas evening, 1849, Frl. von Lindeman spent with the Schumanns, when Robert and Clara played duets, some of the newly-published Op. 85, *Twelve Pianoforte Pieces for Four Hands for Children, Little and Big*. Robert played the *Bear's Dance* with exquisite humour, smiling roguishly while imitating with his hands the clumsy movements of the bear. After the Schumanns settled at Düsseldorf (1850) they never revisited Dresden; but Frl. von Lindeman saw and heard them later at Leipzig, where, she says, they were both overwhelmed with applause, and people were to be heard singing on the way home the melodies they had just heard at the concert.

CHAPTER XIX

From Dresden to Düsseldorf (1850)—Enthusiastic reception and auspicious beginnings—House-hunting trials—Music (public and private) in Düsseldorf—Hiller, and Offenbach—Artist friends.

In the autumn of 1849 Hiller, about to leave Düsseldorf for Cologne to succeed Dorn, wrote privately to Schumann asking whether he were inclined to become his successor at Düsseldorf. There were many matters to be weighed, and Schumann's letters in reply are full of inquiries concerning conditions, artistic and practical, including the likelihood of scope for his wife as well; and there is one inquiry of a special nature in a letter of December 3, 1849. " . . . Lately I was looking out information about Düsseldorf in an old geography book, and there I found mentioned as noteworthy: ' three convents and a lunatic asylum.' To the first I have no objection if it must be so; but it was disagreeable to me to read the last. . . ." And he proceeds to explain that when living at Maxen, near Dresden, some years previously, the chief view from his window included a lunatic asylum, and that this completely spoiled his stay there. " . . . And I thought it might turn out so at Düsseldorf. But the whole notice may be inaccurate and the institution perhaps only a hospital such as every town possesses. I am obliged to avoid carefully all melancholy impressions of the kind. And if we musicians live so often, as you know we do, on sunny heights, the sadness of reality cuts all the deeper when it lies naked before our eyes. At least, so it is with me and my vivid imagination. . . ." After much considering and waiting, and entertaining of other hopes that came to nothing, Schumann finally accepted the offer—the post to be entered upon in autumn of 1850, the salary to date from April 1. In February and March the Schumanns made a concert tour to Leipzig, Bremen, Hamburg, and Altona (with Jenny Lind), returning by Berlin; May and June found them back in Leipzig for the postponed production of *Genoveva*; then came preparations for the removal to Düsseldorf. These were months of heart-stirring experiences, both happy and vexatious, which must be read in the Diary.

Dresden musical officialdom had taken no notice of the presence and activities in its midst of the two great musicians, and it took no notice of their departure. Schumann's choral society arranged a farewell ceremony, concerning which Bendemann told me that during the performance of one of his own part-songs Schumann sat coldly apart. At the end of the second verse he began to thaw, and at the end of the song he said: " Once again, ladies and gentlemen; you made several mistakes, it will go better the second time! " Bendemann was deputed to invite him to a farewell party. He could not make up his mind, and Bendemann said that he would call again next day for his answer. Whereupon Schumann said: " Can you promise me that we shall enjoy ourselves ? " " Well," answered Bendemann, " it is sad for all of us that you are leaving us, but still I can promise you that we shall enjoy ourselves." When the moment came for the Schumanns to shake the dust of Dresden from off their feet they can have had but little to regret leaving, except personal friends—in particular the Bendemanns, who themselves were destined to leave Dresden for Düsseldorf, although not till nine years later, 1859, when Bendemann succeeded Schadow as Director of the Academy. Starting from Dresden on the morning of Sunday, September 1, the Schumanns reached Düsseldorf next evening. Robert was now forty years old, Clara nine years younger; both in their best years (although as it turned out Robert's best creative period was already behind him), with, seemingly, a long-desired opportunity at last in store, and correspondingly great expectations.

The town of Düsseldorf itself, at that time less than a quarter of its present size, was originally laid out as a garden city; but even before Schumann's time had begun to lose that exclusive character, gradually becoming what it has now been for many years, a well-to-do city of manufacturers with all their attendant luxuries. It lies on the right bank of the Rhine with a busy harbour; in its beautiful and varied Park (Hofgarten), where Schumann was so often to be seen walking, especially between his house and the Ratinger Tor, are the favourite Ananasberg and the still smaller Napoleonsberg, the pond and bridge with charming view, including that of the fine old Jägerhof; dispersed through the town many other pleasant leafy and watered public grounds, mirroring ponds, and stately, shady avenues; while a little westwards of the town rises the beautiful wooded eminence, the Grafenberg, with its shady walks and drives and restaurants, a favourite resort of artists as well as others. Bearing in mind Schumann's morbid aversion from the sight of a lunatic asylum, one notes with satisfaction that at that time the now existing one was not yet built.

For the account of the early days in Düsseldorf we must draw largely upon the Diary. These days are also described in letters of Clara's to Frl. Steffen and Frl. von Lindeman, both of whom kindly copied some extracts for me. As far as they go, they coincide pretty closely with Clara's Diary notes, and contain many expressions of her appreciation of the great kindness shown to her and her husband, and of his satisfaction with his choir and orchestra and their goodwill towards him. An enthusiastic reception had been prepared for the two great artists, for the Düsseldorfers realised that they had double honours to pay—to their new Music Director, the great composer, and to his wife, the great pianist. They were met by Hiller and the concert directors, and escorted by Hiller to the best hotel, the Breidenbacher Hof in Alleestrasse, frequented by the aristocracy, high officials, and military, and guarded, accordingly, by a sentinel (Mendelssohn and his family, too, had stayed there), to find rooms ready and decked out with flowers, two laurel bushes at the entrance. Later in the evening Robert was serenaded by the *Liedertafel.* Next forenoon, after a round of ceremonial visits shepherded by Hiller, began a tedious search for quarters—the opening of the first chapter of disillusionments. The following day again house-hunting, and in the afternoon a coffee party on the Ananasberg (a restaurant on a pretty knoll) in the beautiful

Hofgarten, when acquaintance, that grew into friendship, was made with Director von Schadow of the Academy (their friend, Frau Bendemann, was his sister). The same evening, while supping at the hotel, they heard strains of the *Don Giovanni* overture in the next room—a surprise serenade, this time by the town orchestra. "It was a most pleasing surprise to Robert. They played everything very well, and I think Robert will be able to do something with the orchestra." Next day further fruitless house-hunting; and the concert committee came in state to invite the Schumanns to a concert, supper, and ball in their honour two days later. On Friday, September 6, the furniture arrived, and an abode had to be found somehow or other to house the furniture in. Saturday was devoted to unpacking and the three-act festivity in the evening.

The programme lies before me :

CONCERT.

1. Overture to *Genoveva*
2. Three Songs   by
3. *Paradise and the Peri*, Part II ⎱ Rob. Schuhmann [*sic*].

SUPPER.

FIRST COURSE.
Vocal Piece.
FIRST TOAST.

SECOND COURSE.
Vocal Piece.
SECOND TOAST.
Chorus : Festival Song.

THIRD COURSE.
Vocal Piece.
THIRD TOAST.

BALL.

[The words of the Festival Song were a specially-written welcome, in six stanzas, to the noble "Artist-pair," "the richly-gifted Master," and "the Mistress of tones whose sweet sounds transport us to heaven," etc.]

On entering the hall Robert was greeted with a triple flourish of trumpets (*Tusch*), and the *Genoveva* overture began (conducted by " Tausch, pianoforte teacher and player, who came here some time ago recommended by Mendelssohn "), followed by *Du meine Seele, Die Lotosblume*, and *Wanderlied*, and, finally, the second part of the *Peri*. . . . " Herr Tausch conducted quite well ; if only the man were more agreeable personally : there is something in his face to which I cannot accustom myself at all. . . ." It has to be noted that Clara was prejudiced against Tausch from the first. " Then a very lively supper, but none too abundant, so that each fresh course was hailed with a ' hurrah,' which struck us as very comical " (an initiation into Rhineland geniality for the Schumanns !). The speeches, on the other hand, were generous ; that of the assistant Burgomaster, Herr Wortmann, who proposed Schumann's health, began with the Creation, and when this and all the other toasts were ended and the ball began, the Schumanns were tired out and withdrew. Next day, Sunday, fatigue obliged them to forgo an outing arranged by Hiller to see the surroundings of Düsseldorf. Monday was spent in arranging the house ; on Tuesday they moved in, and a time of unspeakable confusion and discomfort had to be gone through, the thought of the cost of removal, far greater than they had expected, adding to the general burden. Poor Clara notes : " Never have I been so worried by material cares as just now, and the fact, too, that I am earning nothing. . . ." The greatest anxiety was that the constant street noises of all kinds made Robert more and more nervous and irritable—there was no quiet place for his work. The Schumanns had thought of Düsseldorf as a garden city, where they could easily find a house with a garden of their own, with quiet and privacy for Robert ; but they found things very different from these expectations, and had to change their quarters several times. Sunday, September 29, was a day with important consequences—they went for recreation to Cologne, which enchanted them with the glorious view from the Belvedere of the Rhine and Seven Hills, but, above all, they were impressed by the great

s

Cathedral, and Robert brought home with him the first inspiration for the E flat major, the "Rhenish" Symphony, completed before the year was out.

To domestic and social duties official work was shortly added. Schumann's duties as Music Director comprised the conducting of the subscription concerts (orchestra and choir), the weekly choir practices, and certain regularly recurring performances in connection with the Roman Catholic church services. On Tuesday, September 17, Robert had his first choral practice, and Clara recorded that he was greatly pleased with the large choir (over one hundred and twenty)—the sopranos in particular sounding beautifully fresh. Robert himself wrote to Whistling, his publisher, on October 10, to the same effect. On October 15 we hear of the arrival from Leipzig of Wasielewski, whose engagement as leader of the orchestra Schumann had brought about. On Sunday evening, October 20,

we, with Wasielewski and Tausch, were at the Eulers', where we had music. Tausch is the best pianoforte teacher here . . . he is certainly not unskilled as a musician, but often very rough as a player, and not very attractive as a man. . . .

On Tuesday, October 22, Robert had the first orchestral rehearsal. Considering the small town, he found the orchestra quite excellent, and was well satisfied. Two days later the first subscription concert took place, of which Clara reported that the hall was fuller than ever before at the concerts, and Robert was received with a triple fanfare on appearing. Beethoven's overture (Op. 124) went beautifully, and it was a special delight "to see Robert conduct with fine repose and at the same time such great energy." Clara played in Mendelssohn's G minor Concerto, and had a great reception ; the singing of Frl. Hartmann (an excellent amateur) was quite inspired, "and there was a general atmosphere of enthusiasm in orchestra and choir such as has not been felt since Mendelssohn's departure. . . ." This comparison of Clara's is misleading, ignoring, as it does, Mendelssohn's successors, Rietz and Hiller, both of whom commanded the devotion and enthusiasm of choir and orchestra in a high degree. Rietz was a potent and a model conductor, and played a highly important part in Düsseldorf musical life, both in concert-room and theatre; and Hiller was always a most popular conductor in the Rhineland, and a very special favourite with the Düsseldorfers. The programme included Schumann's *Adventlied* and his favourite *Comala* by Gade. If, perhaps, everything was not quite as Clara saw and heard it, it was at least certain that everyone, performers and hearers alike, did their best to make the great occasion a success, and the Schumanns were justified in feeling satisfied. And so for once the proverb was wrong, for in this case the beginnings were easy.

As I pointed out many years ago, the Düsseldorf music directors had no very great resources at their disposal; what they accomplished in the way of choral, and particularly orchestral music was due chiefly to their energy and talent as conductors; and Hiller, like his predecessors, bequeathed a well-drilled choir and orchestra to his successor. I have by me a small thin quarto booklet :—*Programme der Concerte des Allgemeinen Musikvereins zu Düsseldorf in den Jahren* 1847, 1848, *u.* 1849 *unter der Direction des Herrn Musik-Directors Ferdinand Hiller.* The first concert, in December, 1847, was in memory of Mendelssohn, a performance of *Elijah*, and Mendelssohn's music plays a considerable part in the following programmes along with Haydn, Mozart, Beethoven, Gluck, Hummel, Spohr, Weber, Schumann (still no Schubert except for the song *Lob der Thränen*), Meyerbeer, Méhul, Cherubini, Gade, Hiller himself, etc., and one composer less likely to be met with in concert programmes of to-day—Offenbach. He appears on June 12, 1848, both as composer and performer ('cellist) with his *Hommage à Rossini, Concertfantasie für Violoncell mit Orchester*; and *Prière et Boléro*. It is a pleasure to make here through Hiller a more prominent allusion to this undoubtedly very notable, if hardly classical artist. Jacques Offenbach (1819–80), son of the Cantor of the Jewish synagogue at Cologne, was one of the most prolific composers of light opera, to whose talent justice has not been done by biographers and lexicographers, who mostly dwell on his musical frivolity and underrate his gifts. Offenbach began as a violoncellist; became conductor of the Paris Théâtre-Français orchestra; published bright and popular tunes, especially for subjects from La Fontaine's fables; ran for a time a small theatre of his own—Théâtre des Bouffes-parisiens, producing chiefly his own compositions, easy and popular; and later was to be heard at more important theatres, the Opéra Comique, etc. He travelled in America, and paid several visits to England, where for a time his music was extraordinarily popular. He wrote an enormous amount of catchy ephemeral music. Offenbach did not live to see the production of his favourite comic opera, *Les Contes de Hoffmann*, which, produced at the Paris Opéra Comique in 1881, became very popular in France, and also in Germany; and within the last few years has been frequently heard on the British stage.

When Mendelssohn came to Düsseldorf some seventeen years earlier he found it " so charmingly diminutive "; and in that respect, as well as in social and artistic respects, conditions had not changed so very greatly—many of the artist personalities of Mendelssohn's time (whom we met in Chapter XII) were still to the fore when the Schumanns came to Düsseldorf.

The Schumanns' relationship to Düsseldorf life was a very different one, for while some of their chief new friends were artists, it cannot be said that pictorial art played an influential part in Schumann's life as it did in Mendelssohn's. Of the artists already named, Hildebrandt, Köhler, Schadow, and Karl Sohn were amongst their most congenial friends, and especially at Hildebrandt's house we hear of music being cultivated.

Clara describes Hildebrandt as a great music enthusiast, but within a year she is complaining that at the meeting of the singing club [started by Robert in the autumn of 1851] at the Hildebrandts' " Robert was very angry because there was so much talking. Good Hildebrandt first and foremost. It is characteristic here—they are always ready enough for talking but not for singing." In a two-hours conversation with Hildebrandt I found him a very charming and interesting man but not specially musical; and although he, Köhler, Sohn, Lessing, and others frequented musical gatherings, none of the painters had outstanding musical qualities. The most important musical amateur, and from the beginning a special friend of the Schumanns, was the notary Euler (but *Notar* connotes more than does our word " notary "); there was also Dr. Herz, the advocate, less intimate; and several other advocates who need not be further specified here. The Schumanns had soon to find out that the taste for working at serious music was not to be expected from their friends, and that only at their own house could they have what they wished. Their pianoforte trio was completed by Wasielewski and Reimers, and after them by Ruppert Becker, son of the Schumanns' old Freiberg friend, and the excellent amateur 'cellist, R. Bockmühl—Tausch, before the breach, occasionally playing the pianoforte part. There was also Albert Dietrich, and his friend von Sahr.

CHAPTER XX

Düsseldorf (1850–54)—Schumann as a conductor—Different points of view—
Tausch : his position and personality.

ALTHOUGH the first concert had seemed such a success, and
the general public were delighted with their new Music
Director, others had no illusions as to Schumann's conducting powers. It must be plainly stated in unqualified
terms that Schumann was entirely unsuited to be a conductor. His mental ailment was gradually obliterating, as
it were, the very abilities and qualities, moral and physical,
that are indispensable for that activity—alertness, authori-
tativeness, concentration, energy, presence of mind, sympathy,
tact, even ability to speak audibly. He lived mentally aloof,
his thoughts busy within him, out of reach of, and out of
touch with, his fellow-men for most practical purposes.
How Hiller, who knew Schumann intimately, could have
thought of him as a possible, not to say suitable, successor is
incomprehensible. Hiller's temperament was easygoing and
amiable, he liked to please everybody ; perhaps he thought
little more about it than that his friend Schumann ought to
have a more worthy *milieu* than he had at Dresden, and that
if he had a regular post and scope he would be stimulated
to rouse himself—but if he thought so he ought to have
known better. To Hiller solely the appointment was due—
the Düsseldorf committee had such confidence in him that
they asked him to find a successor, and empowered him to
negotiate with Schumann, and Schumann's consent sealed
the appointment without further discussion.

Wasielewski, who, as leader of the orchestra and one who
was much in Schumann's society in private, knew only too
well how things were, summarizes matters as they were

during his time ; but although he had on competent authority the facts relating to the final *dénouement* (which took place after Wasielewski had left Düsseldorf), he avoids criticism of them. It is, nevertheless, not difficult to guess what his opinion would have been had he not wished to remain silent, which, at the time of writing, discretion required. Litzmann, on the other hand, writing in 1905 (vol. ii) lets the Diary give a very full account of the troubles as they appeared to the Schumanns ; but knowing the other side intimately, he does not hesitate to say that there were two sides to the question ; that the Schumanns were not able to see things objectively ; and that the other side had an immensely difficult part to play. He, however, hardly adduces the available evidence in enough detail to clear the Düsseldorfers completely of much unjust criticism that has been fastened on them and to show how impossible things were for them ; and it is only fair that this should be attempted, the more since it can be done without gravely blaming the chief participators in the complicated misunderstanding. It was an absolute *impasse*—a great creative genius and noble personality in the false position of having undertaken duties he was physically unfit for, *unaware* of it, and consequently justified in feeling aggrieved at what seemed to him personal intrigue and want of respect ; a choir and orchestra unable to do themselves justice and fulfil their duties for want of an efficient conductor ; a concert committee bound to keep up tradition and provide good concerts for the public, unable to fulfil their duty owing to their impossible conductor ; and a complaining public, unable to see why the concerts should go to rack and ruin to spare a man who, no matter how great he was in other respects, was unsuited for the post of conductor. As the Schumanns did not realize Robert's incapacity and its consequences, the painful step had to be taken by the committee. Whether it could have been more tactfully taken cannot now be said ; but considering the respective temperaments of Robert and Clara a way can hardly be imagined that would not have been taken amiss by them. There were, no doubt, on both sides over-zealous partisans, even deliberate mischief-makers, but these may be discounted : those who had to act in the matter were honourable, well-disposed men, and much of the intriguing so constantly suspected by Clara in particular was of her own imagining. Clara saw with Robert's eyes and heard with his ears ; she regarded him (rightly) as the great creative genius to whom (wrongly) everyone and everything had to be adjusted. For her own sake this was, doubtless, fortunate ; since even had she realized his disability, she would probably not have been able to convince him.

Wasielewski, then, after stating Schumann's disqualifications as a conductor, points out that, on the other hand, he had a highly eminent, artistic personality, whose serious, dignified bearing commanded reverence. And this fact and the other that he found both choir and orchestra in good condition, explain how it was that the earlier period of his Düsseldorf activity had good and pleasing results, the inadequacy of his conducting powers remaining at first unrevealed to the uninitiated. But as time went on and Schumann's condition grew worse and became widely recognized, a general discontent set in which came to a head in the autumn of 1853 (Wasielewski had by that time left Düsseldorf). The committee had to take some step, and after much anxious deliberation it was decided to suggest to Schumann that, for the sake of his health, he should leave conducting alone for a time, except that of his own works —Tausch, who had often before acted as his substitute, being willing to act in that capacity again. The Schumanns took this proposal amiss. Schumann absented himself from the next rehearsal, and the concert having been already advertised Tausch was asked to conduct it ; and from that time Schumann ceased to act as Music Director. After this bare outline of the chief facts I must now try to show briefly the attitude of the chief actors, giving first the Diary point of view with Litzmann's criticism of it, then the point of view of the other side.

Litzmann relates that as early as the end of the first season (spring, 1851) vexations and dissatisfactions had arisen—the

early harmony between the Director and the concert committee, also the relation between the Director and his orchestra
and choir, were already disturbed. He (Litzmann) states
that the first definite note of dissatisfaction to be heard in
public was an article in the Düsseldorf newspaper towards
the end of the first concert season, criticising the conducting
of the concerts. This the Schumanns regarded as an insult
and impertinence, especially as they believed that the writer
was a member of the concert direction, and Clara breaks out :
" The so-called enthusiasts, Euler and Müller among others,
calmly let this happen ; it is a disgrace that they should
quietly acquiesce in such treatment of Robert at the hands
of the Düsseldorfers, instead of shielding him in every way
as they should do in order to keep him." The public had
already become disillusioned, and the feeling had perhaps
been vented in an unsuitable way. In two concerts the
choir had not sung with enough sureness to satisfy Schumann
(in two of his own compositions) ; again, both the Schumanns felt aggrieved by the coldness of the public—in particular his new overture, *Die Braut von Messina*, was received
without any sign of approval. Still, the last concerts of the
season were in part very successful, and the Schumanns
themselves felt satisfied with the results of the first season.
But satisfaction was not the prevailing feeling. And Litzmann goes on to analyse the causes of the trouble, keeping
to generalities. A right relationship between Director and
choir had not grown up. The master's mild and self-absorbed
way was demoralizing for the choir—a good instrument under
a strong conductor. Discipline began to relax, and with the
consequent friction at the practices zeal flagged. The first
practice after the summer interval was poorly attended, and
Schumann seems to have contemplated giving up the choir.
On September 6, 1851, the Diary complains, among other
matters, that " the choir is going down altogether, no zeal,
no love for work . . ." and a few days later Clara again
complains of the want of attention at a practice of Bach's
B minor Mass. " . . . People here have respect neither
for art nor for the Director. And it is said to have been so

always " [Far from it]. Be this as it may, says Litzmann, the outlook was not promising. Although there was no outward rupture during the season 1851–52, the breach between the Schumanns and the Düsseldorfers widened ; and especially relations with the choir grew worse. After a practice of Bach's *St. Matthew Passion*, Clara complains bitterly (March 30, 1852) of the disrespectful behaviour of some of the choir, which made her blood boil, " indeed nothing would please me more than Robert's withdrawal from the choir, for it is a post unworthy of his position " [What of Mendelssohn, Rietz, and Hiller ?]. Litzmann remarks that in such a state of matters even happy events such as the enthusiastic reception of Schumann's B flat major Symphony on May 6, 1852, could bring only temporary improvement, while the slightest friction, intentional or not, revived the opposition and sharpened mere difference of opinion into harsh dissonances. The Schumanns imagined that the concert committee were wanting in the proper consideration due to Robert's importance as an artist, which hurt them all the more because it had been different at the beginning. On the other hand, the concert committee—from which, moreover, some of those very members who had been so eager for Schumann's appointment had withdrawn—found itself painfully situated on account of the public's complaint of the unsuitable conductor. And Litzmann says that to maintain tact in such a conflict, and to prevent a local annoyance, in itself comprehensible, being vented on a great genius whose idiosyncrasy must be respected even at the cost of some inconvenience, is an almost superhuman task, which could neither be asked nor expected of a heterogeneous concert committee. Further, that at that time no one suspected that a certain apathy and dreaminess which sometimes made the Director at his conducting desk forget that he had a duty to perform, also an occasional difficulty of speech, were symptoms of the disintegrating illness—not even when in summer, 1852, Schumann became so seriously ill that the preparations for and conducting of the first two concerts of the next season had to be deputed to Tausch.

After their absence both the Schumanns met with a cold reception—intentionally cold, as Litzmann believes—at their respective first appearances at the winter concerts; and shortly after, three of the choir committee, with the utmost coolness, invited Schumann to give up the post he was unable to fill. Although this was undoubtedly a lapse of some specially tactless persons, which, by the intervention of others, was, as far as might be, made good, the perpetrators making the humblest apology, it was ominous that such a thing could have happened. Litzmann thinks that the temporary conducting of the choir by Tausch may have had to do with it, increasing the desire in certain circles to substitute Tausch for Schumann, the atmosphere in general being pervaded by the propaganda of this set. Then came the 1853 spring Music Festival, when, although Schumann enjoyed a great triumph as the composer of the D minor Symphony, it was noised abroad as well as locally by the press that the master was not up to the mark as a conductor, not to be compared, for instance, with Hiller. All this was gall and wormwood to the unreasoning Clara, who pours out her bitterness in the Diary, asking why good friends such as Dietrich and Dr. Hasenclever keep silence in face of the injustice done to their " honoured master." Upon which Litzmann remarks that we can understand her complaint but cannot recognize it as unprejudiced. Next come complaints about the orchestra.

Bad rehearsal of Joachim's *Hamlet* overture, which is very difficult and would not go at all, all kinds of intrigues coming into play. Forberg ('cellist) ran away, came back later, and nobody said a word about it to him. He should have been turned out again at once; in short, there is no discipline here and no possibility of co-operation between Director and orchestra.

" In these circumstances," says Litzmann, " responsible men cannot be blamed for trying, even at the risk of paining so great and noble a master, to find a new way out and to bring about a compromise to prevent worse and harsher happenings." Let us look, still through the Schumanns' eyes, at the step taken.

"On November 7 [writes Clara], two of the committee, Herr Herz and Herr Illing, came and told me their wish that in future Robert should conduct his own compositions only, that Tausch had promised to take over the rest. It was an infamous intrigue and an insult to Robert, forcing him to resign altogether, and I said so at once to the gentlemen without having spoken to Robert. Apart from the impertinence of taking such a step with a man like Robert, it was also a breach of contract which Robert will in no case tolerate. I cannot say how indignant I was and how bitter it was not to be able to spare Robert this mortification. Oh! they are despicable people here. Vulgarity reigns, and the well-disposed, such as Herr von Heister and Herr von Lezaak, keep back, disapproving but passive. What would I not give to be off at once with Robert, but that is not so easy when one has six children.—Nov. 9. Robert has communicated to the committee his decision not to conduct any more. Tausch is behaving like a rude, ungentlemanly (*ungebildet*) fellow . . . for in the present circumstances he ought not to conduct, but did, although Robert wrote to him that if he did, he (Robert) could not regard him as well disposed. It grows clearer and clearer that Tausch, seemingly quite passive, has manœuvred the chief intrigue. Hammers (Burgomaster) is behaving very kindly in the matter and would gladly intervene if it were possible.—November 10. Concert evening—we at home. Tausch conducting. Robert wrote him a second letter to-day which he is not likely to get framed! . . .

Before looking at the other side of the question we must make further acquaintance with the other chief person concerned—Tausch. We have seen that Clara Schumann had taken a dislike to him at first sight, and when troubles began was therefore too ready to attribute to him motives and deeds for which in justice he could not be held responsible. We saw also that Schumann, who had constantly asked Tausch to act as his substitute, took it amiss that Tausch should have consented to act for him when asked by the committee to do so.

Julius Tausch was born in 1827 at Dessau, where he was a pupil of Fr. Schneider. In 1844 he entered Leipzig conservatorium, where he studied under Mendelssohn and Hauptmann, and in 1846 settled in Düsseldorf on Mendelssohn's recommendation, teaching and playing the pianoforte there. When Rietz left Düsseldorf Tausch became conductor of the *Liedertafel*, on various occasions acted for Schumann at Schumann's request, and sometimes took part in his domestic music-makings; in 1853 he became Schumann's substitute, in 1855 his successor, and conducted at many of the Lower Rhine music festivals at Düsseldorf. In 1878 he conducted orchestral concerts in Glasgow. He retired from his Düsseldorf post in 1889 or 1890 and died at Bonn in 1895. Of his excellent and varied compositions should be mentioned: Op. 1, *Fantasiestücke* for pianoforte; Op. 4, music to *As You Like It*; Op. 9, Festival Overture; Op. 16, *Germanenzug* from *Trutznachtigall*, by August Silberstein, for soprano solo, chorus, and orchestra—" *Germanen durchschreiten des Urwaldes Nacht* " (there is a pianoforte score with both German and English text); *Miriams Siegesgesang*, for solo, chorus, and orchestra, first performed at the Düsseldorf Lower Rhine festival in 1887.

Pauer characterizes Tausch as "an eminent pianist and clever composer." I myself knew Tausch well—he was an out and out good musician. As a lad I played in the orchestra under his baton, and was afterwards his pupil in pianoforte playing and composition (I can still see in my mind's eye his beautiful writing and music writing, large and neat); sparing of words, as a teacher he showed best when exemplifying. Much later in life, when I visited Düsseldorf in 1889, I met him again and he told me much about the Schumann time. A taciturn man, without the gift of smooth speech, Tausch might easily have been guilty of awkwardness, but not of ill-nature or ill-breeding. His main defects were indeed defects of omission. A greater mistake could not be made than to describe him, so guileless a man, as an intriguer; and Clara's other characterization of him as " rude and ungentlemanly " must also be emphatically repudiated. But Clara never fails to speak of him in a derogatory way—he always fares badly at her hands. Tausch's complaisance in carrying out the Schumanns' wishes is indeed quite wonderful; for instance, he was always ready to perform any classical concertos desired by Robert or Clara—*e.g.* Weber, Beethoven, Mendelssohn, etc. He understood and venerated the master. Schumann was,

he said, an amiable character; but he could not brook contradiction, even in trifling matters of opinion; he even took
offence if, when he asked a question, the answer was not to
his taste. In such cases he usually rose and walked away
without saying a word. In the conducting of Handel he
was never quite at home: he took the *allegros* as fast as
modern ones—a performance of *Israel in Egypt* was finished
in two hours. He once said to Tausch that he really did
not know how to beat time there, and asked how he (Tausch)
would do it. Tausch said that he would beat four crotchets.
Whereupon Schumann said with the greatest decision and
excitement: "That should never be done." He conducted
badly from the first, and was often absent-minded. Once at
a mass he went on conducting after the movement was finished
and the priest had begun to intone. At a choir practice the
sopranos were singing several high A's and the effect was
such that it aroused laughter; the sopranos stopped singing
and the other parts gradually followed suit until Tausch was
left playing the pianoforte alone. Schumann noticed nothing
and went on beating time, and Tausch, thinking it was no
use going on by himself, stopped too. Schumann beckoned
to him to come, and Tausch expected a reproof for having
broken off. But no—Schumann showed him a passage in
the score and said: "Look, this bar is beautiful." After
practices Schumann was fond of withdrawing to refresh
himself in the Cürten Hall, and often invited Tausch to
share his half-bottle of champagne—but Schumann was not
immoderate in drinking. When his friend, the musician
von Sahr, was leaving Düsseldorf, Schumann brought him
an autograph souvenir to the restaurant. Schumann apparently thought that von Sahr showed insufficient appreciation
of the gift, for he returned it to his pocket and departed. At
an evening party Frau Schumann and others were playing
the Quintet: nothing pleased Schumann, the *tempi* he thought
all wrong (one of the symptoms of his condition), and he said
to Tausch: "You play it, a man understands that better."
At first Frau Schumann played the accompaniments for
the choir practices. Later Schumann asked Tausch to relieve

her, as the pianoforte drumming tired her too much and was more suitable for a man. Tausch several times played duets with Schumann, whose playing, he said, was slovenly. Tausch liked above all things to spend his time with his fellow-artists at the *Malkasten* (painters' club), and there he found, too, his creative inspiration, especially for his music to *As You Like It*, and for other works.

CHAPTER XXI

The official Report of the *Allgemeine Musikverein* by the secretary, the assistant Burgomaster Wilhelm Wortmann.

The assistant Burgomaster, Herr Wilhelm Wortmann, communicated to me the full report which he, as secretary of the *Verein*, supplied " concerning the relations between *Herr Musik-Director* Dr. Schumann and the *Allgemeine Musikverein*, intended in the first place for the Town Councillors, who wish for information on the subject." It is too long to reproduce in entirety—I draw from it what seems necessary to show clearly what were the difficulties that confronted the *Allgemeine Musikverein*, the *Gesangverein*, and the orchestra, and how they coped with them.

[The *Allgemeine Musikverein*, an independent society with legal statutes, was the body which arranged and was responsible for the concerts (also music festivals and church music), with the co-operation of the orchestra and chorus. It was represented by an administrative committee of citizens, of which Herr Wortmann (the assistant Burgomaster) was the secretary. Schumann's contract was with this society—the Town Council granting an annual supplement of five hundred thalers to his salary, with no conditions attached. The *Gesangverein* (Choral Union) was a separate society, with its own directors, appointing and paying its own conductor (one hundred thalers a year), but was associated with the first-named society. The chorus consisted mostly of amateurs. The orchestra was in the pay of the municipality, and its services were shared by the concerts, the theatre, and any special civic ceremonies.]

The paving of the way to graver misunderstandings was Schumann's procedure with the chorus. The report (after stating that Rietz had left the chorus in flourishing condition, and that Hiller had so won the general confidence that the choice of his successor was left in his hands) relates that at the choral practices previous conductors had accompanied at the pianoforte and their remarks were instructive, clear, intelligible, with the result that the learning of new works for public performance took much less time than was the case with other choirs. The conductors were in constant touch with the members of the chorus and understood how to incite them to perseverance. Dr. Schumann's way was very different. He beat time at a conducting desk, his wife accompanying at the pianoforte. He was extremely reserved with the members of the chorus; it was quite exceptional for him to speak to them. All communications to the chorus—requests for full and punctual attendances, intimations as to rehearsals, etc., were now made by a member of the administration, while Dr. Schumann sat by passively. He thus remained a stranger to the greater number of the chorus and failed to evoke the personal sympathy which readily overlooks this or that shortcoming. The chorus, consisting largely of amateurs of little training, soon missed the countless little helpful and stimulating indications of the previous conductors. In fugal works especially, the entries became uncertain and feeble, and if the leaders of the parts happened to be absent, difficult works could hardly be practised at all. The few remarks Dr. Schumann did make were so softly spoken as to be unintelligible to the majority. It often seemed to the best singers that their conductor could not have heard many of the mistakes, as he took no notice of them, while on the other hand he required frequent repetitions of passages without any indication of what was wrong and how it was to be put right. Thus the learning of new works took an unheard-of length of time and the former results were not attained. Many of the members began to find it irksome and stayed away, and there was often difficulty in raising the necessary number of singers for public performance. The choir, hitherto so flourishing and vigorous, felt its decline, and not a few appeals

T

for help were made to the administration. Dr. Schumann, obliged in the summer of 1852 to travel for his health's sake, left Tausch as his substitute, and the summer months were devoted to the study of Mendelssohn's *Elijah*, which was publicly and successfully performed under Tausch for the benefit of the funds of the choir. On Dr. Schumann's return he spontaneously arranged that Tausch should always take the preliminary practices when a new work was being studied, he himself conducting the later practices and the performances. And he stated in writing his reason for this—that for a creative artist after his day's work it was too great an irritation to direct the preliminary studies of an amateur choir; moreover, Tausch was known to the choir as a capable conductor; he (Schumann) would arrange financially with Tausch and the matter would be settled to everybody's satisfaction. The choir had certainly no objection to the conducting of the practices by Tausch; but when, in accordance with the arrangement, Dr. Schumann again conducted, there were complaints to the directors, and the desire became more and more insistent that Tausch should conduct all the practices.

The directors felt that they must now take action, but they chose a way that was not approved of. They wrote to Dr. Schumann, and, not venturing to question his conducting capacity, ascribed the difficulty to the superficial point of his directing from the desk instead of from the pianoforte like his predecessors, and tried thus to account for the wish of the choir that Tausch should in future conduct all the practices. This letter caused great commotion among Dr. Schumann's friends; Tausch declared that he would leave; it was the middle of the concert season, and the directors felt that, as they had acted not of their own free will but to carry out the wishes of the choir, it was incumbent on them to resign in order to avoid upsetting the local musical conditions. The newly-elected directors were able to negotiate with Dr. Schumann with the result that he handed over to Tausch the conducting of the practices with the corresponding salary, keeping in his own hands the orchestral practices and the public performances. This fortunate agreement was made at the beginning of 1853 and lasted until shortly before the break. Dr. Schumann's conducting of the public concerts was no more satisfactory than his conducting of the practices, but if the unfortunate results did not become earlier apparent it was because of the steadfast loyalty of the administrative committee to Dr. Schumann, the willingness of the orchestra (amateurs and professionals alike) to put up with things as long as possible out of consideration for Dr. Schumann's greatness as a creative musician, and the patience of the public in tolerating the artistic deterioration of the concerts.

The orchestra missed in Dr. Schumann's conducting, firm, dependable indication of the *tempi*, regular time-beating, clear, decided, and intelligible remarks and instruction at rehearsals, constant presence of mind, and all the little signs and hints by means of which a skilful conductor contributes so endlessly to a sure, perfect, and most delicately shaded performance.

After these indications the report goes on to relate that Dr. Schumann was from the beginning unable to assume the attitude of a colleague towards the members of the administrative committee, and it did not suffice him that when he appeared at the meetings for a few moments and made proposals, they were almost without exception and unconditionally agreed to ; in particular, the concert programmes were fixed almost solely according to his choice, but he did not hold himself bound by these fixtures. Away from the meetings he acted quite independently, changed the programmes, ordered music, engaged outside artists, and acted in general as if no committee existed. Again, for many years the arrangement had held that with regard to the theatre and the orchestra (for the orchestra had to serve there as well as for the concerts), the subscription concerts were to take place on Thursdays, and the two corresponding rehearsals on the preceding Tuesday evening and Thursday morning. Thus the relationship of the concerts to the theatre was regulated by the treaty between the town and the theatre director, and collision thereby avoided. Dr. Schumann disregarded this, and required the second rehearsal to be held on Wednesday evening (a theatre evening), because it tired him too much to conduct a rehearsal and concert on the same day. Dr. Schumann tolerated no contradiction, and his wife and friends always urged the chairman of the committee to agree to his wishes so that everything disagreeable might be kept out of his way.

The chairman now found himself in most unpleasant conflict on all sides, and had constantly to mediate and pacify. This extremely difficult position caused several successive resignations of the chairmanship, and the committee became convinced that only a chairmanship conducted on a purely business footing could be permanent, and this would be impossible for an intimate friend of the Schumanns. At the request of the committee Herr *Regierungsrat* Illing consented to undertake the chairman's duties on a purely business footing. After this the following happened. On October 16, the usual High Mass was to be celebrated in St. Maximilian's Church, for which the choir had prepared a mass of Hauptmann's under Tausch. The choir hoped that he would conduct the performance as well, but Dr. Schumann, in accordance with the standing arrangement, desired to conduct. At the rehearsal on Friday, 14, Dr. Schumann was more absent-minded than ever before, consequently the performance was so imperfect as almost to make a scandal, the public even complaining that the choir was lacking in due respect for the Holy Office in presenting such an insufficiently prepared performance. The unfavourable reception of this public performance of a classical work in the practice of which the choir had not been wanting in diligence, could not but have an effect on the choir, and it soon found expression. On Wednesday, October 19, the committee met to make arrangements for the concert on October 27, for which Joachim was engaged. The choral work to be performed was Mendelssohn's *Erste Walpurgisnacht*. Before Schumann appeared at the meeting, the representative of the choir directors intimated that after the happenings of the Hauptmann mass, the chorus refused to appear in public unless the conductor who had taken the practices conducted the performance also. Immediately after this announcement Dr. Schumann made his appearance, and was about to leave after the usual concert arrangements were made. The chairman begged him to wait a moment, as an unpleasing message from the choir had just been communicated which would have to be considered by him. When Dr. Schumann heard the communication he left the meeting without a word, leaving the committee in no little embarrassment regarding the arrangements for the approaching concert, which would affect the whole season. The chairman and the committee member best acquainted with the Schumanns immediately went to their house, and brought about an arrangement that Tausch should conduct small works, Dr. Schumann conducting large ones, and that the *Walpurgisnacht* might be regarded in this connection as a small work, and so be conducted by Tausch. On Thursday forenoon, October 27, was the orchestral rehearsal for the concert on the same evening, Joachim being there to rehearse his violin solos. The first number on the programme was Joachim's *Hamlet* overture, and it was hoped that he would conduct it himself—the work is difficult, with many changes of measure and *tempo*, requiring a skilful conductor no less than a well-rehearsed orchestra. But Dr. Schumann conducted, and in a way that made all previous shortcomings still more deeply felt. The chaos was struggled through somehow, and at the concert in the evening Joachim's perfect playing covered deficiencies in other directions. Joachim's appearance had drawn a large number of subscribers to the concerts, but a Joachim could not be presented every time; moreover, the rest of the performances had to be worthy of the soloist. Many came from neighbouring places to hear great virtuosi, and what would be thought of Düsseldorf's defective performances with their own material? Dr. Schumann's predecessors had brought fame to Düsseldorf, not only by their presence but by what they brought to pass there. Every friend of art must be deeply pained to see the achievements of Mendelssohn, Rietz, and Hiller fall into decay, and a famous name alone could be no compensation. Similar feelings must have possessed most of the committee and had an influence on what followed. On November 5 the committee met to settle the programme for the second concert, and when that business was finished Dr. Schumann left. The others remained to discuss the circumstances, and came to the conclusion that it was not possible to have the concerts in general conducted by Dr. Schumann, but that Tausch should act as his substitute, Dr. Schumann conducting his own works; and a member was commissioned to sound Tausch as to whether he would be willing to act in this relationship to Dr. Schumann.

Next day a formal committee meeting was held and the whole matter thoroughly gone into. Tausch's answer was first intimated—that he was not inclined to subordinate himself to any director as substitute, but that with his high respect for Dr. Schumann he was willing to make an exception and agree to act as his substitute. It was then formally discussed whether the substitution was really necessary, and the chairman put the question : " Must a substitute for Dr. Schumann really be arranged for ? " asking a special friend of the Schumanns to give his vote first. After short hesitation and with perceptible pain came his " Yes," followed by the unanimous agreement of the other members ; and it was also unanimously agreed that Tausch be appointed as substitute. It was next discussed how Dr. Schumann could be gently persuaded to allow Tausch to act for him, and for various reasons it was decided to negotiate verbally. The first proposal, to ask Burgomaster Hammers and Director von Schadow to try to bring Dr. Schumann round to the wish of the committee, was shown to be unsuitable, for in the first place it was feared that these gentlemen, not being conversant with all the motives that caused the wish, might not be readily convinced of the necessity for the step or induced to undertake the commission ; then there would certainly be objections on Dr. Schumann's part which could be met only by those thoroughly familiar with the state of matters. Finally it was feared that co-operation of the Burgomaster would give an official colour to the matter which might hurt rather than soothe Dr. Schumann. For they were most anxious to have an amicable settlement which meantime should, to outward appearance, leave everything as before, frequent opportunity being given Dr. Schumann to conduct his own works and so to appear in public as acting Music Director. The committee then urgently begged Schumann's friend, referred to above, to undertake the commission, but in vain ; and as the next concert was approaching and the first orchestral rehearsal imminent, there was no choice but to vote for delegates. The vote fell on the chairman—*Regierungsrat* Illing, and the advocate Dr. Herz, who at once repaired to the Schumanns' house, but found them out and were asked to return at ten next morning. The delegates talked with Frau Dr. Schumann and asked her to communicate the matter to her husband. Dr. Schumann (the report continues) sent a written answer, unfavourable, and showing irritation, with the specific remark that the communication had been made through his wife [we already know the gist of the letter—Schumann maintained that the step taken by the committee involved a breach of contract, depriving him of his directorial rights ; *see* Litzmann, vol. ii, p. 248].

At the same time Dr. Schumann wrote to Tausch : " If you conduct to-day and as long as we are here, at the rehearsals and concerts, I cannot regard you as well-disposed." But Tausch kept his word to the committee. On Tuesday at 6 p.m. the orchestra assembled to rehearse, and, as by 6.15 Dr. Schumann had not come, the committee asked Tausch to proceed ; he also conducted the rehearsal and concert on November 10, the performance satisfying the public. Neither Dr. Schumann nor the committee having given notice, the contract, says the report, holds good until July 1 (1854). But the conducting of the remaining concerts had to be provided for, and Tausch pressed for the regularizing of his position in the matter. The committee therefore decided to appoint Tausch as substitute for the remainder of the season (1853–54), and to act independently for the following season ; which would give them time to consider the whole position without, on their part at least, dislocating the musical organization of the town. The committee felt that they

owed Dr. Schumann an answer to his letter and they wrote
in the most courteous way, pointing out, among other things,
that a mere inquiry or the simple expression of a wish can
hardly be regarded as a violation of contract or of due respect
(Litzmann, vol. ii, p. 250).   On this followed another letter
from Dr. Schumann, showing unfortunately that he had not
the least idea of his deficiencies as Director, had therefore
not recognized the motives for the committee's action, and
he naturally held to the view that a great wrong had been
done him.

This ends the chronological narrative of the report, but
some of its further observations must be noted.

By the Schumann side, it says, the orchestra as well as the
choir has been blamed for the misunderstandings.   But, it
can with truth be maintained, wrongly.   The orchestra has
never, either collectively or individually (except in the following
isolated case), been to blame with regard to Dr. Schumann,
it has always shown him due respect and praiseworthy patience
at the rehearsals, often fatiguing to the point of exhaustion,
and any other attitude would at once have been properly
reproved by the committee.   The chief members of the
orchestra have, however, offered, in case of need, to make a
formal declaration that Dr. Schumann's way of conducting
makes it impossible for them to play their parts in a way
worthy of artists and of the reputation of the Düsseldorf
orchestra, and in accordance with the reasonable demands of
the public.   But the committee have had no occasion to
require this declaration.   The above-mentioned case was that
of a member of the orchestra who, at a rehearsal for the
first concert, after frequent repetitions of certain parts of the
Joachim overture, left his place and went out of the hall,
returning after a time and playing his part in the remainder.
This man had recently recovered from a dangerous illness
which had left him in an irritable state, which any medical
man knowing the circumstances would understand.   Nevertheless the committee minuted a sharp reproof for this
behaviour and instructed the orchestral committee to convey
it to the musician in question.   [Compare Clara's Diary

entry about the 'cellist Forberg already quoted in this connection (p. 267).] When Herr Wortmann (for the orchestral
committee) performed this duty, the musician said that he was
so exhausted in mind and body by the immoderate repetitions
that he could not have gone on and was obliged to leave the
rehearsal, and if these ways were to continue he must give
up.   Dr. Schumann will hardly maintain that the orchestra
has been wanting in respect for him.   Further, says the
report, it is alleged that there is a Tausch party opposed to
Dr. Schumann ; but it may fearlessly be asked, Where is
this party and who are its supporters ?   Are the committee
members known in their civic life as intriguers and partisans ?
Is Tausch not the musician who has acted as substitute for
both Hiller and Dr. Schumann ?   Have not the municipal
authorities themselves on occasion turned to Tausch as
Dr. Schumann's substitute and found him always agreeable
and willing ?   The committee, therefore, have done nothing
but what the music directors and municipal authorities
themselves have done.

The report sums up in six points :

1. Herr Dr. Schumann is not a municipal official, but is in contract
with an independent legally constituted society.

2. The Town Council granted an unconditional yearly supplement
to Dr. Schumann's salary.

3. The administrative committee, in proposing to Dr. Schumann
through his wife that he should allow the works of other composers to
be conducted by a substitute, have neither put a stop to his activity
as Music Director nor made it impossible.

4. Herr Dr. Schumann, inasmuch as he intentionally absented himself
from the rehearsal on November 8, made a breach of contract.

5. As no notice has been given either by Herr Dr. Schumann or by
the committee, the contract is not cancelled.

6. The committee, driven by necessity, acted not without pain, and
have kept in view on the one hand the proper respect due to the name
of Schumann, on the other hand, consideration for the reputation of
their city and its art. . . .

Burgomaster Hammers, wishing to act as mediator, sent
the memorandum to Schumann on December 5, with a letter
(Litzmann, vol. ii, p. 246) inviting him to send his own account

of the quarrel to a specially-appointed committee of the
Town Council who wished to investigate the whole matter.

No more, however, is heard of it all, and it may reasonably
be doubted whether Schumann would have taken any notice
of the document even had it reached him before he and his
wife set out (November 24) on their concert tour in Holland.

CHAPTER XXII

For two reasons this must be my last chapter—my space
and my strength alike remind me that the time has come for
me to refrain.   It remains, therefore, only to run over some
points of interest in the last few years of Schumann's life, and
to conclude with some first-hand reminiscences given me by
friends or acquaintances of my own who knew him.   They
reveal nothing new, but are additional illustrations and
corroborations, from reliable sources, of the master's well-
known idiosyncrasies.

The Schumanns were, naturally, anxious to leave Düsseldorf; but various letters of Robert's show how far he was
from realizing the state of his health, for his hope was to find
a directorship elsewhere.   Even in 1852, before the worst
had come to the worst, he wrote to the *Capellmeister* at Sondershausen, Gottfried Hermann, then about to leave for Lübeck,
inquiring confidentially about conditions and the possibility
of succeeding him.   To Joachim, undated, but, Jansen thinks,
on November 9, 1853 :

. . . . We are . . . soon going away from Düsseldorf altogether.
What I have long had in mind is settled.   We are tired of these vulgar
goings on.   I have an offer (although a third-hand one) from a town in
which my wife and I have long wished to settle. . . . Meantime we
remain here till July.   All this is for you and Brahms only. . . .

Schumann jots down on November 8 : " Hesitation between
Berlin and Vienna."   On November 10, " Decision for
Vienna."   (Litzmann, vol. ii, p. 244.)   But on December 29

he writes the following letter to Julius Stern in Berlin, who,
some years before, had let Schumann know that if he ever
left Düsseldorf, he, Stern, would like to succeed him.   Schumann's letter is of curious interest as showing his optimism
and remoteness from actuality :

.... What I have learnt since [returning from Holland] is this :
the Town Council, who have the decisive voice in the matter, wish to
retain me in any case for Düsseldorf.   This could only be on condition
that certain ill-disposed and low-minded members of the *Allg. Musikverein* committee are removed from it.   Otherwise, Herr Tausch would
conduct the concerts temporarily, for this winter, but in no case would
he have the prospect of being permanently appointed Music Director.
You have a much better chance of that.   But meantime there is nothing
to do but to wait and see.   In the event of the Town Council not agree-
ing to my conditions they will certainly consult me, and I would with
pleasure propose you as my successor . . . we might then effect an
exchange, I taking your place in Berlin, you taking mine here.   But
these are only thoughts told in confidence to you alone.   As soon as
anything is settled you shall hear from me.

While nothing came of these hopes and plans there were
meantime many distractions and satisfactions, of which two
were outstanding.   The story of the appearance on the scene
of Brahms is well enough known.   Joachim had given him
an introduction to Schumann, who notes on September 30,
1853, " Hr. Brahms from Hamburg " ; next day, " Visit
from Brahms (a genius)."   And he wrote two lines " in
prophetic style " to Joachim : " This is he who should come."
On October 8, " Lively letter to Joachim."   In this letter to
" the Apostle Joseph " chiefly about " Johannes the true
Apostle," Schumann writes of—

the young eagle that has flown so suddenly and unexpectedly from
the hills to Düsseldorf. . . . The young eagle seems to feel at home
in Flatland . . . he has found an old attendant who, used to such young
highflyers, understands how to calm the wild beatings of their wings
without hindering their powers.

On October 8 Schumann began the famous essay *Neue
Bahnen*, four days later he read it aloud to three friends, and
sent it to Joachim for his opinion, writing :

. . . . I have begun to collect and draw up my thoughts about the young eagle; I should dearly like to be at his side on his first flight over the world. . . .

The essay was published before the month was out, in the *Neue Zeitschrift für Musik*, October 28, 1853—Schumann's last essay, a unique recognition and a prophecy still being fulfilled. The Diary itself must be read for the account from the Schumann side of the wonderful brotherhood that ensued.

On November 2, after a month of constant music at the Schumanns', Brahms left Düsseldorf to join Joachim at Hanover; a few days later the trouble with the committee came to a head, Schumann ceasing to act as Music Director from November 10, when he absented himself from the concert; and on November 24 the Schumanns started for a concert tour in Holland which proved a veritable series of triumphs for both Robert and Clara. From Utrecht Robert wrote to Joachim of the success and honours that were falling to their lot, and of the enthusiasm and high level of Dutch musical culture and the great appreciation of his own music. Husband and wife, each rejoicing in the other's triumphs, were fêted in public and private alike; they felt warmed and cheered by it all and looked forward to returning to Holland in the future. By Christmas the family were reunited. In the parents' absence the children were looked after by their friend Frl. Wittgenstein, who treasured and showed me with pride the following characteristic little letter of Schumann's from Amsterdam, December 16, 1853: " Dear children and dear housekeeper, we shall soon see each other again—we expect to leave here the day after to-morrow (Sunday) and to reach Düsseldorf by the Oberhausen train in the evening. If anything unforeseen should prevent us we shall arrive at latest on Monday. We hope to find you all very well, and Mamma will have ever so much to tell you. Mamma is bringing a great deal of fame and lots of gold pieces with her, you will be surprised. Good-bye, then, dear children and housekeeper. We shall meet soon.—Your Papa."

Schumann's compositions during the Düsseldorf years till the end of 1853 were numerous, and, although his creative power was declining, some important works came into being during this last period. Of these a mere mention of the chief must suffice. The E flat major, the "Rhenish," Symphony, Op. 97, composed in the autumn of 1850 and first performed at Düsseldorf, February 6, 1851; the Festival Overture on the *Rheinweinlied*, for orchestra and chorus, Op. 123, composed 1853 and first performed at the Lower Rhine festival of that year; the reinstrumentation of the D minor Symphony, Op. 120, so that it came to be known as "the fourth," although strictly speaking it is the second. Of the considerable quantity of other works—orchestral and chamber music of many kinds—all are of less value, though in varying degree. The overtures inspired by Schiller, Shakespeare, and Goethe; the Requiem and Mass; the Ballads, *Der Königssohn, Des Sängers Fluch, Das Glück von Edenhall*, etc.; the chamber music; these, in spite of their many beauties, all show failing creative and critical power in some respect or other. During the last two months of his Düsseldorf life, January and February, 1854, Schumann was preparing his *Gesammelte Schriften* for publication, and working at the completion—not attained—of his *Dichtergarten*, an anthology of sayings on music from the great poets, which he had begun many years before.

In January (1854) the Schumanns visited Hanover, where Clara played the Beethoven E flat major Concerto and Joachim conducted the fourth symphony and played the Phantasie for violin. (A performance of *Paradise and the Peri* to be conducted by Robert had fallen through.) Everything was successful and happy, but the chief happiness was the renewed intercourse with Joachim and Brahms. While the Diary notes Brahms's taciturnity and Joachim's increased seriousness, it tells also of an evening at Joachim's with Brahms and J. O. Grimm: "Very merry, much champagne drunk." Of this occasion Joachim told me that champagne was suggested, and having none himself he slipped out to a neighbouring hotel to fetch some. This naturally took a little time, Brahms meanwhile perpetrating the joke, long kept up against him, that Joachim must have lost the key of his cellar!

On January 30 the Schumanns returned to Düsseldorf, Robert working so zealously at the *Dichtergarten* that Clara began to be anxious lest he should overtax himself. On the night of Friday, February 10, Robert developed an alarming symptom —he himself notes: " [February] 10. Marked and painful auditory affection." From this the catastrophe was only seventeen days distant. But we must first glance back. Although during the Düsseldorf years Schumann had considerable periods of seemingly satisfactory health, every now and then trouble of one kind or another broke out—the disease was gaining ground without Robert or Clara realizing it. Robert had written of " nervous troubles " to Wasielewski, who describes the manifest symptoms. Above all there was the increasing heaviness of speech. Then all *tempi* seemed to him too fast, he was obviously unable to follow a quick *tempo*. He carried himself heavily, and in intercourse, in spite of his amiability, an unmistakable apathy made itself felt. As time went on fresh symptoms developed, among which must be reckoned Schumann's morbid enthusiasm for and belief in table rapping—one aspect of the spiritualism that was greatly in vogue at the time. There followed hallucinations of hearing which, it was hoped, were passing affections. Through the autumn of 1853 Schumann was wonderfully well (except for a quickly passing alarm at the beginning of the tour in Holland) until the breakdown in February, 1854. The painful story is told very fully in the Diary and bears no re-telling. To summarize it very briefly—the symptoms of February 10, though intermittent, increased for about a week and were followed by intense melancholy and delusions, first of good, then of evil spirits. On February 17 he rose from bed to note down a theme which, he said, the angels had sent him. On the 26th he suddenly begged to be taken to an asylum, and calmly collected all the things he wished to take with him. He was persuaded to go to bed. Next morning he woke in a state of profound melancholy and was working at his variations on the theme (which, Litzmann notes, is printed in the supplementary volume of the critical edition under No. 9, *Thema (Es dur) für Pianoforte*)—

when suddenly [writes Clara]—I had left the room for a few minutes only, letting Mariechen sit with him, to discuss something with Dr. Hasenclever in the other room (but for the last ten days I had not left him alone at all for a moment)—he left his room and went sighing into the bedroom. Marie thought he would come back immediately; he did not come, but ran out in most frightful rain, without boots or waistcoat. Bertha burst in suddenly and told me that he was gone. . . . Dietrich, Hasenclever, all who were there, ran off to look for him, but did not find him; after about an hour two strangers brought him back—where and how they found him I could not discover. . . .

Clara was not allowed to see him; nor did she learn for certain where he had been found until his death at Endenich, when his missing wedding ring occasioned explanations. After a few agonizing days Schumann was taken on March 4, 1854, at his own wish, to the private asylum of Dr. Richarz at Endenich, near Bonn, by his friend and physician, Dr. Hasenclever, and two attendants.

None of the accounts of the precise circumstances of the disappearance agree. Wasielewski says that Schumann was sitting at midday with Dr. Hasenclever and Albert Dietrich, that during conversation he silently left the room, and, as after some time he did not return, his wife went in search of him. Ruppert Becker's version again, a hearsay version, reported in his diary (which he lent me to copy) on March 8, is that Schumann slipped out of his bedroom in felt slippers, went straight to the Rhine, and plunged in from the middle of the bridge. At the entrance-toll of the bridge he had been noticed from the circumstance that, having no money, he had given up his handkerchief as a pledge. Some fishermen who had watched him, on seeing him leap, at once took a boat and rescued him; he is said to have made another attempt from the boat. The homeward journey must have been terrible, eight men bringing him through an excited carnival crowd. Continuing on March 10, Becker adds: " Frau Schumann, who slept during this catastrophe, was kept unaware of it until to-day. . . ." The discrepancies are many; even Clara's own account may be inaccurate, as it was not written down until some time after the events, and it is easily understandable that in the perturbation of that and the following days nobody was able to recall exactly what did happen, moreover, that accounts became altered in passing from mouth to mouth.

For a time hopes were entertained of Schumann's recovery,* and he was able to occupy himself a good deal with music (he wrote at Endenich a pianoforte accompaniment † for the Paganini *Capricci*) and walking, and was occasionally allowed to see intimate friends, especially Joachim and Brahms. But in the autumn of 1855 all hope of complete recovery was abandoned, and in the spring of 1856 news reached poor Clara, in London at the time, that Robert was " irretrievably lost." She returned home, after a three-months' concert campaign in England, on July 6 ; saw Dr. Richarz on July 14, who told her that Robert had not another year to live ; on July 23 a telegram summoned her to Endenich, but the crisis passing, she was urged not to see Robert, and went back to Düsseldorf without having seen him. Unable to endure, however, she returned to Endenich on Sunday, July 27, with Brahms, and saw Robert that evening ; he was able to show sign of recognition and welcome, but could not speak intelligibly. " . . . He seemed to be in converse with the spirits, disliked to have anyone by him for long, then became restless, but hardly anything could be understood. . . ." On Monday, Clara and Brahms were with him or watching him unobserved all day. " On Tuesday [writes Clara] he was to be freed from his troubles ; at four in the afternoon he passed gently away. His last hours were peaceful, and so he passed in sleep unnoticed—nobody was with him at the moment. I saw him half an hour later. Joachim had come from Heidelberg on receiving our telegram, and this had detained me in town longer than usual. . . ."

Schumann was buried two days later, July 31, 1856, in the evening, at Bonn, in the beautiful Old Cemetery by the Sternentor, with solemn music. Joachim and Brahms led the way ; the coffin was borne by members of the " Con-

---

* Wasielewski's Biography contains a report—of pathological and psychological interest—on Schumann's malady, furnished at the biographer's request by Dr. Richarz of Endenich.

† Not published.

U

cordia " society who had serenaded him in Düsseldorf; the Burgomasters were there; and Hiller had come from Cologne. ". . . I had not made it known [wrote Clara in the Diary] because I did not wish many strangers to be present. His dearest friends walked in front : I followed last (unobserved). It was best so—certainly as he would have wished it. . . ." Forty years later—years of devotion to his ideals—on Whit-Sunday, 1896, Clara was laid lovingly beside Robert by their children and faithful friends from far and near, Brahms among them to the last.

The prophetic words of the eighteen-year-old poet Schumann come back to us : " And so it is throughout human life—the goal we have attained is no longer a goal, and we yearn, and strive, and aim ever higher and higher, until the eyes close in death, and the storm-tossed body and soul lie slumbering in the grave."

If we want to understand a man it is better to listen to his friends than to his enemies. Joachim found it difficult to believe that Schumann should have any enemies, and perhaps he had as few as any man can expect to have ; but his ways were at times liable to give offence, and his friendships were not all free from friction. Among the most faithful and comprehending were the Bendemanns, Bendemann even admonishing Schumann on occasion at the risk of offending him. At a party given by the Bendemanns Schumann sat the whole evening by himself in one of the inner rooms—they had several communicating rooms. The pianoforte was in another room, and after playing, Clara joined her husband, who asked, " Who was playing ? " " I." " Really ? " And she wept. When supper-time came, Clara carried wine and food to him in his corner, and later went to him and said, " I feel unwell, shall we not go ? " " But why should we go ? It is so nice here." And they remained. At last Bendemann said to Schumann : " Although it is very impolite of a host to say so to a guest, I cannot help saying that you should have taken your wife home before now." Schumann said nothing but was angry. Next day Bendemann received a letter in which Schumann said in an irritated way that he did not need to be told of his wife's excellences, that he was well aware of them. Bendemann apologized, and the friendship was restored. On another occasion Bendemann called to take Schumann out and found him dressing. After fumbling with his tie for some time he called out, " Clara, my waistcoat." And she brought it, and afterwards his coat. Bendemann reproved him for this, but without convincing him. A conversation with Schumann rarely lasted more than ten minutes. As to likenesses, Bendemann said that the Rietschel medallion is excellent ; the whistling shape of the mouth, however, was in reality more marked—the artist had toned it down. (The Bendemanns never heard any whistling sound, but Frl. Hartmann stated that Schumann not only shaped his lips as if whistling, but did actually whistle—she had often heard it when sitting next him at table.) There is no painted portrait from life of any importance. Bendemann himself made a drawing from a photograph. The Bendemanns possessed a letter relating to the dedication of the *Bilder aus Osten* ; and another, shorter, inviting them to stand godparents ; they are neatly written, only here and there indistinct. Bendemann remarked that the handwriting resembled Mendelssohn's.

Frl. Mathilde Hartmann, an excellent amateur singer and friend of the Schumanns, was the first to sing the Rose in the *Pilgerfahrt*. Soon after the first performance Schumann gave her the poem with a kind inscription, and later the pianoforte score with a dedication. She was much at the house, and as Schumann liked to sit next her at table, Frau Schumann arranged it so. Although he talked little and fragmentarily, sometimes he spoke well—once she heard him talk very finely about painting with a painter sitting opposite him at table. He spoke softly : walked as if he had no bones in his body. Sometimes, after music and supper, there was dancing—Frl. Hartmann had seen him dance with his wife, when he looked like an amiable bear. He was very amiable. " Nobody accompanied me so well, not even his wife."

Herr *Justizrat* Herz (the reader will remember the trying part he had to play in the negotiations about conducting) emphasized Schumann's kindly disposition ; he himself had experienced no brusqueness from him. A letter he received from Schumann after the breach exonerated him from all blame. The step taken by the committee was, Dr. Herz said, necessary, and it was taken with all possible delicacy.

Langhans, my master, told me of his visit to Schumann when passing through Düsseldorf on his way to Paris with Japha (another well-known violinist). They called on Schumann and were shown into a dark room ; after some time Schumann appeared in the doorway, but having gazed into the room he vanished, shutting the door. After a further wait the two art-disciples asked if they had been announced to Dr. Schumann, and learned with amazement that he had gone out long ago. Langhans and Japha played string quartets with Ruppert Becker and Bockmühl, and when Schumann heard that his quartets had been played elsewhere he was vexed at not having been invited.

And now let us hear the wholly congenial and most loyal friend—Joachim. He described Schumann as of noble appearance, and well-disposed and kindly in manner. If anyone or anything displeased him he simply turned away ; he would not engage in exchange of words and argument. When he said, " He is not a gentleman " (" Das ist kein feiner Mann "), it was as much as to say, " I will have nothing to do with him." But he was in general so amiable that it is difficult to understand how he could have enemies. In Düsseldorf he had enemies, which may be ascribed to his distinguished, silent, reserved nature, than which the Düsseldorfers would have resented rudeness less. [This is hardly fair !] Schumann was never witty in conversation, but pleasantly humorous, with a gentle touch of humour (" freundlich humoristisch, so ein leiser Anflug von Humor "). Once the topic of Hauptmann's book *Die Natur der Harmonik und der Metrik*, new in 1853, came up. Joachim said he found it difficult to read as he had not enough mathematical knowledge, and had not got beyond the thirtieth page. Schumann replied :

"Indeed, did you get as far as that? I stuck at the first pages. It is not musical at all." Schumann had spoken or written to Joachim of a beautiful effect in a passage for the horns in his *Hamlet* overture, and Joachim inquired afterwards how they had sounded. "They didn't come in." "Perhaps the parts are not right?" "Yes, I saw to that myself." At the rehearsal the horns failed again. Instead of rating the players roundly Schumann turned sadly to Joachim and said, "They don't come in." Schumann never could conduct, Joachim said. In early days he may have beaten time accurately enough, but he made no remarks on the performances. At the rehearsal of *Paradise and the Peri* Clara (at the pianoforte) said : "My husband says that he wishes this passage *piano*"; and he stood by and nodded gratefully. Repetition without indication. If it did not go then, moral indignation. To the drummer in the A minor Concerto : "Once again ; *once* again ; once again, you must count." And when the drummer came out with angry words Schumann was angry, and said, "That is impertinent." At a performance of one of his own symphonies he stood dreamily with raised baton, all the players ready and not knowing when to begin. Königslöw and Joachim, who sat at the first desk, therefore took the matter into their own hands and began, Schumann following with a smile of pleasure. Of Schumann's musical sympathies and antipathies Joachim had little to tell me. He did not believe in the supposed antipathy to Haydn, but he remembered that Schumann said of the slow movement of a Haydn sonata for pianoforte and violin that one could no longer play such music. In later life he found all *tempi* too fast, and beat time with his foot, keeping back his wife's pace, for instance. In his last works the strong accentuation is striking, also a certain heaviness.

When Joachim visited Schumann at Endenich he talked about books and music, inquiring specially about Rubinstein, whose compositions were being much praised at the time. Then Schumann led Joachim into a corner of the room, and said : "I cannot stay here any longer. They do not understand me." To Joachim's question whether he wished to go

back to Düsseldorf, he answered : " Oh no, that is degradation." At the first visit Joachim thought that improvement
might be hoped for ; but at the second he thought Schumann's
condition hopeless. He was trembling, and when he played
Joachim his own compositions with trembling hands it was
horrible to hear. When Joachim left, Schumann took his
hat and said he would accompany him a little way. But
at the door he stopped suddenly, nodded quickly, and
said abruptly, " Adieu." Joachim inferred that Schumann
imagined that he was being followed by attendants.

Many of Schumann's predicaments had their humorous as
well as their pathetic side, and sometimes he himself derived
amusement from his own weaknesses. For instance, he was
apt to let his baton fall, and my father often told me how one
day at a rehearsal when this had happened, Schumann came
up to him as he stood at his desk, and showing him a baton
with a string attached to it and to his wrist, said with childlike simplicity and a pleased expression of face and voice,
" Look, now it can't fall again ! "

There is still much that I intended to write of ; but having
had my say on some of the special matters that lay nearest my
heart I must be satisfied. Topics that in particular lent themselves to supplementary and corrective treatment were the
personality and behaviour of Wieck ; the Mendelssohn–
Schumann relationship ; the Düsseldorf conditions and difficulties ; the personality and behaviour of Tausch. Many
other matters that must perforce be left alone I meant to deal
with, as Goethe puts it, " not in order to make new discoveries,
but simply to view in my own way what has already been
discovered."

At the beginning I said that the unity, the consistency, of
the master's life must become apparent to every observant
person. My hope is that these chapters may in some measure
contribute to this perception ; to the increased perception,
also, of the nobility and greatness of Robert Schumann as a
musician and as a man.

FINIS

APPENDIX I

* *SCHUMANNIANA*

REMINISCENCES, ANECDOTES, AND DISCUSSIONS

By Fr. Niecks.

To the student of modern literature and art the name of Düsseldorf cannot be unfamiliar. There the brothers Jacobi—Friedrich Heinrich, the philosopher, and Johann Georg, the poet—were born and spent part of their lives; there the dramatist and novelist Karl Lebrecht Immermann resided during the last thirteen years of his earthly career, attending to his official duties, directing for a short time a standard theatre, and producing a splendid array of works— the dramatic myth *Merlin*, the trilogy *Alexis*, the droll tale *Tulifäntchen*, the comic romance *Münchhausen*, his *Memorabilia*, a *Journal of Travel*, and many other compositions besides, in verse and in prose, dramatic, lyric, narrative, satiric, epis- tolary, etc. ; there also first saw the light of day, and received his early education and impressions, one of the most popular and delightful lyric poets, one of the wittiest and most *malicieux* prose writers Germany can boast of—Heinrich Heine. The supreme glories of Düsseldorf, however, do not lie in the fields of literature. To see it under its most brilliant aspect we must turn to the pictorial-art, to which it owes one of the highest honours that ever fall to the lot of

* First published in the *Monthly Musical Record*, January and February, 1884.
It seemed appropriate, some repetition notwithstanding, to reprint this article written fully forty years ago. My husband intended to use in his Schumann articles some of the anecdotes told here, but space forbade the inclusion of more than the story of the baton.

a town—the honour of giving its name to a school of artists. Under the direction of Peter von Cornelius (1822–26), W. von Schadow (1826–59), and his successor, Eduard Bendemann, the Düsseldorf school flourished vigorously. It infused a new spirit, a new sentiment, into its work, and in doing this secured for itself a place in history. As a native of the same town, I cannot pass over in silence the fact that Cornelius, one of the greatest creative geniuses of this century, was, like Heine and the Jacobis, a son of Düsseldorf.

In regard to the art of music as well, the " village on the Düssel " furnishes matter worthy of attention as well as provocative of curiosity. To verify this statement we have only to call to mind the musicians who, during the last fifty years, held successively the post of municipal music director of Düsseldorf. They are :—Felix Mendelssohn Bartholdy (1833–35), Julius Rietz (1835–47), Ferdinand Hiller (1847–50), Robert Schumann (1850–53), and Julius Tausch (1853–1889 or –90). As these names might give rise to misconceptions, I hasten to state that there were by no means great resources at the disposal of these musicians. What they accomplished in the way of choral, more especially of orchestral performances, was due chiefly to their energy and talent as conductors, which, of course, varied very much, and in the case of Schumann were non-existent. It is, indeed, an undeniable fact that in the art of music Düsseldorf always shone with a borrowed lustre. At this moment I cannot remember a single native of the town who has conquered for himself a place among the princes of his art. The only musician who promised to do so, Norbert Burgmüller, died (March 7, 1836) before he had reached maturity. Some of his compositions were published after his death, and they show that in losing him the world lost a tone-poet of great power. " After Schubert's early death none could affect us more painfully than that of Burgmüller." Thus wrote Schumann in 1839, in the *Neue Zeitschrift für Musik*, and he paid the departed a still greater compliment in 1851, when he orchestrated, attracted by its value, an otherwise finished composition of his—the *scherzo* of a symphony.

Of other now well-known musicians who for a more or less long space of time took up their abode at Düsseldorf, I may mention the violinist and conductor, W. J. von Wasielewski, better known by his literary works (*Robert Schumann, The Violin and its Masters, The History of Instrumentation*, etc.); the violinist, composer, and *littérateur*, Dr. Wilhelm Langhans (author of *The Musical Judgment and its Development, The History of Music in Twelve Lectures, The History of Music in the 17th, 18th, and 19th Centuries*, etc.); the violin virtuoso, Leopold von Auer; and the violoncello virtuoso and composer, Jules de Swert.* With the three last-named I had much intercourse, for it was my good fortune to have Dr. Langhans and Mr. Auer for my masters, and to be the tenor player of a quartet of which the latter was the first violinist and M. de Swert the violoncellist.

Connections, however, are also formed by intermediate links, often of the most shadowy nature. My having lived for several years opposite the natal house of Cornelius; my having frequently walked and sat in the garden where the philosopher Jacobi hospitably entertained Goethe; my having bought more than one pencil and note-book within the walls which heard the infant Heine's first artlessly modulated lyrical outbursts and inarticulate expressions of his views of the world—these experiences give me the consciousness of an advantage over less privileged individuals. What could be more natural than that, under the circumstances, I should more thoroughly understand and be more fully in sympathy with the genius of the three great men! And such a puerile feeling of superiority, vague though it be, cannot be reasoned away.

My connection with Mendelssohn, although he had left Düsseldorf long before I was born, is less shadowy. Indeed, he seems to me more familiar and real than many people with

---

* Subsequently M. de Swert was solo violoncellist of the Imperial orchestra at Berlin and professor at the Hochschule, but gave up these posts in 1877. In 1888 he became Director of the Ostend Music School, teaching also at the music schools of Ghent and Bruges. He died at Ostend, on February 24, 1891.

whom I have associated for years.. This can easily be explained. My father, who was a member of the orchestra under all the conductors mentioned by me, had, of course, much to tell of Mendelssohn ; so had several of his colleagues, who, from my thirteenth to my twenty-second year, were also my colleagues. Then I knew many—some only by sight, others personally—whom Mendelssohn regarded as friends. The venerable figure of Schadow still stands before my mind's eye with the clearness of actuality. Eduard Bendemann I saw for years almost daily pass the house where I lived, on his way to the Academy. With the well-known painter Ferdinand Theodor Hildebrandt, who was so fond of talking of his friend Mendelssohn, I had, shortly before his death, a pleasant conversation about the amiable master. The warm summer evening, the pleasant garden where we sat, and the frail old artist with his young enthusiasm, will never be forgotten by me. I mention only men I have known in Düsseldorf, and who, through their own genius and Mendelssohn's letters, are known to the world. For, outside Düsseldorf, more especially at Leipzig, I have come in contact with not a few who were dear to the master, or, at least, had seen much of him—for instance, Conrad Schleinitz, the late director of the Conservatorium, and Ferdinand Wenzel, the late eccentric professor of the pianoforte at the same institution.

But it is time that I should bridle my talkativeness, give over digressing, and take up the principal subject of my reminiscences. Before I set to work, however, I will yet premise that, when I do not state the source from which I derive my information, I rely on what I consider to be good authority—of which I may not be an altogether unqualified judge, seeing that my sojourn in Düsseldorf extended over twenty-three years, that my intercourse with the musicians and amateurs of this and other towns was both long and intimate, and that my musical studies were partly pursued under the guidance of Julius Tausch, the assistant and successor of Schumann.

Schumann arrived in Düsseldorf on the 2nd September, 1850, with his family, and full of joyful expectations ; he left it on the 4th of March, 1854, accompanied by his physician and friend, Dr. Hasenclever, and two keepers. Then followed two years of wretchedness in a private asylum at Endenich, near Bonn; after which, on the 29th of July, 1856, death laid his kind hand upon him.

At the time of Schumann's stay in Düsseldorf I was still a little boy; my personal recollections are therefore few and unimportant. I remember very well my father pointing him out to me as he was slowly walking by himself in the public park (Hofgarten). And I still see the quiet face, the protruding rounded lips (as if he were whistling, or pronouncing O), and the absorbed, absent look. I must often have seen him conduct, but remember distinctly only one occasion—namely, a rehearsal of a mass at St. Maximilian's Church on a Saturday afternoon before some great church festival. The organ-loft, the disposition of the chorus and orchestra, the bearing of the conductor, and the light that fell upon the group through the large windows behind them, form a picture indelibly impressed upon my mind. This was one of the occasions on which Schumann became so entirely oblivious of the work he was engaged on that he let his baton fall. With regard to this point, I must, however, caution the reader. For although I seem to remember the circumstance well enough, I still cannot help feeling a little doubtful about it. Memory often plays such curious tricks. It not only combines different events, but also what we have experienced with what we have been told. It is, however, an indubitable fact that Schumann let his baton fall on several occasions. My father told me often how one day at a rehearsal when this had happened, Schumann came up to him as he stood at his desk and showed him a baton with a string attached to it and to his wrist, and said with childlike simplicity and a satisfied and pleased expression on his face and in his voice, " Look, now it can't fall again ! "

How Schumann's imagination was always busy is shown by the following occurrence :—At the first rehearsal of a new work of his one of the trombone players left out some notes intended by the composer, either because the passage was not in his part, or because he had made a mistake in counting. Schumann duly noted and pointed out the omission. After the same movement had been played at the second rehearsal, the composer turned to the trombone-player in question, who this time had been as silent as on the previous occasion, and remarked : " It is all right now, and sounds very well."

Schumann's absent-mindedness led sometimes to curious encounters and scenes. Let me give two examples. Whilst a pupil of the Leipzig Conservatoire, Dr. Langhans played with some fellow-students a work of Schumann's at one of the evening entertainments of the institution. The composer, evidently pleased with the performance, sent word through Ferdinand Wenzel to the young violinist to come to him. Inexpressibly happy, the youth hastened to the revered master. Imagine his feelings when, on presenting himself to Schumann, the latter remained dumb. After waiting respectfully for a while, the disappointed hero-worshipper ventured to say something ; whereupon Schumann made an effort, and asked him : " What country do you come from ? " and then relapsed into silence. A more interesting case is the following one. From 1849 to 1854 there existed at Paris a concert society, a " Société Sainte-Cécile," founded and conducted by François Jean-Baptiste Seghers. The advancement of the art, not gain, was the object of all concerned in the undertaking. I have been told by a friend of mine who was one of the body that the executants gave their services gratis. M. Seghers and his enthusiastic supporters were especially anxious to make the Parisians acquainted with the best modern works. Among the various new compositions which were brought by them to a first hearing in Paris was Schumann's overture to *Manfred*. The performance, however, gave rise to disagreements between the conductor and some of the players, among whom the Teutonic element was strongly represented. The question was : What are the *tempi* intended by the composer ? To settle the debated points, Carl Witting, who was then preparing to go to Germany, was commissioned to visit Düsseldorf, and in the name of the Société Sainte-Cécile to lay the matter before the

composer. Herr Witting arrived at Düsseldorf, called on
Schumann, was received by him, and explained to him the
object of his visit. When he had ended, and was looking
forward to an answer that would set all doubt at rest,
Schumann, who was smoking a cigar, said : "Do you smoke ? "
" Yes," was Herr Witting's reply. But the composer had
already become—or, rather, had again become—oblivious of
his visitor, for he neither offered him a cigar nor gave him an
answer to his questions. After waiting for some time, Herr
Witting made another attempt to get the desired information,
but with exactly the same result—the words " Do you smoke ? "
followed by silence. A third attempt elicited as little as the
two previous ones, and Herr Witting took his leave of the
composer just as wise as when he greeted him on entering.

Although an eloquent writer, and, as Wasielewski relates,
occasionally expressing striking ideas in his conversations,
Schumann was generally taciturn, and had much difficulty in
finding words for what he had to say. " He could not say
without breaking down once or twice, ' Ladies and gentlemen,
our next rehearsal will be to-morrow at seven o'clock.' "
These are my father's words, from whom I have also the
following anecdote.

Schumann was in the habit of going in the evening to some
restaurant to read the papers and drink a few glasses of beer
or wine. He rarely continued to frequent any house for long,
as he was sure to meet soon with something that annoyed him.
At one time he took into favour Korn's restaurant on the
Hundsrücken. On the very first evening, after a considerable
stay, during which he read the papers, drank several glasses of
beer, and ate something, he left without paying. The waiter
noticed it, and was on the point of going after him ; but the
host, though he did not know his guest, would not permit
this, being convinced that forgetfulness, not dishonesty, was
at the bottom of the singular proceeding. " Let him alone,"
the host said ; " he is a gentleman, take my word for it ; he'll
come back and pay." Part of the host's prophecy was fulfilled ; Schumann came back, but he paid neither the old nor
the new reckoning. The host, of course, thought this

very strange.   His confidence, however, remained unshaken.
To satisfy his curiosity he inquired among his other guests
if they knew the silent gentleman who sat apart from the rest.
Some of them knew the Herr Music Director, and they
advised him to send his account to Madame Schumann.
This the host did after some time, and forthwith came the
money, accompanied with thanks, and the request not to
disturb her husband.

The relation between Schumann and his wife must have been
very beautiful.   We know from his literary works, and, still
better, from his letters, how he loved her, and how she inspired
him.   Those who have lived near them know equally well
how she watched over him, placed herself between the outside
world and him, and prevented, as far as possible, those rubs
which tortured his sensitive mind.   Schumann, on the other
hand, owing to his self-absorption, may have caused her
unwittingly and unconsciously much annoyance, and even
inflicted upon her many a severe pang.   Of the two anecdotes
I shall now tell, the second shows how precious her husband's
approval was to Madame Schumann.   Dr. Langhans met
the composer and his wife at an evening party at the house
of the Preussers in Leipzig.   It is needless to say that there
was music.   Among the works performed was Schumann's
Quintet, in which Madame Schumann took the pianoforte
part.   In all this there is, of course, nothing remarkable ;
but the reader may perhaps think it sufficiently remarkable
that the composer, to prevent the great pianist, his wife, from
hurrying the *tempi*, beat time on her shoulders.*   The next
anecdote describes a scene which took place several years later
at Düsseldorf.   Madame Schumann had played at one of the

---

* Speaking of Leipzig, I may quote a passage from Hans Andersen's auto-
biography which, I think, is little known.   It occurs in that part of the book
which treats of the years 1840–44 : " From Weimar I went to Leipsic, where
a truly poetical evening awaited me with Robert Schumann.   This great composer had a year before surprised me by the honour of dedicating to me the
music which he had composed to four of my songs [Op. 40]; the lady of Dr.
Frege, whose singing, so full of soul, has pleased and enchanted so many
thousands, [was] accompanied [by] Clara Schumann, and the composer and the
poet were alone the audience; a festive supper and a mutual interchange of
ideas shortened the evening only too much."   I have taken the liberty of insert-
ing a few words which, I hope, the not very idiomatic translator will forgive.

subscription-concerts some unaccompanied solo pieces. Her husband sat not far from her, behind the pianoforte. When she had finished there was a general rivalry among the audience and the musicians on the platform to give expression to their delight, which she, however, heeded little, for she saw her husband motionless and cold. " Have I not played well, Robert ? " But there came no response, and she wept whilst the hall was ringing with ecstatic applause.

And now my last ancedote. At Düsseldorf I have often heard that when Schumann was rescued from the Rhine, into which he had thrown himself (on February 27, 1854), he spoke with rapture of the beautiful music he had heard in the river, and was inconsolable that he had not the power to write it down. Whether the story is based on fact, or is a product of the myth-making popular imagination, I cannot tell. The reader will remember the incident related by Wasielewski, namely, that shortly before this occurrence Schumann rose from his bed and asked for a light, as Schubert and Mendelssohn * had sent him a theme which he must write down at once. Afterwards he wrote five variations on this theme. Brahms made use of it in his Variations for four hands, Op. 23.

In the sub-title of these Schumanniana I promised " discussions," which discussions, however, are, strictly speaking, only *a* discussion, and the subject of it is Mendelssohn's opinion of Schumann. That Schumann admired and loved Mendelssohn *cannot* be doubted ; it is patent to all that have eyes to see and ears to hear. That Mendelssohn was well-disposed towards Schumann *need* not be doubted ; indeed, Hiller tells us (*Mendelssohn : Letters and Recollections*, Cologne, 1878,) that Mendelssohn esteemed Schumann highly. What may, however, well be doubted is, whether Mendelssohn fully apprehended Schumann's greatness. Few, if any, writers, have dealt with this question in a satisfactory manner. Most of them are so anxious to free Mendelssohn from any possible blame that they rush into all sorts of inconsistencies and irrelevancies. Spitta, in his interesting biography of Schumann (in Grove's *Dictionary of Music and Musicians*) may be instanced. He writes as follows : " Mendelssohn at first

* But see p. 287.

only saw in Schumann the man of letters and the art-critic. Like most productive musicians, he had a dislike to such men as a class, however much he might love and value single representatives, as was really the case with regard to Schumann. From this point of view must be regarded the expressions which he makes use of now and then in letters concerning Schumann as an author. (See *Mendelssohn's Briefe*, ii, 116; Lady Wallace's translation, ii, 97; and Hiller's *Felix Mendelssohn Bartholdy*, Cologne, 1878, p. 64.) If they sound somewhat disparaging, we must remember that it is not the personal Mendelssohn speaking against the personal Schumann, but rather the creative artist speaking against the critic, always in natural opposition to him. Indeed, it is obviously impossible to take such remarks in a disadvantageous sense, as Schumann quite agreed with Mendelssohn on the subject of criticism." To this statement of the case various objections may be urged: (1) that the passage in Mendelssohn's letter (January 30, 1836) alluded to by Spitta proves that the writer misunderstood Schumann's criticism (*Gesammelte Schriften*, vol. i, p. 139); (2) that it is foolish to despise all critics alike, as the judgments of men possessed of the requisite technical and general knowledge cannot but be highly instructive to the artist, especially when the critic is a creative artist like Schumann; (3) that it is difficult to understand how an artist of Mendelssohn's culture could entertain so low an opinion of æsthetics, and not only of the philosophy of art, but also of the theory of art, as we find again and again expressed in his letters. These were deficiencies in Mendelssohn's mental constitution (or were they merely affectations?) which cannot be explained away. Another deficiency was his inability to comprehend Schumann. I look on the matter as an interesting psychological problem. Nothing could be farther from my mind than to accuse Mendelssohn of jealousy, or any kindred abomination. I simply suspect that he was one of the many great creative artists who, by the nature of their genius, were incapable of appreciating their differently-gifted contemporaries. Let me point out some of the facts from which I have drawn my inference.

Mendelssohn, writing on March 15, 1835, from Düsseldorf to Frau Voigt, of Leipzig, a friend of Schumann's (see
Acht Briefe, Leipzig, 1871), remarks : " May I ask you to
thank Herr Schumann in my name with friendly words for
his friendly present.   I should like to be a few days in Leipzig
that I might tell him how many things in it are to my mind
and please me, and again how other things do not.   Indeed
I feel certain he would become of my opinion if I could
explain to him exactly what I mean.   Among my favourites
is No. 11 in F minor.*   Once more please thank him very
much, and tell him how much pleasure he has given me."   A
passage in a letter addressed to Hiller, and written on April 15,
1839, runs thus : " One morning at a rehearsal somebody
showed me a number of the *Neue Zeitschrift für Musik* (the
editor of which, Schumann, was the whole winter in Vienna)
wherein there was news concerning me."   This sounds rather
distant.   But the main fact is that in the Mendelssohn letters,
published under the auspices of his family, the name of
Schumann does not appear at all, not one of his compositions
is alluded to.   And yet Mendelssohn wrote to his sister
Fanny often and fully about new musical works, and must
have heard, or at least got sight of, many of his great contemporary's compositions.   For had not Schumann by the
end of 1839 written all his important solo pianoforte pieces,
in 1840 a large number of his best songs, in 1841 the first
symphony (which Mendelssohn himself conducted), etc.,
in 1842 the string quartets (dedicated to his *friend* Mendelssohn) and the Pianoforte Quintet and Quartet, in 1843 *Paradise
and the Peri*, etc. ?   I therefore ask, Does not this silence speak
with convincing eloquence ?

* The reference can only be to No. 14, *Estrella*, of the *Carnaval*, which is
in F minor.   The only other early composition by Schumann which contains
a No. 11 is the *Davidsbündler ;* none of the numbers, however, is in F minor.
As the *Carnaval*, although finished in 1835, shortly before the above letter was
written, was not published till September 1837, Mendelssohn must have had
a manuscript copy.   This circumstance would explain the discrepancy with
regard to the number of the piece, as Schumann may have subsequently changed
the order of succession.   The supposition of a slip of the pen on the part of
Mendelssohn would, of course, explain the matter equally well.

X

APPENDIX II

LIST OF THE PUBLISHED WORKS OF ROBERT SCHUMANN

[Based mainly on the Catalogue compiled by Alfred Dörffel as a supplement to the *Musikalisches Wochenblatt* (Leipzig, Fritzsch, 1875). This Catalogue has been drawn upon in the text also.]

PART I. WORKS PUBLISHED WITH *OPUS* NUMBER

Titles, dates of composition and publication, and references.

(Vocal works are for one voice with pianoforte accompaniment unless otherwise indicated.)

Op. 1. THÈME SUR LE NOM ABEGG VARIÉ *pour le Pianoforte.*
Composed 1830. Published 1832.
Pp. 133, **134–6**, 180.

Op. 2. PAPILLONS *pour le Pianoforte seul.*
Composed 1829 (Nos. 1, 3, 4, 6, 8) and 1831 (2, 5, 7, 9, 10, 11, 12). Published 1832.
Pp. 109, 133, **136–7**, 139, 175, 176.

Op. 3. VI ÉTUDES DE CONCERT *pour le Pianoforte, composées d'après des Caprices de Paganini.* First Set. (Second Set, *see* Op. 10.)
Composed 1832. Published 1832.
Pp. 85–6, 110, 133, **137–8**, 139.

Op. 4. INTERMEZZI *per il Pianoforte.*
Two Books. Book I, 1–3; Book II, 4–6.
Composed 1832. Published 1833.
Pp. 110, 133, 137, **139**.

Op. 5. IMPROMPTUS ÜBER EIN THEMA VON CLARA WIECK, *für das Pianoforte.* C major.
Composed 1833. Published 1833. Revised edition 1850.
Pp. 133, 137, **189–40,** 179.

Op. 6. DIE DAVIDSBÜNDLER. (*Davidsbündler-Tänze.*) 18 *Charakterstücke für das Pianoforte.*
Composed 1837. Published 1838. Revised edition 1850.
Pp. 133, 171, **172–4,** 176, 181, 187, 305.

Op. 7. TOCCATA *pour le Pianoforte.* C major.
Composed 1830. Revised 1833. Published 1834.
Pp. 133, 172, **174–5.**

Op. 8. ALLEGRO *pour le Pianoforte.* B minor.
Composed 1831. Published 1835.
Pp. 109, 133, 144, 172, **175.**

Op. 9. CARNAVAL. *Scènes mignonnes composées pour le Pianoforte sur quatre notes.*
Composed 1834 and 1835. Published 1837.
Pp. 133, 137, 169, 172, 174, **175–8,** 181, 182, 184, 305.

Op. 10. VI ÉTUDES DE CONCERT *pour le Pianoforte, composées d'après des Caprices de Paganini.* Second Set. (First Set, *see* Op. 3.)
Composed 1833. Published 1835.
Pp. 86, 110, 133, **137–8,** 139, 172.

Op. 11. GRANDE SONATE *pour le Pianoforte.* F sharp minor.
Composed 1835 (begun 1833). Published 1836.
Pp. 111, 133, 157, 158, 160, 172, **178–81,** 196.

Op. 12. FANTASIESTÜCKE *für das Pianoforte.*
Composed 1837. Published 1838.
Pp. 133, 170, 172, 178, **181–2,** 184.

Op. 13. ÉTUDES EN FORME DE VARIATIONS (*XII Études symphoniques*) *pour le Pianoforte.* C sharp minor.
Composed 1834. Published 1837. Revised edition 1852.
Pp. 133, 144, 169, 172, **183–4.**

Op. 14. TROISIÈME GRANDE SONATE (*Concert sans Orchestre*) *pour le Pianoforte.* F minor.
Composed 1835. Published 1836. Revised edition 1853.
Pp. 111, 133, 172, 179, **184–5**, 187.

Op. 15. KINDERSCENEN. *Leichte Stücke für das Pianoforte.*
Composed 1838. Published 1839.
Pp. 133, 172, 182, **185–6**, 187, 242.

Op. 16. KREISLERIANA. *Phantasieen für das Pianoforte.*
Composed 1838. Published 1838. Revised edition 1850.
Pp. 133, 172, 178, 182, 184, **186–8**.

Op. 17. FANTASIE *für das Pianoforte.* C major.
Composed 1836. Published 1839.
Pp. 133, 172, 178, 184, **188–9**, 213.

Op. 18. ARABESKE *für das Pianoforte.* C major.
Composed 1839. Published 1839.
Pp. 133, **199–200**.

Op. 19. BLUMENSTÜCK *für das Pianoforte.* D flat major.
Composed 1839. Published 1839.
Pp. 133, **200**.

Op. 20. HUMORESKE *für das Pianoforte.* B flat major.
Composed 1839. Published 1839.
Pp. 133, **200–1**.

Op. 21. NOVELLETTEN *für das Pianoforte.*
Composed 1838. Published 1839.
Pp. 133, 178, 182, 185, 187, **201–2**, 213.

Op. 22. SONATE NR. II *für das Pianoforte.* G minor.
Composed 1835 (begun 1833), the last movement 1838. Published 1839.
Pp. 133, 187, **202**.

Op. 23. NACHTSTÜCKE *für das Pianoforte.*
Composed 1839. Published 1840.
Pp. 133, **202–3**.

Op. 24. Liederkreis von H. Heine. Nine songs.
Composed 1840. Published 1840.
Pp. 133, 208.

Op. 25. Myrthen. Song-cycle, twenty-six songs (Goethe, Rückert,
Byron, Moore, Heine, Burns, and J. Mosen).
Composed 1840. Published 1840.
Pp. 133, **205–6, 207, 208,** 257.

Op. 26. Faschingsschwank aus Wien. *Fantasiebilder für das Piano-
forte.* B flat major.
Composed 1839. Published 1841.
Pp. 133, **203.**

Op. 27. Lieder und Gesänge, Book I. Five songs (Hebbel, Burns,
Chamisso, Rückert, Zimmermann). Books II, III, IV, *see* Opp. 51,
77, 96.
Composed 1840. Published 1849.
Pp. 133, 208.

Op. 28. Drei Romanzen *für das Pianoforte.* B flat minor; F sharp
major; and B major.
Composed 1839. Published 1840.
Pp. 133, 182, **203–4.**

Op. 29. Drei Gedichte von Emanuel Geibel. With pianoforte
accompaniment. No. 1 for two sopranos; No. 2 for three
sopranos; No. 3 (*Zigeunerleben*) for small chorus, triangle and
tambourine *ad libitum.*
Composed 1840. Published 1841.

Op. 30. Drei Gedichte von Emanuel Geibel. Three songs.
Composed 1840. Published 1841.

Op. 31. Drei Gesänge (Chamisso).
Composed 1840. Published 1841.
Pp. 133, 208.

Op. 32. Vier Clavierstücke. *Scherzo, Gigue, Romanze und Fughette,
für das Pianoforte.* B flat, G minor, D minor, G minor.
Composed 1838 (1, 2, 3) and 1839 (4). Published 1841.
Pp. 133, 184 (*Romanze*), **204, 205.**

Op. 33. SECHS LIEDER. For four-part male voices. Unaccompanied. (Mosen, Heine, Goethe, and Reinick.)
Composed 1840. Published 1842.

Op. 34. VIER DUETTE *für Sopran und Tenor.* With pianoforte accompaniment. (Reinick, Burns, and A. Grün.)
Composed 1840. Published 1841.

Op. 35. ZWÖLF GEDICHTE VON JUSTINUS KERNER. Song-cycle. Book I, 1–5 ; Book II, 6–12.
Composed 1840. Published 1841.
Pp. 133, 208, 257 (No. 3, *Wanderlied*).

Op. 36. SECHS GEDICHTE. For soprano or tenor, from Reinick's *Liederbuch eines Malers.*
Composed 1840. Published 1842.
Pp. 133, 208.

Op. 37. ZWÖLF GEDICHTE from Rückert's *Liebesfrühling* by Robert and Clara Schumann (Nos. 2, 4, and 11 by Clara Schumann, Op. 12). Book I, 1–7 ; Book II, 8–12.
Composed 1840. Published 1841.
Pp. 133, 208, 209.

Op. 38. SYMPHONIE No. I. B flat major.
Composed 1841. Published, parts 1841 ; edition for pianoforte duet 1842 ; score 1853.
Pp. 133, 150, 206, **216–20,** 266.

Op. 39. LIEDERKREIS. Twelve songs, J. v. Eichendorff.
Composed 1840. Published 1842.
Pp. 133, 206, 208.

Op. 40. FÜNF LIEDER. (Four poems from the Danish of H. C. Andersen ; one from modern Greek, translated by Chamisso.)
Composed 1840. Published 1842.

Op. 41. DREI QUARTETTE. Three string quartets : A minor ; F major ; A major.
Composed 1842. Published, parts 1843 ; score 1849.
Pp. 133, 216, **221–3,** 305.

Op. 42. FRAUENLIEBE UND LEBEN. Song-cycle, A. v. Chamisso. Eight songs.
> Composed 1840.   Published 1843.
> Pp. 133, 208.

Op. 43. DREI ZWEISTIMMIGE LIEDER. Three two-part songs with pianoforte accompaniment (Reinick, etc.).
> Composed 1840.   Published 1844.

Op. 44. QUINTETT. For pianoforte, two violins, viola, and violoncello. E flat major.
> Composed 1842.   Published 1843.
> Pp. 133, 216, 221–2, 270, 302, 305.

Op. 45. ROMANZEN UND BALLADEN. Book I, 1, 2, and 3 (Eichendorff and Heine). Books II, III and IV, *see* Opp. 49, 53, and 64.
> Composed 1840.   Published 1844.
> Pp. 133, 208.

Op. 46. ANDANTE UND VARIATIONEN. For two pianofortes. B flat major.
> Composed 1843.   Published 1844.
> Pp. 134, 216, 224, 226–7.

Op. 47. QUARTETT. For pianoforte, violin, viola, and violoncello. E flat major.
> Composed 1842.   Published 1845.
> Pp. 133, 216, 221, 305.

Op. 48. DICHTERLIEBE. Song-cycle from Heine's *Buch der Lieder.* Book I, 1–8 ; Book II, 9–16.
> Composed 1840.   Published 1844.
> Pp. 133, 207–8.

Op. 49. ROMANZEN UND BALLADEN. Book II, 1, 2, and 3 (Heine and Fröhlich). Books I, III, IV, *see* Opp. 45, 53, 64.
> Composed 1840.   Published 1844.
> P. 133.

Op. 50. DAS PARADIES UND DIE PERI. For solo voices, chorus, and orchestra. (From Moore's *Lalla Rookh.*)
> Composed 1843.   Published, pianoforte edition 1844 ; score 1845.
> Pp. 134, 150, 216, 221, 223–6, 252, 256, 257, 286, 293, 305.

Op. 51. LIEDER UND GESÄNGE, Book II. Five songs (Geibel, Rückert, K. Immermann, Goethe, etc.). Books I, III, IV, *see* Opp. 27, 77, 96. Composed 1842. Published 1850.

Op. 52. OUVERTURE, SCHERZO UND FINALE. For orchestra. E major. Composed 1841 (the Finale revised 1845). Published, parts 1846; score 1854.
Pp. 133, 220.

Op. 53. ROMANZEN UND BALLADEN. Book III, 1, 2, and 3 (No. 3 consists of three songs by Heine). Books I, II, IV, *see* Opp. 45, 49, 64.
Composed 1840. Published 1845.
Pp. 133, 208.

Op. 54. CONCERT *für das Pianoforte* with orchestral accompaniment. A minor.
Composed, first movement 1841; Intermezzo and Finale 1845. Published, parts 1846, score 1862.
Pp. 133, 150, 220, 235–6, 247, 293.

Op. 55. FÜNF LIEDER VON ROB. BURNS. For mixed chorus (unaccompanied).
Composed 1846. Published 1847.

Op. 56. STUDIEN *für den Pedal-Flügel.* Six pieces in canon form for Pedal-Pianoforte.
Composed 1845. Published 1845.
Pp. 111, 134, 241.

Op. 57. BELSATZAR. Ballad (Heine) for voice with pianoforte accompaniment.
Composed 1840. Published 1846.

Op. 58. SKIZZEN *für den Pedal-Flügel.*
Composed 1845. Published 1846.
Pp. 134, 241.

Op. 59. VIER GESÄNGE *für gemischten Chor.* Unaccompanied. (K. Lappe, v. Platen, Mörike, Rückert.)
Composed 1846. Published 1848.

Op. 60. Sechs Fugen über den Namen BACH. For organ or pedal-pianoforte.
Composed 1845. Published 1847.
Pp. 134, 241–2.

Op. 61. Zweite Symphonie. C major.
Composed 1845 and 1846. Published 1848.
Pp. 133, 134, 150, 235, 240–1, 247.

Op. 62. Drei Gesänge *für Männerchor.* Unaccompanied. (Eichen-dorff, Rückert, and Klopstock.)
Composed 1847. Published 1848.

Op. 63. Trio. For pianoforte, violin, and violoncello. D minor.
Composed 1847. Published 1848.
Pp. 134, 242.

Op. 64. Romanzen und Balladen. Book IV, 1, 2, and 3 (No. 3 consists of three songs, of which the third is for soprano and tenor. Mörike, Nos. 1 and 2, and Heine's *Tragödie*, No. 3). Books I, II, III, *see* Opp. 45, 49, 53.
Composed 1841 (No. 3) and 1847 (Nos. 1 and 2). Published 1847.

Op. 65. Ritornelle von Friedrich Rückert. Seven canons for male voices. Unaccompanied.
Composed 1847. Published 1849.

Op. 66. Bilder aus Osten. Six impromptus for pianoforte duet.
Composed 1848. Published 1849.
Pp. 242, 291.

Op. 67. Romanzen und Balladen *für Chor.* Book I, Nos. 1–5 (Goethe, Mörike, Chamisso, Burns). Books II, III, IV, *see* Opp. 75, 145, 146.
Composed 1849. Published 1849.

Op. 68. Album für die Jugend (*Christmas Album*). Forty (later forty-three) pieces for pianoforte. Part I (for small folk), 1–18; Part II (for more grown-up folk), 19–43.
Composed 1848. Published 1849. Second edition with ap-pendix : *Musical Rules for Home and Life*, 1851.
Pp. 82 (*Musical Rules*, etc.), 186, 242.

Op. 69. ROMANZEN *für Frauenstimmen.* Book I, 1–6, with *ad libitum* pianoforte accompaniment (Eichendorff, Kerner, Mörike, Uhland). Book II, *see* Op. 91.
Composed 1849. Published 1849.

Op. 70. ADAGIO UND ALLEGRO. For pianoforte and horn (or violoncello, or violin). A flat major.
Composed 1849. Published 1849.

Op. 71. ADVENTLIED VON FRIEDRICH RÜCKERT. For soprano solo and chorus with orchestral accompaniment.
Composed 1848. Published, pianoforte edition 1849; score 1866.
Pp. 242, 259.

Op. 72. VIER FUGEN. For pianoforte.
Composed 1845. Published 1850.
Pp. 134, 241.

Op. 73. FANTASIE-STÜCKE. For pianoforte and clarinet (or violin, or violoncello). Three pieces.
Composed 1849. Published 1849.

Op. 74. SPANISCHES LIEDERSPIEL. For one, two, and four voices, with pianoforte accompaniment. Nine songs translated from Spanish by Geibel.
Composed 1849. Published 1849.
Pp. 243, 250.

Op. 75. ROMANZEN UND BALLADEN *für Chor.* Unaccompanied. Book II, Nos. 6–10 (Eichendorff, Burns, etc.). *See* Opp. 67, 145, 146.
Composed 1849. Published 1850.

Op. 76. VIER MÄRSCHE. For pianoforte.
Composed 1849. Published 1849.

Op. 77. LIEDER UND GESÄNGE, Book III. Five songs (Eichendorff, H. v. Fallersleben, etc.). Books I, II, IV, *see* Opp. 27, 51, 96.
Composed, Nos. 1 and 4, 1840; 2, 3, 5, 1850. Published 1851.

Op. 78. VIER DUETTE *für Sopran und Tenor* with pianoforte accompaniment (Rückert, Kerner, Goethe, Hebbel).
Composed 1849. Published 1850.

Op. 79. LIEDER-ALBUM FÜR DIE JUGEND. Twenty-nine songs (H. v.
Fallersleben, Uhland, Goethe, Schiller, H. C. Andersen, Mörike,
Kletke, Geibel, etc.).
Composed 1849. Published 1849.
P. 245.

Op. 80. ZWEITES TRIO. For pianoforte, violin, and violoncello.
F major. First Trio, Op. 63. Third Trio, Op. 110.
Composed 1847. Published 1850.
Pp. 134, 242.

Op. 81. GENOVEVA. Opera in four acts, after Tieck and Hebbel.
Composed 1847 and 1848. Published, score 1850; pianoforte
edition 1851.
Pp. 134, 242, **248**, 254, 256, 257.

Op. 82. WALDSCENEN. Nine pieces for pianoforte.
Composed 1848 and 1849. Published 1851.
Pp. 242, 243.

Op. 83. DREI GESÄNGE. (Rückert, Eichendorff, etc.).
Composed 1850. Published 1850.

Op. 84. BEIM ABSCHIED ZU SINGEN. Song (v. Feuchtersleben) for
chorus with accompaniment of wind instruments or pianoforte.
Composed 1847. Published 1850.

Op. 85. ZWÖLF VIERHÄNDIGE CLAVIERSTÜCKE. For children little
and big.
Composed 1849. Published 1850.
Pp. 249 (No. 1), 252 (No. 2).

Op. 86. CONCERTSTÜCK. For four horns and orchestra. F major.
Composed 1849. Published 1851.

Op. 87. DER HANDSCHUH. Ballad (Schiller) for voice with pianoforte
accompaniment.
Composed 1850. Published 1851.

Op. 88. PHANTASIESTÜCKE. For pianoforte, violin, and violoncello.
1. *Romanze.* 2. *Humoreske.* 3. *Duett.* 4. *Finale.*
Composed 1842. Published 1850.

Op. 89. SECHS GESÄNGE. (Wilfried von der Neun.)
Composed 1850. Published 1850.

Op. 90. SECHS GEDICHTE VON N. LENAU, and REQUIEM (Old Catholic poem).
Composed 1850. Published 1851.

Op. 91. ROMANZEN *für Frauenstimmen* (Book II, 7–12). With *ad libitum* pianoforte accompaniment (Kerner, Mörike, Reinick, Rückert, etc.). Book I, *see* Op. 69.
Composed 1849. Published 1851.

Op. 92. INTRODUCTION UND ALLEGRO APPASSIONATO. For pianoforte and orchestra. G major.
Composed 1849. Published 1852.
P. 133, 243.

Op. 93. MOTETTE *Verzweifle nicht im Schmerzensthal* (Rückert). For double male chorus with *ad libitum* organ accompaniment.
Composed 1849. Published 1851.

Op. 94. DREI ROMANZEN. For oboe (or violin, or clarinet), with pianoforte accompaniment.
Composed 1849. Published 1851.

Op. 95. DREI GESÄNGE (from Byron's *Hebrew Melodies*). For voice with harp or pianoforte accompaniment.
Composed 1849. Published 1851.

Op. 96. LIEDER UND GESÄNGE, Book IV. Five songs (Goethe, v. Platen, v. der Neun). Books I, II, III, *see* Opp. 27, 51, 77.
Composed 1850. Published 1851.

Op. 97. DRITTE SYMPHONIE. E flat major.
Composed 1850. Published, score 1851; pianoforte duet edition 1852.
Pp. 133, 258, 286.

Op. 98. LIEDER, GESÄNGE UND REQUIEM FÜR MIGNON from Goethe's *Wilhelm Meister*. First Part, Op. 98*a* : the songs of Mignon, the Harper, and Philine, for voice and pianoforte. Second Part, Op. 98*b* : *Requiem for Mignon*, for chorus, solo voices, and orchestra.
Composed 1849. Published 1851.
P. 252.

Op. 99. BUNTE BLÄTTER. Fourteen pieces for pianoforte.
Composed at different times. Published 1852.

Op. 100. OUVERTURE to Schiller's *Bride of Messina.* C minor.
Composed 1850 and 1851. Published 1851.
P. 265, 286.

Op. 101. MINNESPIEL from Rückert's *Liebesfrühling.* For one, two,
and four voices.
Composed 1849. Published 1852.

Op. 102. FÜNF STÜCKE IM VOLKSTON. For violoncello (or violin)
and pianoforte.
Composed 1849. Published 1851.

Op. 103. MÄDCHENLIEDER (Elisabeth Kulmann). For two sopranos
or soprano and alto, with pianoforte accompaniment.
Composed 1851. Published 1851.

Op. 104. SIEBEN LIEDER (Elisabeth Kulmann).
Composed 1851. Published 1851.

Op. 105. SONATE. For pianoforte and violin. A minor.
Composed 1851. Published 1852.

Op. 106. SCHÖN HEDWIG. Ballad (Hebbel) for declamation with
pianoforte accompaniment.
Composed 1849. Published 1853.

Op. 107. SECHS GESÄNGE (Ullrich, Mörike, P. Heyse, Wolfgang
Müller, Kinkel).
Composed 1851 and 1852. Published 1852.

Op. 108. NACHTLIED VON F. HEBBEL. For chorus and orchestra.
Composed 1849. Published, pianoforte edition 1852, score
1853.

Op. 109. BALLSCENEN. Nine characteristic pieces for pianoforte duet.
Composed 1851. Published 1853.

Op. 110. DRITTES TRIO. For pianoforte, violin, and violoncello. G
minor. First Trio, Op. 63. Second Trio, Op. 80.
Composed 1851. Published 1852.
P. 134.

Op. 111. DREI FANTASIESTÜCKE *für Pianoforte.*
Composed 1851. Published 1852.

Op. 112. DER ROSE PILGERFAHRT. Fairy-tale, after a poem by Moritz
Horn, for solo voices, chorus, and orchestra.
Composed 1851. Published 1852.
P. 291.

Op. 113. MÄRCHENBILDER. Four pieces for pianoforte and viola (or
violin).
Composed 1851. Published 1852.

Op. 114. DREI LIEDER. Three trios (Rückert, etc.) for female voices
with pianoforte accompaniment.
Composed 1853. Published 1853.

Op. 115. MANFRED. " Dramatic Poem in three parts by Lord Byron,
with music by R. S."
Composed 1848 (overture) and 1849 (the rest). Published,
overture 1852 ; pianoforte edition of the whole 1853 ; whole score
1862.
Pp. 134, 231, 235, 236, **238–9,** 300.

Op. 116. DER KÖNIGSSOHN. Ballad (Uhland) for solo voices, chorus,
and orchestra.
Composed 1851. Published 1853.
P. 286.

Op. 117. VIER HUSARENLIEDER by N. Lenau, for baritone voice with
pianoforte accompaniment.
Composed 1851. Published 1852.

Op. 118. DREI CLAVIER-SONATEN FÜR DIE JUGEND. No. 1. *Kinder-
Sonate,* G major. No. 2. D major. No. 3. C major.
Composed 1853. Published 1854.

Op. 119. DREI GEDICHTE (S. Pfarrius). Three songs.
Composed 1851. Published 1853.

Op. 120. SYMPHONIE No. IV. D minor.
Composed 1841, and performed 1841 as " second symphony."
Newly instrumentated 1851, and known as " fourth symphony."
Published, parts, and edition for pianoforte duet 1853; score
1854. 1841 version published 1896.
Pp. 133, 216, 220, 231, 267, 286.

Op. 121. ZWEITE GROSSE SONATE. For violin and pianoforte. D
minor.
Composed 1851. Published 1853.

Op. 122. No. 1. BALLADE VOM HAIDEKNABEN (Hebbel) for declamation with pianoforte accompaniment.
No. 2. DIE FLÜCHTLINGE. Ballad (Shelley) for declamation
with pianoforte accompaniment.
Composed 1852. Published 1853.

Op. 123. FEST-OUVERTURE MIT GESANG on the *Rheinweinlied.* For
orchestra and chorus. (Connecting words by Wolfgang Müller.)
Composed 1853. Published 1857.
P. 286.

Op. 124. ALBUMBLÄTTER. Twenty pieces for pianoforte.
Composed in different years, 1832–1845. Published 1854.

Op. 125. FÜNF HEITERE GESÄNGE (Mörike, etc.).
Composed 1851. Published 1853.

Op. 126. SIEBEN CLAVIERSTÜCKE IN FUGHETTENFORM.
Composed 1853. Published 1854.

Op. 127. LIEDER UND GESÄNGE. Five songs (Kerner, Heine, Strach-
witz, Shakespeare).
Composed 1850 and 1851. Published 1854.

Op. 128. OUVERTURE to Shakespeare's *Julius Cæsar.* F minor.
Composed 1851. Published 1855.
P. 286.

Op. 129. CONCERT *für Violoncell* (A minor), with orchestral accompaniment.
Composed 1850. Published 1854.

Op. 130. KINDERBALL. Six easy dances for pianoforte duet.
Composed 1853. Published 1854.

Op. 131. PHANTASIE *für Violine*, with orchestral or pianoforte accompaniment. C major.
Composed 1853. Published 1854.
P. 286.

Op. 132. MÄRCHENERZÄHLUNGEN. Four pieces for clarinet (or violin), viola, and pianoforte.
Composed 1853. Published 1854.

Op. 133. GESÄNGE DER FRÜHE. Five pieces for pianoforte.
Composed 1853. Published 1855.

Op. 134. CONCERT-ALLEGRO MIT INTRODUCTION. For pianoforte and orchestra. D minor.
Composed 1853. Published 1855.
P. 133.

Op. 135. GEDICHTE DER KÖNIGIN MARIA STUART. Five songs " from a collection of old-English poems translated by Gisbert Freiherr Vincke, set to music by R. S."
Composed 1852. Published 1855.

Op. 136. OUVERTURE to Goethe's *Hermann und Dorothea*. No. 1 of the posthumous works. B minor.
Composed 1851. Published 1857.
P. 286.

Op. 137. JAGDLIEDER. Five hunting songs (H. Laube) for four-part male chorus (with *ad libitum* accompaniment of four horns). No. 2 of the posthumous works.
Composed 1849. Published 1857.

Op. 138. Spanische Liebes-Lieder. Ten songs from Spanish folk-songs and romances (translated by Geibel) for one, two, and four voices, with pianoforte duet accompaniment. No. 3 of the posthumous works.
Composed 1849. Published 1857.
P. 243.

Op. 139. Des Sängers Fluch. Ballad (after Uhland, arranged by R. Pohl) for solo voices, chorus, and orchestra. No. 4 of the posthumous works.
Composed 1852. Published 1858.
P. 286.

Op. 140. Vom Pagen und der Königstochter. Four ballads (Geibel) for solo voices, chorus, and orchestra. No. 5 of the posthumous works.
Composed 1852. Published 1858.

Op. 141. Vier doppelchörige Gesänge (Rückert, Zedtlitz, Goethe). No. 6 of the posthumous works. "These songs should be sung without the accompaniment . . . which is intended only to facilitate their study."
Composed 1849. Published 1858.

Op. 142. Vier Gesänge (Kerner, Heine, etc.). No. 7 of the posthumous works.
Composed 1852. Published 1858.

Op. 143. Das Glück von Edenhall. Ballad (after Uhland, arranged by R. Hasenclever) for male voices, solos and chorus, with orchestral accompaniment. No. 8 of the posthumous works.
Composed 1853. Published 1860.
P. 286.

Op. 144. Neujahrslied von Friedrich Rückert. For chorus with orchestral accompaniment. No. 9 of the posthumous works.
Composed 1849; instrumentated 1850. Published 1861.
P. 243.

Op. 145. Romanzen und Balladen *für Chorgesang*. Unaccompanied. Book III, Nos. 11–15 (Uhland, Burns, etc.). Books I, II, IV, *see* Opp. 67, 75, 146.
Composed 1849. Published 1860.
Y

Op. 146. ROMANZEN UND BALLADEN *für Chorgesang.* Book IV, Nos.
16–20 (Uhland, Burns, Rückert). Books I, II, III, *see* Opp. 67,
75, 145.
 Composed 1849. Published 1860.

Op. 147. MESSE *für vierstimmigen Chor.* Four-part chorus with orches-
tral accompaniment. No. 10 of the posthumous works.
 Composed 1852. Published, pianoforte edition 1862, score 1863.
 P. 286.

Op. 148. REQUIEM. For chorus and orchestra. No. 11 of the
posthumous works.
 Composed 1852. Published 1864.
 P. 286.

PART II. WORKS WITHOUT *OPUS* NUMBER

I

SCENEN AUS GOETHES " FAUST." For solo voices, chorus, and orchestra.
Overture. Part I, Nos. 1–3 ; Part II, Nos. 4–6 ; Part III, No. 7,
Faust's Transfiguration, Nos. 1–7.
 Composed : 1844, Part III, Nos. 1, 2, 3, and 7 ; 1847, revision
of No. 7, the final chorus ; 1848, remainder of Part III, Nos. 4,
5, and 6 ; 1849, Part I, and the first number of Part II, No. 4 ;
1850, remainder of Part II, Nos. 5 and 6 ; 1853, the overture.
Published, pianoforte edition 1858, score 1859.
 Pp. 134, 235, **236–8**, 244, 252.

II

DER DEUTSCHE RHEIN. Patriotic song (N. Becker) for solo voice and
chorus, with pianoforte accompaniment.
 Composed 1840. Published 1840.

III

SOLDATENLIED (H. von Fallersleben).

IV

SCHERZO UND PRESTO PASSIONATO. For pianoforte. Nos. 12 and 13 of
the posthumous works.
 Published 1866. The *Scherzo* intended for the Sonata Op. 14 ;
and the *Presto* as finale to the Sonata Op. 22.

V

CANON on " To ALEXIS." A flat major.

VI

SECHS SONATEN *für die Violine* by Johann Sebastian Bach, with pianoforte
accompaniment by Robert Schumann.
Published 1854.

*   *   *   *   *   *

The Supplementary Volume (1893) to the critical edition contains,
besides the *Scherzo* and *Presto passionato* mentioned as No. IV of the
Works without *opus* number, the following items :

1. A vocal duet and three early songs, two of which were afterwards developed into the slow movements of the Sonatas Opp. 11
and 22.

2. Several variations rejected from or sketched for the *Études
Symphoniques*.

3. The original version of the *Andante und Variationen* Op. 46,
as composed for two pianofortes, two violoncellos, and a horn, with
several variations afterwards rejected.

4. Schumann's last theme (February 17, 1854).
P. 287, 303.

INDEX

(For page references to Schumann's compositions *see* List of Works,
Appendix II, pp. 306 *sqq.*)

INDEX

327